Narrating a Psychology of Resistance

Narrating a Psychology of Resistance

VOICES OF THE *COMPAÑERAS* IN NICARAGUA

Shelly Grabe

OXFORD
UNIVERSITY PRESS

Oxford University Press is a department of the University of Oxford. It furthers
the University's objective of excellence in research, scholarship, and education
by publishing worldwide. Oxford is a registered trade mark of Oxford University
Press in the UK and certain other countries.

Published in the United States of America by Oxford University Press
198 Madison Avenue, New York, NY 10016, United States of America.

Library of Congress Cataloging-in-Publication Data
Names: Grabe, Shelly, 1974– author.
Title: Narrating a psychology of resistance : voices of the *compañeras* in Nicaragua / Shelly Grabe.
Description: Oxford ; New York : Oxford University Press, [2017] | Includes bibliographical
references.
Identifiers: LCCN 2016019770 | ISBN 9780190614256 (hardback : alk. paper)
Subjects: LCSH: Feminism—Nicaragua. | Women's rights—Nicaragua. | Women—Political activity—
Nicaragua. | Women—Nicaragua—Social conditions. | Social movements—Nicaragua. |
Nicaragua—Politics and government.
Classification: LCC HQ1236.5.N5 G73 2017 | DDC 320.082/097285—dc23
LC record available at https://lccn.loc.gov/2016019770

9 8 7 6 5 4 3 2 1

Printed by Sheridan Books, Inc., United States of America

CONTENTS

Conclusion: How a Feminist Fight for Justice from the Majority World Informs Liberatory Knowledge

ABOUT THE ARTISTS

The art pictured on the cover was produced by Favianna Rodriguez, a celebrated interdisciplinary artist based in Oakland, California. Rodriguez is renowned for artwork that deals with issues such as war, migration, globalization, and social movements. Her pieces reflect grassroots struggles and tell a history of social justice through images. She was inspired to produce the image that was selected for the cover of this book during a trip to Lima, Peru, in November 2014, where she participated in a feminist gathering of Latin American women with the Global Fund for Women. The piece depicts empowered women collaborating to transform the world. She invites those serving social justice, radical, and revolutionary causes to use her images for noncommercial purposes. Rodriguez has lectured widely on the use of art in civic engagement and is on social media promoting art and activism. Contact her, follow her on social media, schedule her for a talk, or purchase her work online (http://favianna.tumblr.com/).

The photographs of the women included in the book were taken by Ansley West Rivers, a photographer from Atlanta, Georgia. West Rivers received her MFA from the California College of the Arts and is known for her evocative portraits that document social issues ranging from women's agricultural practices in East Africa to the conditions of U.S. watersheds in the context of industry and global warming. Her art interprets narratives by attempting to recontexualize the stories of the subjects. West River's work has been shown bicoastally in a number of galleries and has been featured in the *New York Times* and *Huffington Post*. She currently resides in the low country of coastal Georgia; you can follow her work online (http://ansleywest.com).

ACKNOWLEDGMENTS

First and foremost, I thank my colleague, friend, and mentor Carlos Arenas, without whom I would have never become involved in the *Movimiento Autónomo de Mujeres* (Women's Autonomous Movement) in Nicaragua in the first place and whose critical thinking helped contribute to the kind of scholar I am today. I cannot thank you enough, Carlos, for your collaboration, influence, and support; you changed both my perspective and my direction in life.

I also thank Abby Stewart for generously, and without hesitation, encouraging and supporting this work only shortly after our initial meeting. The layers of support you have offered over the years have unfolded in ways that have allowed me to explore the stories behind the Movimiento in ways I would have never dreamed possible. Thanks also go to Julia Baumgartner, who provided tireless simultaneous interpretation for the interviews conducted for this book that left me, and the women I interviewed, with the experience as if we had direct, one-on-one, conversations with only each other. And, I thank Ansley West Rivers, who carried video and camera equipment through Nicaragua's rainy season to capture documentation of the power behind the women's voices. To my graduate student, Anjali, I thank you for what began as a budding interest that evolved into critical thought and reflection; for the countless hours of patient conversation regarding the role of psychology in understanding social change; for the gentle pressure to think more deeply about narratives as data; and for the countless reads of this writing: You are the next generation.

I am grateful to my friends and colleagues at the University of California, Santa Cruz, who, in taking an unapologetically justice framework in their work (and lives) provided me a setting from which to wrestle with new concepts and ideas and challenge how I might most responsibly use them. You have provided immeasurable forms of inspiration: Heather Bullock, Phil Hammack, Craig Haney, Aida Hurtado, Regina Langhout, Rosa-Linda Fregoso, Marcia Ochoa, and Eileen Zurbriggen. I also thank Avril Thorne, who so encouragingly believed in the contribution this book could make and who generatively provided the guidance to make it happen. I have deep gratitude for the time, generosity, critical eye, and substantive suggestions provided by Brinton Lykes that served to substantially bring this book more in line with my aims and with those of liberation psychology. And, thanks to my Dad, who single-handedly raised me with an autonomous spirit and never questioned why I was able to make time to return to Nicaragua, repeatedly, when I did not have the same ease in finding time to return home.

Finally, my largest thanks go to the women in Nicaragua, both the women who are included in this book and the women I have met over the years who have described moving from an "object" to a "subject" as a result of a feminist platform for action that has revolutionized lives and has the potential to serve as a model for women the world over interested in transforming societal structures that marginalize those most at risk.

PREFACE

Bridging Activism and Academic Research: My Position

As researchers, we inevitably bring our own stories to bear on the research process (White & Dotson, 2010). From the outset, I realized that my interest in the women's social movement in Nicaragua was partly about my own experience and interests as a woman from a working-class background, raised by a single father. It was also driven by my desire to focus on women's communities as sources of feminist protest and as sites where women negotiate counter narratives that challenge dominant power structures. Much of my exposure to feminism occurred after my PhD training when I clandestinely located feminist texts in used bookstores as an intern in psychiatry and read authors such as Nawal El Saldawi and bell hooks, whose critical perspectives pointed me in unforeseen directions that challenged my silence. I went from turning pages in the shelter of a bookstore to rapidly moving those conversations into my life and work. I had already finished graduate school, and as a mainstream research psychologist, my shifting lens was repeatedly labeled "radical" within academia. With the label came the suggestion that my new interests bordered on irreverent. As a result, I increasingly found my home and my people in the activist community, and like other women participating in social movement research, it seemed as though the work I was to become involved in chose me, rather than me choosing it (Shayne, 2009; Taylor, 1998).

A year after receiving my PhD in clinical psychology, I became involved in local community organizing surrounding women's rights. I coorganized events with another community member who was the director of an organization that began in the 1980s to oppose the Reagan administration's military intervention in Central America, including the U.S.-backed Contra war in Nicaragua. Despite that Nicaragua had experienced over a century of U.S. political and military intervention and interference, I knew embarrassingly little about it. The director of the organization, Carlos Arenas, invited me to accompany him on a social delegation to Nicaragua that was focused on women's empowerment. Although I was strongly committed to women's issues and involved in local community activism, the trip seemed a bit far afield from my focus as a psychologist, and I suspected, given my limited knowledge of Latin American politics and culture, and my inability to speak Spanish, that it was perhaps even inappropriate for me to be part of the delegation. Carlos convinced me those were the very reasons I should go.

During my first trip to Nicaragua in 2005, we visited several key women's rural grassroots organizations that were working to transform gender inequity. One of the organizations, *Xochilt Acalt*, facilitated rural women's access to land as a means to alter structural gender inequities in a manner that would transform women's subordination. Both the leaders and the members of the organization took countless risks to boldly and brazenly challenge gender norms, with what appeared incredible effectiveness. Despite that our initial conversations with each other during my first visit to Nicaragua included "solidarity" language, I had yet to contribute anything substantive. However, as I listened to the mechanisms of change that were being articulated by women who participated in Xochilt Acalt's *Programa Productivo*, I found the social scientist in me asking whether research findings might play a role in their efforts toward social justice. A determinedly emphatic response indicated that, yes, being able to empirically demonstrate the efficacy of the programs being administered could afford their efforts more credibility with people in positions of power.

I returned to the United States to inform a senior (feminist) colleague that I aimed to pursue collaborative research with a feminist organization in Nicaragua that was engaging in radical and, I believed, demonstrable change that enhanced gender justice. A fair dose of skepticism was expressed. To be fair, we were located in a mainstream, quantitative, R1 (a university that engages in extensive research activity) environment where using the F-word (i.e., feminism) positioned one in an "alternative voices" box. However, I remained certain I could uphold the standards of my discipline and develop a sound research partnership with the leaders of the Nicaraguan organization.

I began writing grants and pursued funding to run a quasi-experimental study examining the effects of land ownership on women's empowerment and receipt of violence. In planning the research, I was candid with my collaborators at Xochilt Acalt that I knew little of Latin American politics, I was not trained as an international (or feminist) field researcher, I did not have a nuanced understanding of gender oppression in their region, and I could not speak Spanish. Within academia, these disclaimers would often be read as incompetence. However, my collaborators noted astutely that *they* were, of course, the experts of knowledge in these areas. We thus began a longer-term collaboration and have since collected and disseminated data, with support from the National Science Foundation, demonstrating that landowning not only empowers women but also reduces their receipt of psychological and physical violence (Grabe, 2010, 2012; Grabe & Arenas, 2009; Grabe, Grose, & Dutt, 2015; Grose & Grabe, 2014).

Over time, I became increasingly committed to deepening my understanding of the people and region, as well as my role in it. I traveled with Witness for Peace to learn more about U.S. interventions in Latin American foreign policy, spent a summer in Central America taking language classes, and visited other parts of revolutionary Latin America to increase my breadth of knowledge. Although a common and justified concern with transnational work is that Western feminists are deploying a universal Western feminism, I entered into these relationships with no formal training in feminist studies and, rather, became a student of activists who have devoted their lives to social change. In doing so, I learned a women of Color,[1] decolonial, and rural feminism that largely influences most of the work I do today. In this way, I violated the traditions of mainstream science by *not* arriving with ready-made theories or a research agenda driven from the literature. I went into these relationships, though unaware at the time of something called "scholar activism," to use my tools and training in active engagement with and in the service of a progressive social movement (Sudbury & Okazawa-Rey, 2009). I assumed and accepted I may be burning my academic bridges. Nevertheless, I heeded the advice of my colleague, and by then friend, Carlos to familiarize myself with relevant literatures informed by sociology, economics, and feminist studies so that I would also be able to produce scholarship that would be situated in and contribute to the academic literatures on these topics (e.g., Agarwal, 1994; Deere & Leon, 2001; Kabeer, 1999; Naples & Desai, 2002).

Years later, after having secured a position as an assistant professor at the University of California at Santa Cruz, precisely due to my focus on scholar-activist collaborations, I returned to Nicaragua for the current project. Although my collaboration with Xochilt Acalt was a community-driven feminist project that aimed to use research toward liberatory processes, I was also motivated to document the voices involved in the broader *Movimiento Autónomo de Mujeres* (Women's Autonomous Movement)—a multisector, coordinated mobilization of women that had weathered unremitting power differentials characterized by patriarchy and capitalism. The initial intention for this project was to produce a documentary film on the women's movement. However, the idea for this book began when I first met Abigail (Abby) Stewart, a feminist psychologist from the University of Michigan, at the International Society of Political Psychology conference in San Francisco in summer 2010. I attended a talk she gave that detailed the Global Feminisms Project (GFP).[2] During the question-and-answer session, I asked why a Latin American country was not represented in the archive. Abby indicated they had not yet established a collaboration that included a group in Latin America with its own investment in documenting women's activism. In short order, I introduced myself and my connection to the Movimiento to Abby, a partnership ensued, and I put together a team that could travel through Nicaragua to conduct and film interviews that would contribute to the growing database housed at the GFP.[3]

The first person I invited to the team was, of course, Carlos Arenas. Carlos, trained as a lawyer who focused on human rights activism, had, at that time, been working in solidarity with the Movimiento in Nicaragua for years. He was on board, and we began planning for the interviews to occur in summer 2011. In the midst of planning, Carlos suggested that I also consider publishing a book based on the interviews that we would be conducting for the archive. Although work of a similar nature surrounding the role of women in the Nicaraguan Revolution and the birth of the women's movement had already been published by Margaret Randall (1981, 1994), many years had passed, each creating an ever-more-marginalizing situation for women due, in part, to the political conservatives in power.

Nevertheless, I shucked the idea with profuse excuses about being a *gringa* who had never lived extensively in Nicaragua. In one of the only direct and firm responses I had ever received from Carlos, he replied, "Stop apologizing for your position." Of course, his choice of words rung deeply because, by this stage in my career, I had an academic understanding of feminist reflexive engagements with positionality and knew there were more responsible ways to engage it than hiding from it. Moreover, the story that ultimately needed to be told was not about me and my limitations—as had been candidly told to me in 2005 when my collaborators at Xochilt Acalt informed me of our relative roles in community research projects. I could decide not to write the book or I could, instead of apologizing for my position, understand better how to work with it.

I knew documenting the experience of social movement actors for this project would demand a methodology different from the large-scale survey designs and quantitative analyses that I had mastered and were more widely valued within my discipline. In this case, feminist thinking and practice would require eliminating the boundaries of division that "privilege dominant forms of knowledge building, boundaries that mark who can be a knower and what can be known" (Hesse-Biber, 2007, p. 3). Therefore, I used the oral history method because it allowed the women to serve as storytellers who narrated and interpreted their world and their experience in it (Riessman, 2005).

As the reader will be able to observe through the reproduction of the narratives in this book, the breadth and depth of the women's stories and their social locations as grassroots organizers, journalists, Nobel Peace Prize nominees, labor union leaders, and rural organizers make abundantly clear that the women interviewed for this book are active agents of a vibrant social movement. Before interviewing them, I read as much as I could find about each of them and the organizations in which they worked. I prepared relatively parallel questions for each woman to ensure that I could facilitate the telling of their personal stories because most of them have become accustomed to telling the story of the Movimiento and not their own.

The interviews were supplemented with semistructured interviews with various organizations (these are not reproduced in this book). At other times, I treated some of the same activists as key informants, for example, when I met with Sofía Montenegro[4] over dessert and she candidly spoke with me about the movement's politics and challenges. Three prior trips to Nicaragua (2005, 2007, and 2008) and a follow-up trip in 2015 also opened up a broader understanding of the emergence of the women's social movement as well as what the current obstacles and challenges were to sustaining a coherent base and place from which to mobilize action.

To collect the 15 interviews conducted for this project, I hired a team. The translator, Julia Baumgartner, was a U.S.-based activist who traveled to Nicaragua regularly for solidarity work and was familiar with feminist organizing in rural areas. I also invited an award-winning artist and documentarian, Ansley West Rivers, who filmed the interviews that we were conducting and photographed the women. Each of us read extensively before the trip and met every morning during our visit to discuss our aims and each evening to discuss how the interviews went. I hired a driver, Juan Pablo Membreño, who was a feminist sympathizer and who knew the city and surrounding areas as well as the challenges of reaching this many women in the short amount of time we had. Most residences and businesses in Nicaragua do not have addresses or house numbers, and it sometimes takes extraordinary effort, patience, and persistence to find a location, never mind to find it on time. If we were to have given the project completion to chance, it would never have been completed; instead, we gave it to Juan Pablo. And, finally, although Carlos was not in the field with us, he checked in regularly via cell phone and email to help ensure that we were keeping our scheduled appointments and staying in regular contact with the leader of the Movimiento, Juanita Jiménez, whose story is reproduced in the first chapter.

Although the aim of this book is to have women's voices in Nicaragua contribute to a growing understanding of feminist liberatory knowledge, their voices are clearly being filtered through my own social location and my production and interpretation of the interviews (Collins, 1989; Riessman, 2005). Nevertheless, two distinct interests, that of the researcher to gather information and that of the activists to improve their capacities for political action, were able to meet temporarily to create an exchange that I hope holds the possibility to contribute to social change. I am forever indebted to these women for opening my perspective and understanding of commitment to social action and justice.

Notes

1. Following the suggestion of Aída Hurtado (1996), Color is capitalized because it is used in reference to specific ethnic groups (e.g., Chicanos, Asians, Blacks, etc.), whereas the reference white is often not used to refer to specific ethnic groups, but to many groups.

2. The GFP (http://www.umich.edu/~glblfem/) is a collaborative international project, housed at the University of Michigan, that conducts, examines, and archives interviews with women involved in feminist activism, social movements, and women's studies departments in various countries. Currently, the archive consists of interviews with women from China, India, Nicaragua, Poland, the United States, and now Brazil.

3. Abby Stewart provided consultation on the design and method that was used by most of the other researchers who had contributed to the archive. The GFP at the University of Michigan contributed $5,000 toward the data collection for this project, as well as transcription, translation, and uploading all of the completed interviews for open access through the website (http://umich.edu/~glblfem/).

4. Sofía Montenegro is widely considered one of the most prominent feminist activists in Nicaragua. She was a leader in the mobilization of the Movimiento Autónomo de Mujeres in the early 1990s and remains one of its key figures. Her *testimonio* is reproduced in Chapter 2.

Narrating a Psychology of Resistance

Introduction

TRANSNATIONAL FEMINIST LIBERATION PSYCHOLOGY AND FEMINISTS' STORIES OF SOCIAL JUSTICE IN THE *MOVIMIENTO AUTÓNOMO DE MUJERES* OF NICARAGUA

> *If our objective is to serve the liberation needs of the people of Latin America, this requires a new way of seeking knowledge, for the truth of the Latin American peoples is not in their present oppression but rather in the tomorrow of their liberty.*
>
> —IGNACIO MARTÍN-BARÓ, *LIBERATION PSYCHOLOGIST*, 1994

> *I always had this . . . calling for justice, for justice when it comes to inequalities, and to me gender inequality is the cruelest form in society because well even though there are institutions, even though there are laws, there is still that mentality well, I mean they don't accept women as equals. And well these are strong cultural barriers and you have to fight against it, using litigation, for example, or through political action.*
>
> —JUANITA JIMÉNEZ, *ELECTED REPRESENTATIVE OF THE* MOVIMIENTO AUTÓNOMO DE MUJERES, 2011

The *Movimiento Autónomo de Mujeres* (Women's Autonomous Movement) in Nicaragua emerged, like many other Latin American social movements in the 1970s and 1980s in the context of dictatorial regimes, as a marginalized and restricted movement (Alvarez, 1990; Shayne, 2004). It is now characterized as expansive and diverse, with feminist agendas being found in multiple sectors (e.g., civil society, legal, nongovernmental, agricultural). Although much has been written about social movements from a sociological perspective, this book examines the *psychology* of resistance and change by using the voices of the *compañeras*[1] to contribute to knowledge that will allow for a better understanding of liberatory action aimed at transforming societies in the fight for social justice. Investigating psychosocial processes behind resistance is critical to understanding a commitment to justice and the development of subjectivity that is necessary for enacting the political activity required for

1

social transformation. Psychology, in particular, is positioned to engage in a systematic exploration of the links between social and political conditions that determine how, why, and under what circumstances resistance emerges (Moane, 2003). This book documents voices within the women's Movimiento in Nicaragua—a coordinated mobilization of women that has weathered unremitting power differentials characterized by patriarchy and capitalism—to examine how psychological processes that emerge in response to sociopolitical oppression can lead to gendered justice.

During over a 40-year period in Nicaragua (1936–1979), the Somoza dictatorship had what was considered the most heavily U.S.-trained military establishment in Latin America and was internationally condemned for its human rights violations (Walker, 1985). In the 1970s, the Sandinista National Liberation Front (*Frente Sandinista de Liberación Nacional*; FSLN) mobilized in opposition to the dictatorship to improve the situation of people in a region marked by egregious social and economic inequalities. The Movimiento Autónomo de Mujeres was, in part, birthed out of the Sandinista Revolution when many women first asserted the need to engage in a struggle for social justice by joining efforts with the FSLN to overthrow an authoritarian capitalist model imposed by a dictator and an imperialist ruling class (Kampwirth, 2004). Women's participation in the Revolution to overthrow Somoza was lauded as more substantive than nearly any other revolution during the time. Women made up approximately 30% of the FSLN combat forces and were appointed to senior positions in the newly established ministries after the FSLN formally gained power in 1979 (Kampwirth, 1996; Molyneux, 1985).[2]

The FSLN mobilized many thousands of women in support of its struggle, in part because the levels of suffering and national corruption were so high that men and women from across all class backgrounds and ages were actively seeking opportunities in which to participate in opposition (Randall, 1994). The Association of Women Confronting the National Problem (*Asociación de Mujeres ante la Problemática Nacional*; AMPRONAC), although conceived by the mostly male leadership of the FSLN, was founded in 1977 as a women's organization that intended to combine a commitment to overthrow the Somoza regime with that of struggling for women's equality. At its peak, AMPRONAC had attracted over 8,000 members (Molyneux, 1985). Shortly after the fall of Somoza in 1979, AMPRONAC changed its name to AMNLAE (*Asociación de Mujeres Nicaragüenses Luisa Amanda Espinoza* or the Luisa Amanda Espinoza Association of Nicaraguan Women) to honor the first woman who died in the war against Somoza. Although women participated in the revolutionary struggle in unprecedented numbers, it was also true that the FSLN imposed a singular focus in defense of the Revolution that restricted women's organizing and demands to those that supported the aims of the socialist agenda and silenced women's concerns surrounding gender inequality and injustice (Jubb, 2014; Molyneux, 1985; Randall, 1994).

Women's attempts to advance an agenda sympathetic to feminist concerns were thwarted throughout the 1980s, when women's rights were largely marginalized by male leaders in favor of the national agenda, which at the time included weathering the Reagan-imposed trade embargo and the U.S.-backed Contra war (Kampwirth, 1996, 2004; Molyneux, 1985). Because the United States viewed the Sandinista agenda as a threat to its own economic interests, Reagan administered the Central Intelligence Agency (CIA) to recruit and support counterforces (i.e., the Contras) with over $20 million in aid, representing the CIA's most ambitious paramilitary action of the decade. Despite that women were involved in nearly all aspects of the war during the Revolution, male *compañeros* demonstrated neglect and often outright dismissal of matters of particular concern that were being raised by women—such as domestic and sexual violence and reproductive rights (Molyneux, 1985; Randall, 1994).

As such, many women came to understand gender oppression as profoundly cultural, crosscutting all public and private discourses and spaces—including those of the male-dominated Revolution, where women and their "issues" were too often consigned to the sidelines. Therefore, by the late 1980s a fledgling women's movement had begun to organize within Sandinista Nicaragua—driven by women whose experiences gave them an increased consciousness surrounding inequity, yet for whom the dominant ideology served to subjugate. As the hierarchical, patriarchal culture prevalent on the Left came to be identified as part of the problem, early feminists declared the need to invent new ways of doing politics. In particular, questioning the social roots of women's disadvantage led many women to consider a political separation from the FSLN to formulate their own agendas based on the rights of women.

A catalytic event in 1990 contributed to the transition toward political autonomy that many women were seeking. In the 1990 presidential election, the Sandinistas were voted out of office and replaced by the U.S.-backed candidate Violeta Chamorro, whose administration subsequently promoted neoliberal policies that worsened the already-existing threats to gender justice (Kampwirth, 1996). Although the new administration proved to create conditions that were even more limiting, several women seized the moment and made an official break from the Sandinista party by mobilizing a national meeting (the "We Are 52%" festival) to publicly denounce the violation of women's social and economic rights in Nicaragua. This initiative was followed by the first National Feminist Conference in 1992, with the title "Diverse But United," to declare the autonomy and political independence of women's organizations that were mobilizing after the election.

In mapping a model for an autonomous movement, feminist activists were revealing a strategic design whereby actors from different social locations could meet to enact politically effective means for transforming dominant power relations. At this crossroad, understanding and rejecting the social obstacles to actualizing women's rights appeared to form a key starting point for feminist groups to mobilize. At the same time, women's personal experiences of marginalization within the Revolution appeared to influence an inclusive strategy for collective mobilization that was reflected in cross-class and urban-rural alliances (Grabe & Dutt, 2015). By 1992, several women's organizations had mobilized into a network under the umbrella name Movimiento Autónomo de Mujeres to represent one of the largest, most diverse, and most autonomous feminist movements in Latin America (Kampwirth, 1996).[3]

To this day, as an organized coalition of women, individuals within the Movimiento Autónomo de Mujeres continue their struggle to transform institutional and political structures in their fight for gendered justice. Not surprisingly, across several disciplines, numerous forms of prior scholarship have already written about this social movement. For example, several authors, who have spent extensive time in Nicaragua, have contributed key texts that contain important levels of detail and analysis that examine how the Revolution in Nicaragua led to the rise of a feminist movement and why certain women became feminists as a result of their experience (Kampwirth, 1996, 2004; Randall, 1981, 1994). Other forms of scholarship have examined specific autonomous organizations that emerged after the Revolution (Mendez, 2005). These prior publications have been invaluable in documenting that women in Nicaragua are not mere victims, but rather have worked to resist oppression and fight injustice for decades. Yet, what remains missing from this contribution is scholarship aimed at understanding the *psychology* of resistance: In other words, what are the psychological mechanisms and methodologies that emerge from the margins that determine the kind of social action that leads to liberation and justice?

To date, processes of resistance that have fueled individuals committed to collective action aimed at social justice for women have received only limited attention from the discipline of psychology. This may be in part because much of mainstream Western feminist psychology has, with few exceptions, largely neglected the voices of marginalized women and women of Color in understanding feminist dynamics of resistance and oppression (see Cole & Stewart, 1996; Grabe, Dutt, & Dworkin, 2014; Hurtado, 1996; Lykes, Beristain, & Pérez-Armiñan, 2007; and White & Rastogi, 2009, for exceptions). In fact, recently it has been suggested that the liberatory potential of feminism within psychology has fallen short because of its grounding in (neo)colonial legacies of hegemonic[4] feminism (Kurtiş & Adams, 2015). For example, much of mainstream feminist work in psychology has developed theories and understandings of gender oppression in Western, educated, industrialized, rich, democratic (or WEIRD; see Henrich, Heine, & Norenzayan, 2010) contexts and imposed those perspectives across varied settings for understanding what has been conceptualized as "universal" gendered oppression (Kurtiş & Adams, 2015). Moreover, and not unrelated to the first point, mainstream feminist psychology has largely employed methodologies that involve sampling predominantly white undergraduate college students studying at U.S. universities.

These approaches to understanding gendered injustice are problematic not only because they develop understandings that might not be applicable across varied local contexts but also because they tend to treat women in "majority world"[5] settings as powerless (Kagitcibasi, 2002; Kurtiş & Adams, 2015). This book attempts to break through the strongholds of marginalization imposed by mainstream socialist agendas, neoliberal governments, and universalizing feminisms to elevate the voices of the compañeras in the Movimiento Autónomo de Mujeres in the production of feminist liberatory knowledge.

Much prior research in the academic disciplines that address women's injustice has taken and identifies a linear approach that identified discernable problems (e.g., violence, food insecurity) and empowering outcomes (e.g., newly administered laws, interventions). This book instead examines how the psychosocial *processes* involving resistance are critical to creating transformative change that is necessary for justice. In the case of the women activists in the Movimiento, a key question centers on the relation of their personal narratives to methodologies that lead individuals from positions of marginalization to greater subjectivity. In other words, how do citizen subjects—people who can and do use their social locations to create liberatory change—emerge (Sandoval, 2000)? To answer these questions, rather than focusing theory and analysis on the privileged few, the analysis of feminist activist stories from Nicaragua will employ a *transnational feminist liberation* psychology to understanding how individuals transform the societies in which they live (Grabe, in press). Because a major aim for this book is to understand how psychology can contribute to efforts toward social justice in a global context, within each chapter of the book feminist activists' lived experience in Nicaragua is treated as a legitimate source of knowledge. Concepts found in the theoretical framings of transnational feminism and liberation psychology, and which are used to interpret women's stories throughout the chapters in this book, are detailed next.

Transnational feminism: A framework for understanding marginalization. Although problems related to patriarchy have long concerned women and feminists throughout the world, transnational feminism, specifically, arose during the 1980s out of the interplay between global and local practices influenced by neoliberalism that were denying women's rights, permitting exploitation, and reproducing subjugation (Alexander & Mohanty, 1997; Naples & Desai, 2002). In response to violations that were becoming increasingly exacerbated in this context, the political mobilization and feminist activity that were emerging at that time reflected diverse modes of resistance, operating from different strategic spaces and subject positions within society (e.g., civil society, participation in social movements, academia) to address the range of women's growing concerns globally (Ferree & Tripp, 2006; Kabeer, 1994; Montenegro,

Capdevila, & Sarriera, 2012). The mobilization and collective identity behind transnational feminism, therefore, is not rooted in the notion that women have universal experiences; rather, it is rooted in a shared criticism of how neoliberal economic policies and governments create structural conditions that limit women's rights in their respective locations (Moghadam, 2005).

Pioneering scholars in transnational feminism have suggested that because a multiplicity of knowledge and practice emerges from local perspectives, there is and must be a diversity of feminisms—responsive to the varying needs and concerns of women throughout the world and defined by them for themselves (Alexander, 2005; Grewal & Kaplan, 1994; Mohanty, 2003a; Sen & Grown, 1987). In Nicaragua, there was an explosion of feminist analysis and consciousness raising surrounding gender after the 1990 electoral defeat of the Sandinistas (Randall, 1994). Feminists in Nicaragua came together in ways not yet seen before, in part because they were mobilizing not only outside the parameters of patriarchal society but also outside the parameters of a growing neoliberal context that reflected the extreme marginalization imposed by global capitalism (Randall, 1994). Understanding how the women's positioning in this context shapes and is shaped by their activist work can further inform theories of feminism and prescriptions for social change.

In U.S.-based literature, feminist scholars have drawn attention to how inequities and imbalanced power relations related to multiple aspects of one's social identity (e.g., race/ethnicity, social class, sexual orientation) can intersect to have an impact on women's well-being (e.g., Anzaldúa & Moraga, 1983; Collins, 1990; hooks, 1984; Hurtado, 1989). Critical race theorist Kimberle Crenshaw (1989) coined the term *intersectionality* to underscore how multiple aspects of one's identity can be experienced simultaneously in an additive manner in the experience of marginalization. Transnational and decolonial feminist scholars suggest that, in addition to other marginalizing factors such as race/ethnicity or sexual orientation, women's experience in the majority world is also inextricably linked to systemic inequities of global power (e.g., colonialism, globalization; Bose, 2012; Grabe et al., 2015; Lugones, 2010; Narayan, 1997; Sen & Grown, 1987).

The idea of intersectionality in this book therefore uses a *transnationally intersectional* approach to the study of gendered justice by taking into account the theoretical perspectives offered by women of Color and Third World feminisms,[6] which argue that gender oppression operates through unfavorable social systems such as global capitalism that exacerbate or maintain violations of women's human rights (Crenshaw, 1989; Grabe & Else-Quest, 2012; Lugones, 2010; Mahalingam, Balan, & Haritatos, 2008; Sen & Grown, 1987). For example, in Nicaragua, women's experience of gendered injustice has been influenced not only by the dominant political culture within Nicaragua but also by decades of U.S. military intervention and economic policies and practices that have consistently denied women's rights—all of which serve as powerful intersections between the local and global that have consistently led to the suppression of women's human rights. Taking a critical view of how marginalization in the context of globalization can inform our understandings of liberatory action requires that feminist psychologists expand their investigations to include women from the majority world who are confronting gendered injustices that are reproduced or exacerbated in local and global processes.

Liberation psychology. Although investigating structural patterns of inequality has long been the task of political and social theorists, liberation psychologist Martín-Baró (Martín-Baró, 1994) argued that psychologists, in particular, should reframe standard methods to consider that the root causes of oppression lie in the structures and ideologies that underlie inequity. According to liberation psychology, psychological analysis of oppression should involve a systematic exploration of the links between social and political conditions and psychological patterns, with explicit emphasis on taking action to improve those conditions (Moane, 1999, 2003). Among critical feminist scholars across disciplines, there has also been growing interest in the relationship between neoliberal transformations and an oppositional consciousness that develops among individuals in subordinated positions (Sandoval, 2000). Sandoval suggested that oppositional consciousness develops when those engaged from the grassroots are positioned to identify, develop, control, and marshal the knowledge necessary to create social change. Similarly, Mohanty (2003a) states that

> in the crafting of oppositional selves and identities, decolonization coupled with emancipatory collective practice leads to a rethinking of patriarchal, heterosexual, colonial, racial, and capitalist legacies in the project of feminism and, thus, toward envisioning democracy and democratic collective practice such that issues of sexual politics in governance are fundamental to thinking through questions of resistance anchored in the daily lives of women. (p. 8)

In writing about methodologies that can expose resistance to and rethinking of social structures, Sandoval (2000) proposed a "science of oppositional ideology" that would allow for the investigation of new "citizen subjects"—individuals who have developed an oppositional ideology and are engaged in resisting structures of social domination. The formation of citizen subjects is similar to processes of subjectivation introduced by Foucault (2005). Foucault argues that because "subjects" are typically constituted through the exercise of power or subjection, alternative forms of subjectivity allowing for the construction of the subject through practices of autonomy and freedom from authority are necessary (Milchman & Rosenberg, 2007). Because liberation psychology has become an increasingly utilized approach to understanding how individuals develop critical perspectives that become directed toward social change, the discipline of psychology has the potential to be the social "science" of oppositional ideology proposed by Sandoval that can investigate how alternative forms of subjectivity produce citizen subjects (Burton & Kagan, 2005; Martín-Baró , 1994; Moane, 2003, 2010). As the feminist narratives of resistance in the following chapters reveal, through various stages of action and reflection women involved in the Movimiento developed a subjectivity from an autonomous grassroots perspective that allowed them to challenge the structural and ideological conditions that limited the situations in which they lived their lives.

To systematically explore the links between intersecting structures of social domination and psychological resistance, several concepts from liberation psychology are used to analyze the women's stories in this book. Brazilian social theorist Paulo Freire's (1970) concept of *conscientización* refers to a process in which those working to create bottom-up social change participate in an iterative, ideological process whereby analysis and action develop together in a limited situation. In Freire's understanding of liberation, he argues that individuals are most likely to change their own circumstances by simultaneously working to challenge the social structures that disadvantage them (Brodsky et al., 2012; Moane, 2003). Among the first steps in this process is the development of critical understandings of how adverse social conditions undermine well-being (Prilleltensky, 2008). However, within community psychology, processes surrounding political consciousness and resistance have often been encompassed in the construct of empowerment (Zimmerman, 2000). Yet, early conceptualizations and investigations of empowerment within psychology focused primarily on individual factors, thereby giving limited attention to context and social structures (Perkins, 1995; Riger, 1993). Moreover, many empowerment interventions within community psychology typically have not been designed to transform inequitable social structures, but rather to help "victims" (Prilleltensky, 2008).

Similarly, a majority of international development interventions aimed at empowerment utilize a "rescue narrative" by intending to rectify injustices experienced due to "tradition" that women, in particular, are presumably unable to confront without outside help (Alexander, 2005; Cornwall, 2003). Furthermore, in recent decades, international agencies have co-opted and depoliticized the concept of empowerment that was once used by progressive social movements to facilitate a struggle for social justice and apply it instead to the context of broad-based neoliberal economic development strategies (Cornwall & Brock, 2005; Perkins, 1995).

Therefore, despite the intent to improve the social conditions in which people live their lives, empowerment approaches have been limited in demonstrating how those with less structural power take action within social contexts that maintain inequity. Thus, there is increasing reason to believe that focusing solely on empowerment may not offer the most comprehensive framework for evaluating struggles for social justice among some of the most marginalized populations of women (Brodsky et al., 2011).

Thus, there is an urgent need to move beyond empowerment to focus on a "psychology of resistance" that captures the ways in which women develop their subjectivity through critical awareness and challenge power-based structural constraints as they become citizen subjects acting collectively to resist and rethink structures of social domination (Lykes & Moane, 2009; Moane, 2003; Sandoval, 2000). Critical psychologists argue that it is through awareness and dialogue of "limited situations" that possibilities for change are explored that give rise to conditions of action (Moane, 2010). In this way, *resistance* to oppressive structures is not necessarily the end goal of political struggle or an outcome, but rather a beginning—an emergent behavior that moves toward justice and liberation. Decolonial theorist María Lugones defines resistance as the tension between "subjectification (the forming of the subject) and active subjectivity, that minimal sense of agency required, without appeal to the maximal sense of agency of the modern subject" (2010, p. 746). In the context of large systems of global inequality, a liberation psychology approach to resistance may be well suited as the science of oppositional ideology because it recognizes that "limit situations," or circumstances that constrain people's lives, are also places where possibilities begin (Martín-Baró , 1994; Montero, 2009; Sandoval, 2000).

Critical psychologist Maritza Montero (1994) suggests that the understandings that emerge in limit situations are used to *problematize* social conditions, in other words, to view conditions, rather than individuals, as problems that require solution. Problematizing social conditions results in *deideologizing*, or reconstructing understandings of lived experience based on rejecting dominant ideologies that justify social oppression (Montero, 1994, 2009). As the lived experiences of the women included in this book illustrate, each woman, in her own way, problematizes the social conditions surrounding inequity and rejects the dominant ideologies that serve to continue the subjugation of women. In addition, as they narrate in their stories, problematizing injustice also begins a process of conscious mobilization leading to transformations in understandings of certain phenomena (e.g., sexism; Montero, 2009).

The stories women tell in this book demonstrate how processes of problematizing and deideologizing led to mobilized actions taken among members of the Movimiento. Because concepts of conscientización, problematization, and deideologization are central to understanding how a psychology of resistance develops, they are used to analyze how women's oppositional ideology moves to committed action aimed at change. An overemphasis in traditional psychology, to date, on topics such as empowerment and agency, may have precluded an optimal understanding of how the social conditions in which people live their lives influence the actions taken to transform the social and psychological patterns associated with injustice. In contrast, a transnational feminist liberation psychology is well positioned to examine how citizen subjects develop methodologies to transform the social structures of domination.

Geraldine Moane was among the first scholars to articulate a feminist liberation psychology that takes into account the effects of both globalization and activism surrounding women's issues when linking women's well-being to structures of power (Moane, 1999). Although work in this area is in its nascent stages, Lykes and Moane broke the ground in 2009 by identifying researchers who were interfacing feminist psychology with the work of feminist social movements to focus on liberatory processes in their investigations in India, Guatemala, Pakistan, and Portugal (e.g., Chaudhry & Bertram, 2009; Crosby, 2009; De Oliveira, Neves, Nogueira, & Koning, 2009; Madrigal & Tejeda, 2009; White & Rastogi, 2009). Although a small, but growing, literature since that time has begun to apply this theorization to the development of women's liberation in the context of gendered inequity elsewhere (Brodsky et al., 2012; Dutt & Grabe, 2014; Grabe et al., 2014), the role of psychology in understanding how women's lived experience contributes to liberatory knowledge remains seriously underexplored. This book draws on the ideas of a transnational feminist liberation psychology to focus theory and analysis on marginalized women from the majority world to inform the production of liberatory psychology knowledge.

Praxis, epistemology, and method. Another key element of liberation psychology is that of praxis, or the juncture where theory and practice meet. Praxis was defined by Freire as "reflection and action upon the world in order to transform it" (1970, p. 33). The idea of praxis has been used to suggest that psychologists should be critical of working with professionals and experts in positions of power and work, instead, alongside the people (Martín-Baró, 1994; Prilleltensky, 2012; Prilleltensky & Prilleltensky, 2003). In *Activist Scholarship: Antiracism, Feminism, and Social Change,* Sudbury and Okazawa-Rey (2009) suggest that "the production of knowledge and pedagogical practices through active engagements with, and in the service of, progressive social movements" (p. 3) defines activist scholarship. Because an underlying goal of activist research is a reconfiguration of knowledge production that shifts power and control into the hands of the oppressed or marginalized (Fals Borda, 1988; Sandoval, 2000), the epistemological position taken in this book is that feminist activists in a majority world setting are a resource to rethink conventional scientific wisdom and illuminate concepts related to the broad project of liberation (Martín-Baró , 1994; Swarr & Nagar, 2012).

Feminist approaches to epistemology share in common that women's lived experiences are legitimate sources of knowledge and that feminist thinking and practice require eliminating the boundaries of division that privilege who can be a knower and what can be known (Hesse-Biber, 2007). Thus, the underlying goal of collaborative community-based research is to challenge the assumptions about knowledge production and raise questions about the purpose of research. Therefore, attention should be given to whose voices are privileged in the production of scholarship attempting to create a space for the expression of subjugated knowledge and in doing so transforming oppressive social structures (Fals Borda, 1988).

To identify the key leaders of the Movimiento whose stories would be included in this book, I relied on suggestions from the elected leader of the Movimiento, Juanita Jiménez, and Carlos Arenas, thus building a key sample of participants in the women's movement as identified by movement activists themselves. Although the data collection for this book was designed in accordance with Mohanty's (2003b) assertion that understanding women's struggles for justice must involve illuminating "Third World" women's engagement with resistance to oppressive regimes, my social location as a white, middle-class, highly educated, monolingual woman writing from the United States underscores unequal and complex relationships between me and the women included in this book. In particular, because the United States has a long history of economic exploitation and armed conflict in Nicaragua, my government is deeply implicated in many of the repressive stories told by women in the Movimiento. Recognizing and understanding how these power asymmetries may manifest in the research collaboration was key to this being a liberatory feminist project (Grewal & Kaplan, 1994 Mohanty, 2003a).

I attempted to engage the issues surrounding our differing social locations by directly confronting the ways in which power shapes the research process (Mendez & Wolf, 2007). As discussed in the Foreword of this book, my involvement in the Movimiento began with scholar-activist collaborations first established in 2005 that made transparent who the "authorities of knowledge" (i.e., the activists) were. At that time, the research collaboration was with a community-driven, rural feminist organization that was interested in using research toward an agenda aimed at social justice for women. Findings from this research were used by the organization to support and bolster their community involvements and by me to put forward models in psychology for understanding transformative change (see Grabe, 2010, 2012, for detailed discussions of the collaboration and findings). The meeting ground for me and activists in the current project was the mutual awareness that there was a demand for the dissemination of feminist liberatory knowledge in the context of the political subjugation of women's voices. All of the interviews were preceded by a conversation that involved disclosure of my prior research interests and involvement in Nicaragua as well as my political commitments and motivations for this project; each woman was given copies (in Spanish) of the research I had conducted in the past. The methods I have chosen to use in the projects I have worked on in Nicaragua have undoubtedly been influenced by my own interests and position as a researcher, but relevant to the inquiry in each project has been the notion of standpoint epistemology—or the idea that women's status as a subordinate group enhances the production of knowledge (Hesse-Biber, 2007).

During a field visit to Nicaragua in 2011, I conducted 15 interviews with female political activists who were considered key leaders in Nicaragua; 12 of them identified as members of the Movimiento Autónomo de Mujeres.[7] The method used for the interviews in this book centered on the use of *testimonios*, a form of oral history or life story that is an explicitly political narrative describing and resisting oppression (Chase, 2003; Latina Feminist Group, 2001). Testimonios have been widely used with Latin American activists involved in revolutionary movements (e.g., Menchú, 1984; Randall, 1981, 1994). The women I interviewed were former guerrilla commanders during the Revolution; occupied ministerial or congressional positions; or were heads of human rights counsels, journalists, grassroots organizers, academics, labor union organizers, Nobel Peace Prize nominees, and rural feminists. Nine of their *testimonios* are included in this book.[8] Although much prior scholarship on feminist activism has concentrated on the middle class (including prior work in Nicaragua; Randall, 1994), the women included in this book have diverse backgrounds that reflect the complex identities that result from globalization: Approximately a quarter of the sample were from poor backgrounds disenfranchised through years of U.S. economic exploitation and dictatorship; approximately two thirds of the sample came from Sandinista-sympathetic households; one woman was from the autonomous Atlantic Coast; and others came from households with at least one parent being a Somoza supporter. This sample is reflective of the Movimiento's Diverse But United strategy and demonstrates how democracy has thrived within the Movimiento. In addition, to gain a fuller understanding of processes related to gendered justice in Nicaragua, I visited 15 organizations[9] that were either involved in the Movimiento or conducted work related to women's human rights.

To facilitate rapport and ease, the interviews were scheduled in a location of each woman's choosing. Sometimes this was her home; sometimes it was her office. Before beginning the interviews, each woman received an explanation of how her story might be used and disseminated (i.e., through the Global Feminisms Project [GFP], journal manuscripts, and this book), and each was given a list of the other interviewees in order to indicate the identity of other participants. All of the women agreed enthusiastically to participate in the project and have their stories reproduced.

Because the interviews employed the style of oral history, I began all of the interviews with questions related to the women's childhood and early family life. These initial background questions were followed by questions such as, "What was your first political experience?" By the end of the interviews, the focus shifted from personal experiences to a more analytical discussion of the women's movement in general or the current focus of work within their organization in particular. This style follows, nearly identically, the format used by the other researchers in the GFP and those used by other feminist scholars who previously interviewed feminist activists in Nicaragua (i.e., Kampwirth, 2004;

Randall, 1994). In addition, so Western assumptions about feminist identity were not made, and because women in the majority world often have to contend with the accusation that feminism is a foreign import, I directly asked the women whether they identified as feminists, and what that meant to them, so that each could define it for herself. Because these questions guided topics and thereby contributed to a co-construction of knowledge, they are reproduced in italicized font throughout each interview in the following chapters of this book (Lykes, 1997; Riessman, 2005). The interviews, which occurred through simultaneous translation, lasted approximately an hour and were audio and video recorded.

Although narratives represent storied ways of knowing, they require interpretation when used as data in social science research (Riessman, 2005). I initially struggled with this method and how to analyze the material. For example, I questioned whether it would be better to maintain the transcribed *testimonios* in their entirety or to select sections or quotations to analyze. Because this was a new methodology for me, I read a lot about qualitative feminist research and had, what were at times vociferous, debates with colleagues regarding which was the "better" approach. It became clear that for researchers who collect narratives through intensive interviews, a central question is how to listen to and treat the interviewee as a narrator, both during the interviews and while interpreting them (Chase, 2003).

Implicit in any discussion of how the researcher treats the narrator's voice is the role of the researcher's voice. One interpretive option for authors is to develop what some scholars call an "authoritative" voice in writing by presenting excerpts or summaries of interviews with the researcher separating his or her voice from narrators' voices on the grounds that the researcher has a different point to make than the narrators (Chase, 2003). At the other end of the continuum, some researchers attempt to push the narrator's voice into the limelight. This approach is more characteristic of how Latin American *testimonios* are treated and what I chose to do in this book. Several scholars have written about the importance of testimonio as a crucial means of bearing witness and inscribing into history those lived realities that would otherwise not be documented (the Latina Feminist Group, 2001). Moreover, using *testimonios* in this way is also critical for breaking down essentialist categories because it is through the telling of life stories that majority world women can narrate a more nuanced understanding of the intersectional processes linking sociopolitical events to the psychology of resistance (the Latina Feminist Group, 2001). As such, I chose to maintain the *testimonios* as stories, reproducing nearly two thirds of the original length in the text. The transcripts, in their entirety, can be downloaded in English and Spanish, and the filmed *testimonios* can be viewed at the GFP website.[10]

Although the reproduction of the *testimonios* included in the chapters in this book attempts to privilege an activist standpoint (Maddison & Shaw,

2007), it is also the case that what I have chosen to concentrate on within each testimonio has been filtered by my own social location that involves the power and privilege afforded to a white woman working from a university in the United States. In addition to editing the length of the *testimonios* by approximately a third, another barrier to the full expression of participants' voices in this project was the necessity for translation. Although cultural interpreters and translators are frequently essential players in community-based research processes (Lykes & Coquillon, 2006), the women were interviewed through the assistance of a translator. The interview responses were transcribed in Spanish. The Spanish transcriptions were translated into English by a research assistant for the GFP through the Institute for Research on Women and Gender at the University of Michigan.

Summary and organization of the book

The method in this book is different from other academic work because it shows the immediacy of people's lives with an intensity that academic word can seldom accomplish. The women's *testimonios* demonstrate the particular ways in which inequalities manifest, but more so document the important connection of these inequalities with the creation of political subjects and agents who seek change but do so within the constraints of powerful economic, political, and social relations that operate on local and global levels. Although the analysis that accompanies each interview provides a depth and context that is often impossible to obtain with quantitative data, the text of the interview allows audiences to witness dialogue in a unique way.

The book is organized into three sections mapping to major areas of focus through which members of the Movimiento have mobilized to enact change: democratic participation; legislation and human rights; and agricultural organizing. Within the sections, each chapter contains a reproduction of one woman's testimonio, is titled to reflect the relevant theme her story helps illustrate, and includes an analysis rooted in concepts taken from transnational feminist liberation psychology (i.e., conscientización, resistance, oppositional ideology, problematization, deideologization) to further develop our understanding of the "psychology of resistance." Although it is not my intent to reduce each woman's life to a single theme, a depth of focus into each woman's story allows us to see more clearly how the abstract constructs of theory operate in women's lives and become enacted in social change within each sector. Although each of the interviews used in the current book can stand alone to reflect unique psychosocial experiences, these interviews are also ultimately framed by common political experiences that reflect how intersecting political agendas help contribute to theorizing about feminist liberation. In the pursuit of producing knowledge aimed at creating social justice, women's own voices have the potential to document how women are enacting justice on the ground, rather than abstractly defining it in scholarship.

This book details the way in which a psychology of resistance—enacted by women in a social movement that was first contained through a social-ist revolution and later confronted a neoliberal power structure that has consistently denied women's rights—has fueled efforts aimed at justice and political transformation. Given the global dominance of neoliberalism, con-structing liberatory knowledge from activists within a vibrant, coordinated, and feminist movement that has survived the presence of neoliberal politics has the potential to map a model of oppositional consciousness and activity that has the potential to transform societies. Although the women's *testimonios* included in this book are inevitably embedded in the Nicaraguan context, as well as located in a particular point in time,[11] they offer insights that transcend the particular site and are of relevance to activists and scholars interested in liberatory projects elsewhere.

In the effort to create knowledge that challenges rather than supports hegemonic practices, we must constantly be attentive to histories, experi-ences, and perspectives that are unnoticed, unfamiliar, too easily neglected or misrepresented. The women's voices in this book bring to the foreground the necessity to define human action as the construction of possibilities within boundaries or limited situations. This book is interested in women as social actors in their own right and in the subjective meanings that women assign to events and conditions in their lives in an effort to break the strongholds of silence and, instead, create space for majority world women's experience and perspectives to be privileged in the construction of a counter narrative that more accurately reflects a just world.

Notes

1. In many Spanish-speaking countries, the word *compañero* is used to reflect politi-cal solidarity with someone who is a partner, colleague, or classmate. In Nicaragua, it is often used to refer to those united in struggle. *Compañera* is the feminine form of *compañero*.

2. A timeline of significant events relevant to the social context, and which are refer-enced in many of the women's stories, is provided in the Appendix.

3. Through the mid-2000s, the organization *Red de Mujeres Contra la Violencia* (RMCV; Women's Network Against Violence) served as the organizational space for the Movimiento, mobilizing a membership of 150 women's organizations throughout the country. In 2006, after years of debate and analysis regarding the hostile political setting that feminist activists continued to confront, activists within the autonomous movement founded an official organization with the title of the movement that would allow the move-ment a "public face" and would be dedicated to opening up political institutions to the participation and rights of women. The term *Movimiento Autónomo de Mujeres* was trans-formed into the official name of one organization reflecting the movement on International

Women's Day, March 8, 2006. As such, the movement now exists as both a social movement *and* an organization.

4. The term *hegemonic* is used following the suggestion of Kurtiş and Adams to refer to dominant forms of global feminist discourse that originate in Western settings and become applied universally in diverse local contexts.

5. Given that the commonly used terms *developing* and *Third World* are often used by so-called First World nations to describe the relatively low economic well-being of another country in a manner that implies inferiority, the term *majority world*, borrowed from Kagitcibasi (2002) and Kurtiş and Adams (2015) is used in this book because individuals from developing countries constitute the majority of the world's population.

6. Despite the earlier cautioned use of the term *Third World*, women writing from the perspective of the majority world or Global South often position themselves as "Third World feminists" to highlight the need for postcolonial and transnational analyses of women's lives in a manner that reclaims use of the term *Third World* (Mohanty, 1984).

7. Mónica Baltodano, Vilma Núñez, and Dora María Téllez were the three leaders who did not identify as members of the Movimiento, but for whom transcripts and filmed interviews are available at the Global Feminisms Project. They were each treated as key informants for the book. Baltodano, born in 1954, was one of three women to hold the title *guerilla commander* during the war. She was imprisoned for nearly a year during the war and after was appointed as vice minister of regional affairs, a councilor of Managua, and served as a deputy in the National Assembly from 1997 to 2002 and from 2007 to 2012. Núñez, born in 1938, was a member of the FSLN and participated in the anti-Somoza struggle until she was imprisoned for these efforts in 1979. After the Revolution, she served as the first woman on Nicaragua's Supreme Court. Núñez founded the Nicaraguan Center for Human Rights in 1990 but was unofficially banished from the FSLN after running for president against Daniel Ortega and defending Zoilamérica Narvaez's charges of sexual abuse. Téllez, born in 1955, is a historian and well-known icon of the Sandinista Revolution. In 1978, at age 22, Téllez was third in command during the Sandinista takeover of the National Palace. After the Revolution, her posts included vice president of the Council of State, political chief of Managua, and minister of health. After leaving the FSLN, she founded the Sandinista Renovation Movement in 1995. In 2004, she was appointed as a Robert F. Kennedy Visiting Professor in Latin American studies at the Harvard Divinity School. However, she was unable to obtain an entry visa to the United States because the PATRIOT Act classified her as a terrorist due to her involvement in the Revolution.

8. Due in part to space limitations and saturation among the other interviews, *testimonios* from three women who represented important organizations within the Movimiento, Eva Molina of the *Colectivo de Mujeres de Matagalpa*; Luz Marina Torres, of the *Casa de La Mujer in Managua*; and Soccorro Chavez, of the *Xochilt Acalt Women's Center* were used to inform the larger context but were not included in the book.

9. The 15 organizations were CENIDH (Centro Nicaragüense de Derechos Humanos, Center for Nicaraguan Human Rights), CINCO (*Centro de Investigación de la Comunicación,* Center for Communication Research), *Colectivo de Mujeres Itza, Colectivo de Mujeres La Corriente,* Colectivo de Mujeres de Matagalpa, *Colectivo de Mujeres 8 de Marzo, Federación de Mujeres Productoras del Campo,* FIDEG (La Fundación Internacional para el Desafío Económico Global International Foundation for Global Economic Development), *Fundación Popol Na, Grupo Venancia, La FEM,*

Movimiento Autónomo de Mujeres, *Movimiento Maria Elena Cuadra*, Red de Mujeres Contra la Violencia, and Xochilt Acalt.

10. Complete transcripts in English and Spanish for all of the women included in this book can be read, along with interviews with women from Brazil, China, India, Poland, and the United States, online (http://www.umich.edu/~glblfem/). The GFP project was designed with scholarly goals at its core; therefore, with permission from the GFP, the interviews are available for future research and teaching across disciplines.

11. As with any context, there have been changes within the Movimiento between the time the *testimonios* were conducted and the publication of this book. Most notably, Matilde Lindo, whose testimonio is included in Chapter 4, passed away unexpectedly from a heart attack on January 20, 2013. Her contribution to the Movimiento is deeply missed.

SECTION ONE

Citizen Democracy and Knowledge

LEVELING THE PLAYING FIELD BY CREATING PARTICIPATORY SPACES

Sociologists have written that globalization—or the restructuring of the global economy since the 1980s and 1990s—differs from that of the past because it now involves ordinary citizens and social movements vying for power, not merely governments and elites (Ferree, 2006). Moreover, as citizens challenge their national governments for democratic participation, they are often doing so at the intersection of the global and local by reflecting democratic forms of responding to the top-down challenges posed by a world economy. Social movement theorizing has also given rise to the concept of the "political opportunity structure," which pertains to the political structures in which grievances emerge and collective action is possible (Moghadam, 2005). At the transnational level, the political opportunity structure can vary substantially from that provided at the local level alone (Ferree, 2006).

Although women's engagements in and use of these structures have been understood politically, they have yet to be understood *psychologically*. Psychologists maintain that inequities that lead to marginalization are not only a political issue, but also always psychological and pivotal in attaining progress (Prilleltensky, 2008). The following section is aimed at understanding how the psychology of resistance led some women within the *Movimiento Autónomo de Mujeres* to create strategic structural changes that would allow for women's citizen democracy—in other words, the political participation of ordinary citizens in their society.

Nicaraguan women's mobilized resistance began at first in the effort to fight for social justice during the Sandinista Revolution. However, the class-based approach of the male-dominated *Frente Sandinista de Liberación Nacional* (FSLN; Sandinista National Liberation Front) to winning the Revolution denied women's strategic gender interests at the same time that it brought them together (Molyneux, 1985). On emerging from the Sandinista period of the 1980s, some feminists proposed to break with the dominant ideology of the FSLN by creating a movement that would make space for feminist organizations that were politically autonomous but were united in their struggle for the promotion of women's political participation. The incentive for strategically creating this space resulted from problematizing how male domination during the Revolution created conditions that subjugated women. The continued success of this space would rest on deideologizing dominant styles of leadership by rejecting authoritarianism and instead prioritizing collective action and decision-making within the women's movement (Lacombe, 2014). This generation of women officially broke with the revolutionary party in two foundational events that marked the beginning of the Movimiento Autónomo de Mujeres: the We Are 52% Festival, which took place in 1991, and the Diverse But United meeting held in 1992. The 52% festival reflected a conscious production of resistance by establishing that the female majority was generating activities of a new citizen subject that was politically autonomous from both the ruling and revolutionary parties.

The collective action generated by this Movimiento was marked by multiple debates regarding the type of organizational model the movement was to use to facilitate greater citizen democracy among women. At the outset, they established a reticular, horizontal model considered to be participatory and mobilized around the discourse of women's human rights (Lacombe, 2014). Networks were set up intending to break the dominant structure of hierarchy that had been employed by FSLN-affiliated organizations and with the purpose of sharing experiences and resources (Lira & Martinez, 2009). In mapping a model for an autonomous movement, feminist activists were committed to a strategic design whereby differing oppositional ideologies could meet to reflect politically effective means for transforming dominant power relations. For example, women mobilized in a manner that privileged democratic participation by holding meetings and initiatives aimed at diversifying women's participation and recognizing that women's different social locations (e.g., social classes; rural vs. urban) would bring different demands and a different strategic effort and therefore heavily emphasized collective processes.

One of the major networks within the Movimiento, the Network of Women Against Violence (*Red de Mujeres Contra la Violencia*), provided the strategic space to advance and diversify women's citizen democracy. The Network emerged in the 1990s as an umbrella organization for the broader women's movement by becoming an activist space that mobilized a membership of 150 women's organizations throughout the country and received national and international media attention for involvement in two cases in particular.

In one case, several of the Network's members supported Zoilamérica Narváez, Daniel Ortega's adoptive daughter, when she reported having experienced sexual abuse and harassment at his hands for a period of nearly 20 years.[1] In another case, many members of the Network were involved in the defense of "Rosita," a 9-year-old girl impregnated as the result of child-hood sexual abuse who received a then-legal abortion in 2003. Members of the Network supported Rosita in order to promote the cause of therapeu-tic abortion, which was subsequently criminalized in Nicaragua in 2006. In 2007, a church-backed nongovernmental organization associated with Daniel Ortega prosecuted nine of the women involved in the Rosita case, charging them with a criminal offense of aiding and abetting abortion.[2] Two of the members of the Network who were involved in this case are included in this section of the book (Juanita Jiménez and Yamileth Mejía). Their case was supported by Amnesty International in the United States until charges were eventually dropped. These examples of engaged citizen democracy (i.e., the political participation of ordinary citizens) on behalf of the defense of women's rights brought the Network into the limelight as one of the most visible and engaged organizations that was advocating for women's full and equal participation in political contexts that were directly relevant to the rights of women.

The process of autonomy and emphasis on democracy that drove the efforts within the Movimiento, even in the face of opposition, represent forms of resistance to dominant power structures. Writing in the Central American publication *Envío* in 2002, Sofía Montenegro (whose *testimonio* is included in this section of the book) explained the following:

> The women's movement is a social movement because it proposes to transform culture and the political system, and demands the inclusion of half the nation. We women demand democracy as well as development, because there can be no development without democracy, no equity in a sea of authoritarianism. The fight to include women is thus a fight for democracy as a precondition of development. We are demanding a kind of development that includes the majority and takes into account the par-ticular conditions by which women have been excluded. This requires the creation of mechanisms and arenas for democratic debate.

In 2003, women from different spaces within the Movimiento met to discuss the increasingly hostile political setting that feminist activists were confronting and to brainstorm how to strengthen their solidarity (Lacombe, 2014). As a result of these discussions, activists within the broader move-ment decided to found an official organization with the title of the movement that would be dedicated to opening up political institutions to the participa-tion and rights of women. Securing the legitimacy of this organization was inspired, in part, to protect spaces that could continue to "level the playing field" by providing opportunities for women's citizen participation. Although the Movimiento Autónomo de Mujeres had previously been used to refer to the diverse membership of individuals and organizations that constituted a social movement, the Movimiento Autónomo de Mujeres was adopted as the official name of an organization representing the broader movement on International Women's Day, March 8, 2006.

Although this move was intended to strengthen women's struggle for democracy, their efforts have continued to be met with unremitting obstacles and abuses of power. For example, in addition to the criminal charges brought against women in the Network in 2007, investigations were also undertaken into the financing of the organizations that some of the same women who were subjected to the criminal inquiry in the Rosita case were involved. In October 2008, Nicaraguan authorities raided the offices of the Center for Communication Research (CINCO) and the Movimiento Autónomo de Mujeres, confiscating files and computers containing financial records with the intent of shutting down both organizations (the *testimonios* from the leaders of these two organizations are included in this section of the book). Once again, no criminal activity was discovered, but the repression being issued by the Ortega administration was clearly meant to limit the political opportunity structures that feminist activists were attempting to create.

Certainly under conditions of extreme oppression, high levels of solidarity among the marginalized are often witnessed. Yet, at the same time, women's interests as equal participants in democracy will be expressed differently based on their various social locations. Understanding these various locations, and the psychological mechanisms that emerge from them, is imperative for understanding how true liberatory change becomes enacted. According to critical psychologist Maritza Montero, "Politics should be understood as the possibility and impossibility for . . . actions and knowledge to be known and implemented so as to affect the distribution of power and domination" (2009, p. 150). Montero explained that a *polis* (meaning "city" in Greek) is described as a space where people gather, organized according to the norms they create to facilitate living in a collective realm. Therefore, the possibility of overcoming structural inequity inherently involves participating in these spaces by playing an active role in controlling resources and decisions in one's community (Zimmerman & Rappaport, 1988).

In the following section, issues related to citizen democracy are defined by four women working from different social locations but sharing a common goal that the structural inequities prohibiting free and equal access to knowledge and education need to give way to spaces that will allow for women's full participation in society. In other words, the *testimonios* in this section all problematize the social conditions surrounding access to knowledge and opportunity and view them as limit situations that require solutions. Although the psychosocial processes related to liberation are inherently interconnected (e.g., *conscientización*, resistance, problematization, deideologization), this section focuses slightly more on problematization, in particular, to allow for an in-depth focus on how viewing social conditions as problematic can lead to the creation of democratic spaces for women.

Notes

1. Ojito, M. (1998). *Conversations/Zoilamerica Narvaez; a victim of sexual abuse in a prison of political ideals.* *New York Times*, March 29. Retrieved from http://www.nytimes.com/1998/03/29/weekinreview/conversations-zoilamerica-narvaez-victim-sexual-abuse-prison-political-ideals.html

2. All nine women were well-known human rights defenders and worked with a variety of nongovernmental organizations. They had extensive combined experience in the promotion of sexual health issues and women's rights. Three of them have testimonios included in this book: Juanita Jiménez, Violeta Delgado, and Yamileth Mejía.

Juanita Jiménez

1

Problematizing the Struggle for Freedom Through Contradiction

Freedom should be wide enough so that every person can decide
what to participate in and what to build towards or construct.
—*TESTIMONIO* FROM JUANITA JIMÉNEZ

When the *Movimiento Autónomo de Mujeres* registered its organization with a "public" face in 2006, Juanita Jiménez was elected as its leader. Jiménez is a lawyer and longtime activist who has focused primarily on women's human rights. In the 1990s, she played a critical role at the Network of Women Against Violence (*Red de Mujeres Contra la Violencia*, the organization that served as an umbrella space for the Movimiento, as a movement, prior to its founding as an organization itself in 2006) by reforming and advocating national laws related to women's human rights. She was particularly active in protesting the 2006 law that outlawed all forms of abortion in Nicaragua and was outspoken in protesting the application of this law in a pregnancy that threatened the life of a 9-year-old girl. Jiménez was subject to persecution by the Ortega administration for her defense of women's rights in this case, which led Amnesty International to promote a campaign on her behalf. In recent years, she has turned her focus toward citizen democracy and the ability of women to participate in public decision-making regarding their human rights. In 2011, she was among 100 women leaders honored by the U.S. government in celebration of the 100-year anniversary of International Women's Day.

Jiménez was born in 1967 in Masaya, Nicaragua, about 35 miles from the capital city of Managua. She began her political career as a youth focused on economic inequality when she was active in clandestine opposition and the radical student movements of the 1980s (as were many other women interviewed for this book). After finishing high school, Jiménez joined the *Frente Sandinista de Liberación Nacional* (FSLN; Sandinista National Liberation Front) army and received a scholarship to study law. She was assigned to military tribunals and served in the military courts as a lawyer between 1987 and 1992. Jiménez, as with many youth in revolutionary Nicaragua, is from a family whose parents were mixed supporters of the Revolution—her father was a

Somoza sympathizer and her mother supportive of the Sandinistas. Jiménez highlights the contradictions in her upbringing at the outset of her testimonio and quickly draws parallels to the contradictions within the country. These contradictions would prove, over the course of her lifetime, to create both opportunity *and* obstacles to Jiménez's ongoing struggle for women's democratic participation.

It is through experiencing these contradictions that Jiménez began to problematize the struggle for freedom to participate in society. Over time, she developed an oppositional ideology that widely extends notions of freedom so that the marginalized may benefit from their social and political rights. The iterative process by which she makes meaning of her position and develops action in response to her awareness underscores how focusing only on empowerment outcomes would fail to accurately capture how women engage structurally embedded injustice to participate in the transformation of society. The following testimonio by Juanita Jiménez characterizes how women who were reacting to a patriarchal regime embedded in a system of global capitalism fashioned a distinct feminist platform that valued radical democratic practices and organized autonomy:

> *Juanita, tell me some things about your early years, your childhood, what kind of family you grew up in, some things that you remember from when you were young.*

I'm Juanita Jiménez. I was born in the city of Masaya, which is a city about 35 kilometers from Nicaragua's capital, in a humble *barrio*[1] that is called Países Bajos[2] and it's kind of between the indigenous barrio of Monimbó and the rest of the city of Masaya. In my childhood, well I kind of have dual origins. On my maternal side, it's a very humble family, artisans in Masaya. My grandmother is indigenous; she is from the original settlers of the area of Monimbó. And on my paternal side, my father was a man from the city's oligarchy. . . . On my father's side, it's a—we'll say a family with more economic resources.

And I think that what impacted me most from childhood was inequality, being able to see and, well, live with two realities. With the reality of my maternal family, very humble people with lots of limitations and the reality of my paternal family, with a lot of money, with a lot of land, with a lot of resources, with abundance. And this was a contradiction in my own life from a very young age. I think this would be a very important impact in my life. Since I was a girl, my mom handled my care and upbringing, and this made me feel a part of that poor barrio and I was able to interact with that community. . . . Although my studies, because I was the daughter of this man, they wanted to guarantee that I study in the private school there in Masaya and this connected me to families with more money.

So then this is me. Well, a life of contradictions from a young age in a city, characterized by being very dynamic, a city of artisans, with half the population conserving the culture of the ancestral communities, and this combination made me not disassociate myself from this reality in Nicaragua and of my country. You know, it's a country full of contradictions.

I was born in 1967. As a young girl I still have memories of the Somoza dictatorship, and I lived through the revolutionary process of the insurrection of the Monimbó barrio in Masaya, to see the struggle of the least-protected communities and of the people yearning for freedom and also looking for equality for citizens. And in this context I lived through this whole revolutionary struggle in which members of my mother's family participated. I also saw what the inequality of Somoza entailed because my father's family was supportive of Somoza. They were forced to flee the country. And in that sense my family was divided. One part was expelled from the country for being people that yielded to the Somoza project. And my mother's family that were Revolutionaries, people that fought in the insurrection and that established themselves as leaders in the process of the Revolution.

I was 12 years old during the anti-Somoza fight and the triumph of the Sandinista Revolution. In my childhood, because of my identity with my mother's family, I gave up being in a private school and decided to go to a public school. For secondary school, I went to a public institute, and there I started a process for student leaders and through this youth group I participated in the revolutionary process of the eighties. I have a history of leadership starting with the student groups, in the Sandinista Youth.[3] After graduating as a lawyer, I worked in the courts at the end of the '80s, in the military courts. I lived through the war in the context of the Revolution, the counterrevolution.[4] This context and the contradictions that it invoked, and it gave me a perspective on life, on justice, on what people aspire to, and that many times these projects aren't able to culminate in the improvement for the majority.

Juanita, can I ask you to back up and tell me a little about your experience when you were participating in the Sandinista activity?

I was 12 years old in '79 when the Revolution triumphed. So I was ready for secondary school—for high school. So from a very young age, I was at the front of the groups that the student movements organized to increase production. I led the youth battalions in my region, in Masaya, in what was the fourth region to go harvest cotton. The region also had coffee plantations, and there was also a deficit of labor to harvest the coffee. In that context, the students took it upon themselves to do the harvesting.

Because of my age they didn't take me as a literacy tutor.[5] This is something that really made me suffer because I wanted to participate and to teach people to read, but I was just coming out of primary school so I wasn't the right age to be able to go teach literacy. So since I couldn't be involved in the literacy campaign of the '80s, I became an assistant to the literacy teacher in my barrio. I also received military training. Women also had to learn to use the weapons and I went when I was really young. I was mobilized in war zones, you know, picking coffee. This was a very difficult experience because it meant living very close to the war and what that implies. I had to say goodbye to some very young friends of mine who went to war in that context. Some went voluntarily, but later when the war heightened, others were forced to go; and all those contradictions—they all impacted my life, too, developing in me a sense of justice in my life because I don't think anybody can be forced to do what they don't want to do. I mean freedom should be wide enough so that every person can decide what to participate in and what to build towards or construct or in what things not to participate.

In what kind of activities did you start to get involved in in the early nineties?

In '90, particularly because of the birth of my daughter, I was still officially in the army's structure because I was part of the military courts. It wasn't until '92 when I officially left the military structure and began to work independently as a lawyer.

My husband was named judge of a city in Nicaragua that is in the center of Boaco. The IXCHEN Women's Center[6] was there, which is a women's organization that came out of the structure of the Luisa Amanda Espinoza Women's Movement, and they were looking for a lawyer to help women victims of violence or cases related to violence. I accepted that job. In some way I had to help people.

In the military courts I had already had experience for how the different ways in which the judicial system treats women, so I was more or less aware of the inequality within the scope of justice. Arriving to IXCHEN was like an opportunity to work to improve the injustices. I was representing cases of violence, of sexual abuse, cases of alimony, but also some cases of social injustices that existed in that town. For example, there are many ranchers or farmers, and many people are stripped of their land in unjust ways. Because they didn't have access to a loan, they would borrow from someone and then they ended up having their land taken away. Women were victims of this as well. I became interested in this other type of injustice and I was winning civil cases, penal cases, and this made me well known as a lawyer in that city, one that worked not only for the poor, but for women. I think that was my first encounter with feminism because it was through this organization that I participated in educative and reflective processes and studies of feminism.

And later they offered me a position in Managua. In Managua I had the opportunity to participate more directly in the process of creating the Network of Women Against Violence. I had the luck of participating in the process of starting to organize with police authorities.

And what year was that that you started to organize the Commiserates?

The stations were founded in '93; the first station was created in Managua's Fifth District. I think that was where I became involved in the feminist movement and also deepening my theoretical understanding of feminism. But in daily practice I think I always had this vocation or calling for justice, for justice when it comes to inequalities, and to me gender inequality is the cruelest form in society because, well, even though there are institutions, even though there are laws, there is still that mentality, well, I mean they don't accept women as equals. And well these are strong cultural barriers and you have to fight against it, using litigation, for example, or through political action.

So I worked as a lawyer with IXCHEN for almost 15 years in Managua, directly taking cases. I can credit on my resume that I was the first person to win a case for psychological damage. They had reformed the law and psychological harm had been included,[7] so I said well, yes, there's a law and it has to be upheld. Being in IXCHEN I was elected by the Network's assembly to be one of the delegates on the National Commission for the Fight Against Violence. I participated because of my technical knowledge of the processes to create awareness among the justice officials, and this pushed me to work on a series of training processes with the judges, prosecutors, police officers.

In the Network I was in the position of executive at the beginning and later I ended up in the coordinating commission of the Network, so my involvement in the process of political participation and the processes of reforming the laws has come from me taking this position.

Juanita, did you ever experience any threats or consequences for positions you took on certain issues or cases?

I have been subjected to two investigations with the intent of criminalizing me. I'm part of the list of nine feminists that were accused for illicit association to commit a criminal offense and aiding and abetting the crime of abortion. It was a very difficult experience because I think that Nicaragua's feminist movement, the women in general in Nicaragua have been very strong. We've had our strengths and our fights and our battles. But it's not the same when you are leading a struggle as when you are defending yourself because of this struggle. For me personally, it was hard because it didn't only put us at risk of losing our individual freedom and the possibility of being imprisoned. That's hard. I mean you are in search of justice and soon you feel like the mechanism for justice is being used against you. This puts into question the whole process that, well in a country that supposedly should be democratic, where the authorities respect the laws. It also has a negative effect on the society; it exacerbates machismo because if—let's say an authority, or the powers of the justice system don't respect rights and run over women who defend rights, then an aggressor in his house feels he has the liberty to attack because the law won't do anything. So for me, to be in this context, that political persecution, I mean more than the individual risk, it also puts Nicaraguan women at risk.

It's absurd because you are struggling to defend women's lives. Taking away therapeutic abortion means that you now are denied the possibility of terminating a pregnancy to save your life. The law went backwards and criminalized it.[8] To accuse us for trying to re-establish this right or this section of the law, so that women can save their lives—they want to criminalize you for this. It's really hard. It's very negative for the society. It takes us back many years on the advances that, as a movement, we have accomplished.

For people outside of Nicaragua that aren't familiar with the abortion case in which you were charged, can you tell us what some of the criminal charges were against you personally?

Nicaragua's Penal Code had established a section, 169 years ago, that has been called therapeutic abortion—it's the termination of a pregnancy when the life of the woman is at risk. This practice had a lot of support coming from conservative government.

Nicaragua entered into a process of modernizing the Penal Codes, supposedly with the idea of making them more humanistic, with more guarantees, and in this process of debate—they began to discuss the complete criminalization of abortion. The arguments have never really been about legality; rather they were more religious and guided in particular by leaders of the Catholic Church. Nicaragua is a secular state; it's not constitutionally ascribed to any official religion and governed by the rule of law. This means that rights and the law prevail above any religious dogma.

Nonetheless, in 2006, with the framework of this debate about the new Penal Code, the party that is currently in the government[9] began to negotiate with leaders of the Catholic Church and facilitated an immediate reform to the current code and eliminated the exception of therapeutic abortion from the code. The Nicaraguan feminist movement began to fight to keep the elimination from happening because we are talking about fundamental rights. This required a lot of political mobilization from the movement, and all of the Nicaraguan feminists and other social sections like the medical societies and human rights organizations have been involved.

In 2007, with the current government's arrival to power, nine of us feminists were criminally accused of illicit association to commit the crime of abortion. The actions they included in this accusation were any and all political action by the women's movement to make therapeutic abortion legal again. Because the Constitution gives us the right to express ourselves and mobilize ourselves, it's illogical that they try to criminalize political activism. Without a doubt, there was an intention to intimidate the women's movement and in particular to socially discredit it.

The intention was to criminalize the women's movement, as part of a general strategy against Nicaraguan civil society on behalf of the current government, but with an emphasis on the movement because it's been a very active movement with a history of relentless struggle. A movement of which part of its leadership declared itself in opposition to the initial candidacy of Daniel Ortega because he's someone that is suspected of abuse—for having sexually abused his daughter. Also, we always said that this accusation was a form of payback, because the movement, the leadership in particular, which I was a part of, we supported Zoilamérica Narváez, Daniel Ortega's stepdaughter, when she accused him of sexual abuse.[10] And the movement as a whole, to show unity and autonomy, supported those allegations even though he [Ortega] was the leader of the Sandinista Front and he had a history that went back all the way to the days of the Revolution, as did many of us.

Nothing came of this accusation, but it meant two and a half years of investigation. They had the intention of putting us in jail, but it led to national and international activism, and there were also condemnations from different human rights committees; Amnesty International carried out important activism to prevent the criminalization of the movement and of the leadership.

Juanita, I know that some of those efforts were to really shut down the movement, but can you say a little bit about how it impacted your own life? How did those criminal charges affect your personal life?

Well it has an impact because it entails risk for individuals. The biggest risk was the loss of freedom. If they jailed us for defending rights, we were going to go to jail.

For me, the solidarity gave me a lot of strength, the support of the women on a national and international level. This gave legitimacy to my work but I can't deny that it had an impact on my family because the family feels at risk that you could be detained. I have a daughter that, of course she wouldn't have liked for her mother to go to jail. She's my daughter, and it hurts her, the threat that I could be imprisoned.

I felt that aside from the injustice, it involved confronting power in a direct way and in a way that was disproportional for us. But we were also conscious of the context of persecution that existed or that well persists in this country. It totally violates the institutionalism and denies any kind of action in the legal environment. Because the law isn't valid, the only thing that matters is authoritarianism and the intention of using power against someone who you want to abuse, who you want to eliminate, or who you want to repress or sanction because you don't like them or simply because they project themselves as someone who is opposed to your ideas or opposed to your government.

So that was very difficult, but for me, it gave me a lot of strength, a lot of strength and many lessons about the cause, that it's a valid cause despite the risks. I think that we won the battle and we won it positively, but we also weakened the image of absolute power that they wanted to set up in the country. We feminists also gave a lesson—that in this context of machismo—people aren't willing to give up their freedom.

The second accusation I confronted was against MAM in particular, and against CINCO, the Center for Communication Research, of which Sofía Montenegro[11] is the executive director, and she is another very important feminist leader. In that accusation the intention to criminalize the work that we did and to halt our struggle was more evident. In this accusation it was indicated that the women's movement was illegal and that we were in alliance and executing a governmental project that was the first project that we had achieved through the allocation of democratic governance funds. What we promoted through this project was for women to exercise their rights as citizens. But you know, that can be very threatening to formal powers because if you give women tools and they begin to see that it's not only their particular rights, but that other rights—their political rights—are as important, such as the right to eat, the right to work. This implied that there was activism from the women around defending democracy.

I think that those in power didn't like this, particularly this government, and it pressured and structured a new attack against all of civil society, but with an impressive viciousness on the women's movement. In this context we were accused of money laundering. Those are crimes that belong to organized crime. I think that it was a show of power on the part of the state and on the part of the current government wanting to delegitimize the possibility that you obtain funds for the development of this activism. This was very perverse and was tough because it implied the utilization of authoritarian power in a stronger way, particularly the justice system, it's very serious. I had to confront the process of arbitrary search warrants to the offices of the Autonomous Movement. We had a search warrant that was conducted with a police display as if they were searching the house of a drug trafficker.

It was very hard for the citizens, but I also think it was a wake-up call for the Nicaraguan society. Even though some sectors don't identify with feminism or the topic of abortion, for example, an outrage of this kind, which was in 2008—I think society was very coherent and said, "No, this isn't right." They weren't able to carry it out because the cost was high, particularly for those in power because the level of national and international condemnation was very strong, and I think that this sounded the alarm so people realized that no authoritarian regime can be positive for the country and even less so for the Nicaraguan people that have fought so much for freedom and that have fought so hard to find a democratic model that we can all coexist.

Juanita, can you talk a little about how you went from your work with the Network to starting here at the organization for the Autonomous Movement?

The movement initiated a process of evaluation of the Women's Autonomous Movement with the understanding that since the '90s we had been working to reclaim the feminist agenda that had been ignored in the '80s. In that process of reorganization, of evaluating what had happened in the last 10 years, we're talking about 2003, we made ourselves available for this evaluation to do a series of debates about how we wanted to organize ourselves, how we should strengthen our strategies and how to construct a document, a platform that we could share with the feminist logic and with the two fundamental axes which are the autonomy and equality for women.

This process carried on for almost 3 years of debate, analysis, and restructuring of the Women's Autonomous Movement and it concluded in 2006. In 2006 there was a refounding. On March 8, 2006, the Women's Autonomous Movement was refounded and it was decided to give it a public face. We decided to create a minimum structure and I was elected.

Why were you elected?

They elected me because I have been participating in the different spaces of organizing the movement. Sometimes they tell me that one of my characteristics is that I believe in collective processes, but they should be truly collective. It shouldn't be that one person decides for the rest. In the Network I wagered a lot in creating this structure that feminists wanted so much and that the rest of us resent of patriarchy: that verticalism, that authoritarianism that is reflected in their organizational structure. It is possible to create mechanisms where we can all make decisions, where we can all decide about a platform for complete action. I think where I have participated and I represented others well—I was recognized before my peers and that's why I was elected as part of the structure of the Women's Autonomous Movement.

They offered to me a paid position to coordinate this movement. For some it would seem that I'm the executive director, but the reality is that in the structure I'm part of is a collective coordinated authority. I have now stayed as an executive to guarantee a spokesperson and to continue strengthening that space a bit with the coordination of different requests and different organizational forms for the movement.

What are some of the current issues women are facing that the organization is trying to address now?

Well, today one of the principal challenges that we see is simply the existence of the movement. From this perspective, you find yourself in a position of resistance or resisting the intentions of the formal political powers of wanting to delegitimize you or of wanting to politically eliminate you. So one of the biggest challenges of the movement is its own subsistence, continuing to keep yourself in a key position. But the other key aspect for us is actually the struggle for democracy because I think that a person only realizes the risks and the values of the processes when you lose them or when you are at risk of losing them. And I think that this is what is happening here in Nicaragua.

As I said, we initiated a peace process in '90 and wanted to begin to construct a model that wasn't, um, "Revolutionary"[12] because it had different ideological intersections but was projected in the necessity of a democratic model where we could all participate, but also a democratic model where we could have clear rules and legal security for all. In that context of peace building, women advanced because, if we were constructing democracy for all, then we also demanded democracy for women.

There isn't institutionalism that secures fundamental rights. So for us, who believe in equality and believe in democracy, we believe that the current priority is the power of the fight for democracy to position our feminist agenda as one of the interests of the women's movement.

What are some of the strategies that you're using to rescue democracy for women?

One of the strategies has been the construction of citizenship, citizenship for women, because there's a big deficit in Nicaragua. In Nicaragua, the society, even at an educational level, hasn't guaranteed the understanding of fundamental rights. Here people don't even know the text of the political constitution. So you can't defend your rights if you don't appropriate those rights. And you're imprisoned by leaders or you're imprisoned by populism when you aren't sure that the right to eat or the right to education aren't handouts, they aren't charity from anyone, but they're fundamental rights and the government has to guarantee those rights.

In the different territories we've facilitated a lot of information through workshops, forums, and debates about what democracy is. We are distributing it in text—it's the political constitution in small format that we call it the pocket or purse edition, because we want women to be able to have it, to know what people are talking about when they mention the constitution, what people are talking about when they mention rights. It's not that someone is doing you a favor regarding a right, but rather that rights are already established there, and that you have to understand to be able to defend them.

This is a fundamental strategy; the other is to promote the organizational part. Nicaragua has the characteristic that for adverse contexts whether it's war or natural disasters, people are able to come together to improve their environment. How do we enhance all of these abilities using women? Women can lead, yes, but we also want women to be recognized for this leadership capacity, from her own potential in the community. To work on women's leadership is another important axis for us, and we have been developing these processes at a territorial level.

Juanita, can you tell us very briefly about the history of the Women's Autonomous Movement?

Well, the movement has its origins in the context of the Revolution. The revolutionary context made it easy for people to organize. The difficulty in that context is that you organized around a single model that was the party of the Sandinista Front. The Luisa Amanda Espinoza Movement, for example, is the organizational predecessor of the women's movement. It was a movement totally within the logic of the FSLN's mass organizations. The whole agenda was a function of the agenda of the Sandinista party where women's rights were never the priorities. It was always said that since we were at war, later they were going to look into the rights that women demanded.

At the end of the '80s there was a process of autonomy. There was a demand for the particular feminist agenda and since it never took off with the revolutionary model, many leaders of the movement that were organizing around the Revolution started the process of creating other types of organizations apart from the Luisa Amanda Espinoza Movement. They started forming collectives. In 1992 they held a big meeting that was called the Festival of the 52%. It was about a declaration of autonomy in search of its own identity as a movement. And that's where they begin to talk about the Women's Autonomous Movement in the logic that autonomy is the principal issue to be able to progress as its own movement, as an indigenous and independent movement, as a movement that follows the agenda of its own women. This implied many political costs because many leaders were expelled from the party,[13] for example. But undoubtedly the movement decided to organize in its own way.

Starting in '92 they decided to take on different organizational forms. There were like two possibilities, one was more organic and the other was by networks. The majority decided to organize in thematic networks, and that's where the Network of Women Against Violence, the Network of Women for Health were developed, there were like 10 networks for education—different topics, different axes, you know, within the platforms of the feminist movement. Others decided to articulate themselves in what was the National Feminist Committee, of which Sofía Montenegro was one of the leaders. They believed it was necessary to work around strengthening the feminist identity with the platform.

Generally, all of the expressions that were used by feminists and were autonomous of whatever kind of expression, whether it's a party, church, or any group with power, the emphasis was on autonomy from the Sandinista Front. We took this on as an autonomous women's movement in its distinct organizational expressions—be that networks, specific organizations, or groups or collectives, specifically feminist or women's rights groups.

In '98 there is a kind of a fork in the road because, well, the accusation of Zoilamérica Narváez against the leader of the Sandinista Front in '98. '98 is pretty important for us because the coherence of the movement was proven. It's a movement that, whether we like or not, has its ideological force aligned with the ideas of the progressive left, so for it to accuse the leader of the Sandinista Front of sexual abuse isn't easy. This involved the movement taking a stance. I think this was a test of the autonomy of the feminist leadership in Nicaragua, and I think we passed the test because we decided to back the accusation and push for justice in the case of Zoilamérica and we demanded that Daniel Ortega had to be put through the justice system because if he had committed such a serious crime, well then he had to face justice. In that context I think the movement came out much stronger and much more legitimate in the eyes of other sectors of society that probably identified with the right or ideologically identified with their faith and that weren't very close to the movement. Despite the consequences of the attacks and the outrage that we've gone through, I think that what happened in '98 is a period that marks and definitely strengthens what would be the autonomy of the women's movement.

The Autonomous Movement, as an organizational space, was founded in 2006 out of the particular necessity of having a small space and strengthening the feminist platform. This doesn't delegitimize the Network of Women Against Violence or the regional networks or other parts of the movement that consider themselves feminists and that assume autonomy. They form part of the richness of the movement as a women's movement and a feminist movement here in Nicaragua. The organizational diversity is positive as far as making it easy for women to ascribe to different parts of the organization; it doesn't matter if you can be in a community if you are there connected with other women in a specific organization and you fight for your rights, well all of this contributes to this collective feminist identity in Nicaragua.

Juanita, I'd like to ask you to talk about feminism a little bit but not feminism from the perspective of the movement. Can you tell me what feminism means to you?

Well for me—I'll tell you, for me feminism is an inspiration to fight for equality. Feminism is like a platform for concrete action, and it seems to me that it's the strength of the inspiration for social justice. As I said, I assumed my identity as a feminist in the practice, in the search for justice for women. But later I realized that this justice, well, it's not going to be complete if there isn't social justice and if society doesn't recognize us women as equal. So in the end I see it as an inspiration for this fight in favor of equality for rights and in favor of justice, in general, for women.

You've talked a lot about the different organizations and networks that are linked together in Nicaragua. Are you also organized with regional networks or feminist organizations in other countries?

Feminism in Latin America has strengthened in the last decade. I think that feminism, even though it isn't socially recognized in Latin America, has played an important role in different social changes that have been promoted in the region from the perspective of the military dictatorships to the peace processes and the search to strengthen democratic institutionalism, in a region where one of its deficits has been institutionalism and the rule of law. I think that Latin America has suffered from not having government that guarantees rights in the sense that you find solid democratic bases. This also has to do with the deficit of citizenship that I was explaining to you. Feminism in this context has contributed to strengthening all of these processes that have been developing. In Latin America we have been organizing a series of regional meetings that allowed us to physically meet but also to renew debates, analysis, and to value political action or the difficulties on exercising our rights that we women have in the region.

And this has also allowed us to strengthen feminism from the logic of Latin Americans because it's not the same to be a feminist in our countries that are lacking so much, as it is in a country with guarantees and strong institutionality. It's harder. So then I think that we have been constructing a feminism through practice and through the Latin American reality, and since they coincide, it's what brings us together. When they attacked us Nicaraguan feminists, to see women from other countries firm in their repudiation of Daniel Ortega's visit to their country—throughout the world and particularly in Latin America—they repudiated him for attacking us, for attacking feminism and for wanting to criminalize us. It was very nice for me because it meant that we are related, and that despite the borders, feminism is not only an abstract solidarity but also a coherent activism that we share.

We are very connected to feminism. We have very strong connections with the Mexican [feminists] and with the South American [feminists]. We are a bit closer with the Central American [feminists] because of regional issues, and this has allowed us to experiment with different organizational forms on a regional level. This also projects us to Europe and the United States as a strong grassroots feminism. I think that in contexts where forces that have traditionally been of a Latin American leftist nature have gained power, feminism is like the Achilles heel because feminism has liberating ideas and it shares a vision for social justice and justice for women. [Feminism] has been very critical of how those governments that have been identified as leftist in the region have used their power, and this also indicates a contribution from feminism about the coherence for alternative models to which we have aspired for decades, but there is still a lot missing.

I think that's a perfect note to end on. I want to thank you again, Juanita, for your time today and for participating in the project.

Well, thank you because you've allowed me to share my story.

It was an honor to hear your history.

From the outset of the description of her childhood, we can understand Juanita's position as a woman from the majority world whose experience is inextricably linked to the systemic inequities of global power. She began her interview articulating contradiction and a deep awareness of economic inequality. She was aware of disparity from a young age, in part because her parents occupied very different social locations in a divided country. Her mother's indigenous background reflects the reality of Nicaragua's colonization by Spain, and her father's family supported Nicaragua's dictator, an oligarchical ruler who was both militarily and financially supported by the United States. Juanita's early experience developed at the juxtaposition of the two realities that emerged from these social locations—one an elite resourceful experience that afforded her a private education and another that afforded her the intimacy of care and community that created a sense of belonging in the barrio.

At a young age, the comfort Juanita could take from her social privilege gave way instead to identifying with her mother's side of the family. Her concerns about asymmetry and inequality began to shape activist engagement and revolutionary activity when she was just 12 years old. For example, although

Juanita could have chosen to go a route privileged by her education and the benefits afforded to her based on her father's social class, she withdrew from private school and joined the Revolution. Therefore, at a time when many youth throughout the world are attending secondary school, Juanita began her involvement with youth battalions organized by a revolutionary army in opposition to a U.S.-backed and funded Contra rebel group. As a young girl whose experiences were intimately tied to a context of globalization, Juanita became engaged in the political struggle that was developing in a country torn by war and revolution by attempting to construct solidarity between her own experience and those who she witnessed struggling around her. Juanita's problematization of struggle led her to be a fervent supporter of the Revolution and a member of the Sandinista military because she believed the revolutionary efforts would lead to a more just society. Before even coming of age to graduate high school, Juanita's position in the global context of neoliberalism contributed to a heightened sense of contradiction in her life.

Despite her impassioned desire to contribute to the revolutionary anti-Somoza fight, Juanita's participation in the war positioned her to question the very nature of justice and freedom. As a child engaged in war, Juanita suffered the loss of very young friends, some of whom were forced to join the insurrection against their will. The contradiction she identified in this situation—that she could voluntarily enlist whereas others could not—developed into an oppositional belief that freedom should be wide enough that all members of society should be able to decide what to participate in. Juanita's early experience with the Sandinistas therefore fueled an ideology that problematized the notion that the marginalized should struggle for the freedom to participate freely in society, whether that society is governed by a dictatorial regime or a socialist revolutionary party. The contradiction she articulated between her support for the Revolution and her interest in democratic citizen participation illustrates a growing ideological opposition. Juanita's experiences of this contradiction generated an interest in the law as a mechanism to uphold the people's rights, with Juanita deciding to study law as a means to pursue her sense of justice. Because Juanita's law degree was obtained through funding and training by the revolutionary party, her first appointment to practice law was in the military courts.

Consistent with choices she had made during her youth, observations Juanita made regarding inequity during her time as a military lawyer led her to step off this privileged track. In particular, in the military courts Juanita was able to see firsthand the way the judicial system treated women, driving her instead to take a position with a nongovernmental organization working on women's rights. Juanita's work at the IXCHEN Women's Center demonstrates how developing a deeper understanding of the structural inequities that impose injustice on women and poor farmers led her to continue rejecting the struggles of the oppressed *and* to adopt a role in working to improve injustices by convicting aggressors in civil cases. Although Juanita's childhood interest in injustice began with a focus on economic inequity that was rooted in global abuses of power, her experience as a lawyer forced her to confront the ways in which economic disenfranchisement intimately intersects with patriarchal power to put women at a uniquely disadvantaged position. Juanita's experiences to this point reflect direct political action in opposition to oppression, but it is her introduction to feminism that seemed to deepen her awareness of structural inequity and provide a context for collective involvement that creates a platform for action that will drive the remainder of her story.

As Juanita began her involvement in the feminist movement, she articulated a transition between identifying injustice and problematizing the *ideologies* that operate to sustain and perpetuate injustice for women. This is illustrated when she indicated that although criminal charges against perpetrators of violence are important, the real project is in creating a society that can simply guarantee better conditions for women, a society that offers a structural or institutional context that allows for individual freedoms. Rather than view the cases that came before her as isolated, Juanita began to problematize the top-down nature of how legal rights are violated. In doing so, Juanita began to see the problems women were confronting as "cultural," not personal, and she shifted her focus from fighting individual cases of injustice to taking an interest in political action that can transform the structures that marginalize women's freedom and participation. The tension between the forming of a subject and active subjectivity that Lugones (2010) wrote about gave way here to a maximal sense of agency when Juanita rejected the dominant ideologies that tolerate the injustice associated with privilege and refuted the notion that true freedom can be obtained on a case-by-case basis.

Juanita's political activism, like other women in the Movimiento, did not come without cost. The experience of contradiction in Juanita's life proved meaningful once again: As a lawyer who searched for justice through the legal system, Juanita experienced legal persecution when the administration attempted to criminalize her political action. Moreover, the very leader of the administration (Daniel Ortega), under whom she served as a revolutionary youth and later a military lawyer, was the same leader who persecuted her for legally defending women's rights. Juanita described her experience of political persecution as a "limit situation," astutely observing the limiting conditions of political power at the same time viewing how the very patterns that have limited women's life circumstances have also served to further develop possibilities for women to collectively defend democracy. For example, by criminalizing political activism, the administrative was, in effect, prohibiting women's capacity to democratically participate in legislative areas that were directly relevant to their reproductive health.

Throughout Juanita's story we therefore witness how the experience of contradiction shaped Juanita's views from an early age and how contradictions in her experience as a revolutionary and later a lawyer were shaped by and shaped her activist work. Although Juanita was trained as a lawyer who has used the parameters of law and legislation to fight for justice, in sharing her story of personal political persecution Juanita also recognized the limits of the law. In particular, Juanita's experiences of working from the margins resulted in a belief that a collective, mobilized effort is not only necessary, but to be successful, must come from "different ideological intersections" than those from which the current administration operates. Through collective engagement with other women fighting for similar rights, Juanita developed a model of praxis or action that can serve as the methodology by which to strategically inform a construction of citizenship and democratic participation for women in Nicaragua. Juanita and her *compañeras*[14] problematized the processes of verticalism and authoritarianism that have functioned to marginalize women from spaces of democratic participation in the current government and instead engaged in collective processes in which everyone can be involved in decision-making and in which legal security for all is a goal.

In active resistance to absolute abuses of power by political leaders and lawmakers, two alternative principles guided Juanita's praxis: political autonomy and equality for women. Given that political persecution ravaged the country during the dictatorship, and has been and is currently being used to actively silence women's voices by "revolutionary" political parties, transformative change would require that the collective aims of feminism are privileged over affiliation with a political party (regardless of whether the party may otherwise reflect the interests of the "Left"). Juanita's proposed praxis involved prioritizing women's leadership and feminism as a platform for action, rather than a political party, as a position from which to address injustice. In other words, Juanita recognized that to create a mechanism by which everyone, including women, can make decisions, then a fundamental strategy for transformation must include positioning the feminist agenda over party-affiliated interests. This strategy would involve what she called "organizational diversity" as a number of different political means, outside traditional political party affiliation, by which women can be engaged in the fight for their rights. Alternative processes to enhance democratic participation should be inherently collective, which, for Juanita, meant, "it shouldn't be that one person decides for the rest." Juanita's praxis reflects the oppositional ideology developed in youth that was reflected when she said, "Freedom should be wide enough so that every person can decide what to participate in and what to build towards or construct." However, no longer a 12-year-old girl, Juanita accepted an elected position as a leader of the *Movimiento Autónomo de Mujeres* to facilitate a necessary strategic space from which women can mobilize and engage their citizen participation. In helping to create this strategic space for women, Juanita enacted an ideology that has developed over her life course—an ideology in which she believes that all individuals deserve to participate and benefit freely in society without struggle.

Juanita's ability to problematize the political domination and control that marginalizes freedom reflects processes of *conscientización*—ideological analysis and action—that are necessary in the production of citizen subjects who can and will resist structures of domination. In particular, Juanita illustrates how resistance to structures of domination cannot be interpreted based only on experiences rooted in patriarchy or capitalism as they occur in a local context, but that as globalized subjects who are susceptible to both local and global abuses of power, women can mobilize around a collective interest in liberating individuals from oppressive governments by sharing a vision and praxis for social justice that will employ alternative models of leadership. Juanita concluded her testimonio by suggesting a strengthening of feminism "from the logic of Latin Americans, because it's not the same to be a feminist in our countries that are lacking so much." By taking a transnationally intersectional perspective to rejecting the dominant ideologies that justify political authority in her society, and demonstrating alternative modes of subjectivity that operate based on freedom rather than authority, Juanita positions herself to take direct action in creating the available spaces for women to democratically participate within society—in effect transforming political institutions.

Notes

1. *Barrio* can technically be translated to English as "neighborhood"; however, the word *barrio* carries a connotation more specific to a working-class neighborhood.

2. This translates as "low country."

3. It is in these youth groups that Juanita meets Violeta Delgado, whose testimonio is included in Chapter 5.

4. The term *counterrevolutionaries* referred to those opposing the Sandinistas. Contra was used to name the rebel groups that opposed the FSLN government following the 1979 Revolution. The Contras were financially and militarily supported by the U.S. government.

5. The Sandinistas had a National Literacy Crusade between March and August 1980. The illiteracy rate in Nicaragua dropped from 50.3% to 12.9% in 5 months.

6. IXCHEN is a civil-society nonprofit organization that opened its first women's center in 1989 and was running six centers as of 2016. The organization aims to promote sexual and reproductive health among women and specializes in violence against women from a gender perspective in defense of human rights for women.

7. Juanita was referring to the amendment made to the Penal Code in 1996, with Law 230 protecting victims of domestic violence.

8. Prior to 2006, the law permitted therapeutic abortion in Nicaragua as long as the woman and three doctors consented to it. In 2006, the Nicaraguan Assembly passed a bill

further restricting abortion. The new law outlawed abortion in all circumstances, making Nicaragua only the sixth country in the world to do so.

9. Daniel Ortega was the president of Nicaragua at the time of the interview.

10. In 1998, Zoilamérica Narváez, Daniel Ortega's stepdaughter, accused him of sexual abuse from the time she was 11 years old until a few days before she filed the complaint. She went to court and was represented by Vilma Núñez (whose *testimonio* is included in the Global Feminisms Project; http://www.umich.edu/~glblfem/). This was a pivotal moment in the FSLN: Subsequent divisions in the party are often partially attributed to these accusations. Because the women's movement supported Zoilamérica, many see Ortega's aggressive political persecution of members of the Movimiento as payback.

11. Sofía Montenegro is widely considered one of the most prominent feminist activists in Nicaragua. She was a leader in the mobilization of the Movimiento Autónomo de Mujeres in the early 1990s and remains one of its key figures. Her testimonio is in Chapter 2.

12. Juanita is not referencing revolutionary ideals, in general, but rather distinguishing the women's process from the Sandinista's.

13. The FSLN party.

14. *Compañero* is used to reflect political solidarity with someone who is a partner, colleague, or classmate. *Compañera* is the feminine form of *compañero*.

Sofía Montenegro

2

Resisting Exclusion with Oppositional Participation

I was excluded from hearing what the males in the house were talking about, particularly if they were talking about politics because that was not, you know, ladies' business.

—TESTIMONIO FROM SOFÍA MONTENEGRO

In the search to strengthen democratic participation, the *Movimiento Autónomo de Mujeres* (Women's Autonomous Movement) places emphasis on bringing the social and political factors that have an impact on people in Nicaragua to public awareness. Sofía Montenegro, a journalist and one of the most well-known feminist activists in Central America, held an influential position with the official Sandinista daily newspaper, the *Barricada*, until she was fired for her interest in publishing dissenting political views. She held a position at the newspaper from 1979, when the Revolution triumphed, to 1994. During that time, she became a prominent feminist activist and traveled widely throughout the Americas, Europe, and Asia serving as a spokesperson on the situation for women in Nicaragua.[1] She was in charge of the *Barricada*'s editorial page from 1985 to 1989.

During the Fourth Latin American Feminist Congress held in Mexico in 1987, Montenegro was part of a delegation of women who returned to Nicaragua aiming to create spaces outside the *Frente Sandinista de Liberación Nacional* (FSLN; Sandinista National Liberation Front) party for women to incorporate feminism into popular mass movements. On their return from Mexico, Montenegro was one of the principal organizers of the Party of the Erotic Left (*Partido de la Izquierda Erótica*, or PIE), a group of women who introduced women's issues into different areas of influence (e.g., government, media, etc.) and were successful in promoting gender equality as a constitutional value (Kampwirth, 2011).[2]

Born out of the same efforts following the Feminist Congress in Mexico, Montenegro founded the publication *Gente* in 1989 as a popular weekly supplement to the *Barricada* to disseminate information relevant to the

45

concerns of women. Montenegro would eventually be fired when the FSLN asserted control over the editorial policies of the paper. Montenegro went on to cofound and direct the *Centro de Investigación de la Comunicación* (CINCO; Center for Communication Research), a Managua-based think tank that focuses on communication, democracy, and public opinion in Nicaragua.

Montenegro was born in 1954 in the city of Darío, in the Department of Matagalpa, approximately 60 miles from the capital city of Managua. She spent her teenage years in the United States and, after returning to Nicaragua, studied journalism at the *Universidad Nacional Autónoma de Nicaragua* in Managua and joined the Sandinistas, while still a student, in 1978. Montenegro was from a Somoza-supporting family, with a father and brother of high rank in the Army who excluded her from political conversations occurring in the home.

From this context, she went on to become a journalist who actively participates in the larger political conversation within the country to strategically counter the exclusion of marginalized voices from democratic citizen participation. The following testimonio by Sofía Montenegro demonstrates how an ideology that developed in opposition to having one's voice excluded from political participation creates a strategic platform for action that would develop multiple venues for the inclusion, rather than exclusion, of various perspectives in the production of communication and knowledge that would more transparently contribute to liberatory change in Nicaragua:

I'd like to start by thanking you again for giving so much of your time. I know you've been asked these questions countless times, so thank you for participating again. I'd like to ask first for you to go back and talk a little bit about your personal history and things that you might remember that were formative from your childhood or things you remember about your family.

Okay, I'll try [laughter]. Well, I am Sofía Montenegro. I am 57. I think I got involved in feminism at a very early age. I was 15 or something and have memories of being different because I was a woman. I am one of the smallest children of nine brothers and sisters. And six of them were males, so therefore I think I was quite conscious that there was a difference in treatment between my brothers and myself and my two other sisters. I told in an interview to Margaret Randall[3] that one of the recollections I have was a discussion with my mother about why my brothers could do this and why I couldn't? And my mother's answers were always, "Well, it's because you're a woman." And this was constant, you know. I wanted to find out what a woman was all about, and I think this established the curiosity to find out about myself and why the difference, because I couldn't understand it as a child. I only understood that they could go out into the streets any time and I couldn't. And I had a lot of rules that didn't apply to them and I had the hardest work in the house, even though we had help. In the house, my mother always tried to prepare me to be a wife. That meant to do all the chores in the house, help the maids, learn how to wash and to iron, to make food, and to keep the house tidy. But my brothers didn't have to do that, and I always thought it was unfair because they were bigger, they were stronger, and I was very small and tiny and, and skinny. As a child I couldn't understand why we women had to have the burden and they didn't have any. And when I became a teenager, things became more strict, in the sense that I couldn't use shorts anymore. So I had to wear dresses; I was becoming a *señorita*, a young lady, and I should behave like one. So, this meant more restrictions, and I was absolutely fed up that I couldn't get up and go out in a bicycle in the streets, etcetera. And I always had in the background that there was this political turmoil in Nicaragua—

How where you aware of that, as a child?

Because my father was a major in Somoza's army, and I also had a brother who was a lieutenant colonel in Somoza's army, so there were guns around and uniforms and the stress of having the guerrillas. The Sandinista Front hadn't come to power, but I always remember that there was something going on in the mountains: the guerrillas. They [her family] always spoke about politics in a hushed voice, and obviously I was excluded from hearing what the males in the house were talking about, particularly if they were talking about politics because that was not, you know, ladies' business. I think that was after a big massacre in which my brother was shot.[4] It was famous. 1967. They decided that I should go out and study abroad, and that's the way I got into the United States to finish high school.

I arrived in the States in a moment in which there was the Pacifist movement and there was the Feminist movement, which was going strong, obviously. I went to Florida. Not much was happening there, but I watched TV and I began to get curious to see all these American women; I said "wow!" and I began to read. By the way, that's the way I learned English from reading with a dictionary and reading the feminists. I was, I don't know, 15, 16.[5]

And who were you reading? Which feminists?

I was reading, the first book which struck me, because it was the same thing I always told my mother and what my mother told me, it was *Born Female*.[6] This was the first book I read, and it was very quite complex for me. This brought me to Kate Millet's *Sexual Politics*[7] and all the famous books. Then I read, Shulamith Firestone[8] and all the rest. And they always sent me the footnotes, to some gentlemen. They were called Karl Marx and Friedrich Engels, and that's the way I got introduced to Marxism.

I had no idea you know, who these guys were but they kept on mentioning them, and I began to get interested to know a little bit more. That's the way I taught myself to find out about capitalism. I remember that I read Zillah Eisenstein,[9] and it opened my eyes forever. I became a feminist that way. Not through an organization, and not through any contact. I was an isolated teenager, and the only thing I had was the books. But eventually I couldn't take it any more in the States and I wanted to come back to Nicaragua. At the beginning, I didn't know much what to do, so I went to study in Bellas Artes, in the school of painting.[10] I wanted to be a painter.

And how old were you at that time?

I came back when I was 18 maybe? But I kept on reading—on feminism, on politics. But in the school, the School of Bellas Artes it's called, there were poets and painters and sculptors, and these people were always talking about politics, particularly the painters, and the teachers. And I began to hang around with the group. They were so heated, the discussions of what was going on, that I decided, well, I just realized that I didn't want to paint the world, but change it. That's the reason I decided to get out of painting school and go to the university. Since I was not going to be a big combatant hero, who would fight, 'cause I was just a woman, I could only use my words and my intelligence. I decided to study journalism. I entered the university, and everybody was organizing and I started journalism amidst this agitation. And then I made contact with people in the Front,[11] and that's the way I got involved with the Revolution.

Were you accepted as a woman student in journalism?

Yeah, the thing was that, most of the time we spent in protests, and I began to make political work for the Association of Students in the university. At that time everything was censored, was forbidden. It was very dangerous to have a political book. I remember that the list of forbidden titles that the government had was as big as the Bible. So you had to smuggle the books. Since you could not sell it in the open, all the students had to read philosophy typed in stencils.

Were some of the titles you were reading, like Karl Marx—

The Capital,[12] I copied it [laughter]. And copied 11 theses of Feuerbach[13] and Hegel and countless things because we were a team of students who typed and then printed and sold it for 10 pesos to make these books accessible. I also read General Vo Nguyen Giap[14] from Vietnam, who was the mastermind and strategist of the Vietnam War. He wrote a book that was called *Lucha del Pueblo*, the *People's Struggle*. We had to work a lot to promote the political thinking.

The student organization you were affiliated with, were they part of the Front or were they separate?

No, they were separate. Only the best could go to the mountains, because that was the place where they recruited the future guerrilla fighters. But, you have to have a commitment to do a different sort of voluntary political work, which was very risky. The university was an autonomous area; it was like an island of freedom during Somoza's time. It's the only thing they had of the ground,[15] but when you went out of the university you were in trouble, you know, because they were waiting outside for you. But years later, things got heated and complicated; they intervened into the university with helicopters and everything. A lot of people got killed. That was my younger years.

You started to say that journalism was your, the way you started to become involved in the Front. Can you talk a little about your involvement with the Sandinistas?

Through the university and through friends I met, who still up to this day are my friends and have survived, like myself, who were from one of the tendencies in which the Sandinista Front was organized and divided, which was the Proletarian Tendency. It was basically rural, mostly middle class and intellectuals. The other tendency, the Popular War, was at the mountains, and what is called and known as the *Terceristas*, which is from where Ortega comes. We don't come from the same faction [laughter].[16] We used to call them *duchistas*[17] and reckless, irresponsible, militarists who wanted to make a coup.

These friends, they recruited me and they persuaded me that I belonged better in the Proletarian Tendency, so I started working with them. That's the way I got involved. They began to give me tasks, and I had to drive underground people in and out of town and move things around and be a courier, etcetera. I spent most of the time doing that until eventually the insurrections came. We had a big discussion with Ortega's faction, because the two insurrections were a failure and a lot of people got killed, which proved our point, you know, that it was risking too much to *sublevate*[18] the cities without weapons and without organization and that there was going to be a massacre. But, there's no way out but to fight. I decided that in the end, the Sandinista Front was right—the only way to deal with Somoza was by insurrection and by force. So I joined the thousands; that's basically the story.

And what were some of your first activities? Were you able to put your jour-nalism training to work?

Well, at the beginning, yes, because I began to use my credential as a student of journalism. I was hired by some people as a stringer for some foreign journalist who either did not speak Spanish, did not know the way around, or they wanted someone to help them to make contacts and to do interviews in Spanish. At the same time, I used this possibility to find out what was going on, on the side of the regime, because I could go to the press conferences. I had this pass in which I could move in different parts of the country. Mobilization was quite restricted, but journalists could move around better. And I saw what happened through this, the combats and the insurrections in Masaya and Estelí. Obviously this had an impact and consolidated my decision that it was a necessity to get rid of the dictatorship, no matter what. At the end, well you know, Somoza fell and the Revolution had its victory and the people in the tendency in which I was were given the task to print the paper for the Revolution, the *Barricada.* It was later the Revolution's official newspaper. We built it on the ruins of Somoza's paper. I was there from Day 1 of the Revolution.

And what was that experience like for you?

Well I spent basically 10 years, and maybe even a little bit more, from the whole Revolution, from 1979 to 1994, building the paper and doing whatever it takes to make it. I spent more than a decade—14 years—in the paper. I was first a journalist, then I was promoted to be head of the international page, then I was editor of the editorial page, and then I was given the task to diversify the supplements of the papers, then was named the director of *Gente,* and so forth.

And how did Gente *diversify the newspaper, can you say something about that?*

The main agenda of the paper was production and defense, so it was very boring, because you could only talk about defense and production, you know, because this was the big necessity of the society and the country. Then we decided that life must go on, even in the midst of the war, and you have to diversify and think of not only the collective and public needs, but the individual needs, differentiated needs. I was involved within the movement from Day 1, too, the women's movement, building the women's movement. My life since then has run parallel between building the movement and building the paper or the communication process.

And what was your role in getting Gente *started?*

I designed it.

Can you talk about that?

It was a little bit before the fall of the Revolution, in the elections of 1990, and we thought that the war was going into a peace process. We had to prepare for a postconflict society; we had to stop doing partisan journalism so the people of different walks could recognize themselves in the paper. We needed to create civilian society and focus on the reintegration and cohesion of society. And a women's movement had emerged, and it was obvious that in this future democratic, civilian society, after the war, women will have to have to have a very strong voice. *Gente* was designed as a way to prepare the mechanism for that, but addressing a mixed audience, that is men and women, and particularly to make it appeal to the young.

And how did it go over when you proposed that idea for Gente? *Were people excited about it or did you experience some difficulties surrounding it?*

Well, people liked it; it was a hit from the very beginning. It became very popular. But, there were some people in the party who raised eyebrows because I had the first open sexuality section. You could talk about real problems that people had and questions on gender and sex and things you didn't talk about in the Revolution. That's the reason it was called "People," you know, it was about real people and people's needs, not political needs. This was basically the idea. Being a feminist was not a thing that the Revolution, that the commanders, liked. So I was always quite in trouble because of that, 'cause I was outspoken, I was a feminist out of the closet. Nobody, I mean, in 1979 there were perhaps only a dozen or so feminists in this country, and all the rest of the women, as far as they went, was to think in class terms. To make everybody understand the dimension of gender was a whole political battle.

What were some of the troubles you experienced as a woman trying to introduce these ideas?

Well, feminism was, you must remember, that the way of thinking of the traditional Left in Nicaragua was basically that the Revolution was necessary and emancipation of women will come almost by itself. They saw no need for women, as an organization of our own. So, the first big battle was to win the right to have our own organization. It took a couple of years, but at the end we won. We won, and a group of us who were demanding that we were not the servants of the Revolution, and we needed a room of our own[19] inside the Revolution, otherwise we couldn't push our interests. The second thing was when we began to push what was called the gender perspective, or the feminist perspective, on all other issues. Some people accused us of being, particularly me because I was the one who was public and I was writing things, of making political diversions and promoting bourgeois thinking. Obviously I was a suspect because I studied in the United States, I have read all these crazy women, and I had the French, and this and the other, and I was an intellectual, and I was from a liberal profession, and obviously I was a *petit bourgeois*[20] that could be very dangerous for the masses. The milieu of the journalists is always something I fit in. We got along well and they laughed a little about the things I said that they found preposterous and absurd or whatever. But all in all, I had a space in the paper.

Did you ever experience having anyone trying to silence you or keep you from writing what you were writing?

Absolutely.

What was that like? Can you tell me a little bit about that?

I had a big fight with Daniel Ortega. It was 19__ . . . I don't remember, one eighth of March, I remember that. And they forbid me to talk, to write about women's issues. But it was basically him. This is the reason some people don't understand why he has taken this position today.[21] He had that position in the '80s. I remember; I was there. It only has exacerbated with age because now he has become even worse. I'm not surprised, I am absolutely not surprised because he was the one who said that—one organization, only, of women. You must remember that they didn't want women to have their own organization. We got it. When we got it, we started building the organization, which was called AMNLAE.[22] And then a group of feminists worked to conspire inside the structure to push things. We were just a bunch of feminists, I mean we were about 10 or something. And we were pushing to influence, to build, to write the constitution and this and the other. One of the things we thought was important was to give this one-organization-only sort of scheme to pass to the movement strategy which is diverse, pluralistic, uneven and unequal. The idea for the leaders of the Revolution was that the only women who mattered were the ones who belonged to the peasants or to the proletarians, and the question was what are you going to do with all the rest of us who are not neither peasants nor workers—who are technicians, are intellectuals, from the city? Women, the urban women, the liberal—the ones who work in liberal professions? This is the reason we insist that this classist view of society which the only women that matter were these so-called *fuerzas motrices de la Revolución*[23] were peasants and workers, and the rest are all petit bourgeois who have to get themselves proletariatized,[24] and this was dangerous thinking from my point of view. So, our proposal was that the condition of women was basically the same, but the situation of women was not the same, and this should not necessarily mean a conflict. You couldn't oppose the politics of difference, could not be of confrontation; you have to include. You have to make a sort of wide alliance between the women of the fields, the peasants, and the urban women, each one with their own demands and specificities and different levels of situation, of gender situation.

Were you able to write about these issues in the Barricada *or* Gente?

Yeah, to make the allegation that we need to change from this vertical vision, subordinated vision of a women-only organization to a diversified movement, an autonomous one in which each group of women would organize for what they needed. I mean, you could be your own small organization; if you were Black or you were from the Atlantic coast, you organized as a feminist, as a woman, to fight racism but also fight machismo, and that was the same thing for everybody. So we started organizing against the will and the resistance of the males in the mass organizations, a Women's Secretariat.[25] For example, workers in the field began to push to organize in the unions, professional guilds, associations of professionals in all of it, in health workers, you name it, state workers—to organize this Women's Secretariat.

Across different sectors?

Mmhmm. And the idea was that we could have this good philosophical idea that we could have the unity of feminism on one end, with the diversity of real women coming from different walks of life that are fighting for a common ground. And this would push the women's energy and presence beyond the borders of the secluded, isolated, organization of women. It was necessary to have first an organization of our own, but not to stay there like nuns, but to go beyond the *claustro,*[26] beyond the convent, getting to the world and that was the strategy at that time. Well, we succeeded, they failed, because I'm here [laughter].

You're living proof.

I'm the living proof that we succeeded.

When did you stop working for the newspaper and why?

1994. We had been discussing with the leaders of the Revolution the necessity of giving the paper its autonomy because being an official organ of the party was a straightjacket for thinking, for acting, because nobody could write anything. This was killing any possibility of doing good journalism and having credibility on our own as journalists. Finally, the National Directorate accepted that we were right, and they said okay, prepare the paper to be an autonomous paper. Make it professional; prepare the people, your staff, for that task because when peace comes—because everybody was waiting for peace—we're going to need this, another role for the paper.

The only one who opposed that decision of the National Directorate of the Sandinistas was, guess who? Daniel Ortega! He opposed it since 1990. And we decided—and this is something that Comandante Ortega didn't like either—that after the fall of the Revolution, we opened the paper, particularly to all the Sandinista audience who wanted to know what the hell went wrong with the Revolution. And we, as editors, saw that it was the right of the Nicaraguan people to know and to discuss because these people have lost thousands of people in that war, and they deserve the truth, the right to question and the right to know. That was the position of Carlos Chamorro[27] and myself, and the rest of the staff. We demanded explanation from the leadership, particularly from Daniel Ortega. Everyone had to assume the collective and personal responsibility for whatever failure you consider the Revolution. Immediately after that, when the debates started and people began pointing fingers and responsibilities and so forth, Daniel Ortega thought that it was extremely dangerous for his own leadership and tried to shut this process down. That's where the conflict started. They began—his wife is now First Lady for the second time, Rosario Murillo—began a campaign, a violent campaign, just like now,[28] that was in 1991 or something, against the paper and particularly against Carlos and myself, accusing us that we were oligarchs, that we were bourgeois, that we were sold to the United States and to the imperialists and blah, blah, blah. Obviously, the idea was to shut us down, and we resisted, they persisted, until the Congress was decisive for the Sandinista Front. They decided to take over the paper.

And what did you do after the newspaper? Where did you work next?

To the streets! [Laughter.] No, we went unemployed, and it was a long struggle because we decided that if we couldn't democratize the Front at that moment, it was going to be very difficult afterwards. What came after that was a big push against anyone who opposed the Front and who wanted a democratic political organization and not a tool of power for any other *comandantes.*[29] So, Ortega not only crushed the rest of the party, he crushed his own colleagues, the other comandantes who had an opposition. And he took over the paper, he took over the Front, he took over everything, and to tell you how he did it that's a book in itself, but to make a long story short, that was what happened. In the end, in the Second Congress he arranged things inside the Congress so that the opposition was in such a weak situation that he could crush the opposition inside the Front.

After that, they decided that since we were the traitors and whatever, they have to *defenestrate,*[30] when they throw you out the window. They took over, and they expelled the head of the whole paper. It went back again to become an official paper of—in this case not any more of the Sandinista Front, but of Daniel Ortega and his wife, until they destroyed it; it doesn't exist anymore. It went bankrupt, and people refused to buy it and it just went down. I went out and I wasn't employed for a year and a half or something, and I was very angry, I wanted to kill all the bastards with my bare hands, that's how angry I was. And then I, we decided to build this, what you see, we came and created this Center for Research and Communication to start all over again and build small media, independent media—absolutely independent media—we self-decided never to go back to work for anyone: party, boss, anything. And we started CINCO, which is an NGO[31] that deals with investigation research on communication, culture, and politics.

What are some of the current issues that you're trying to address right now?

Well, so far the problem of the *ni-ni*,[32] which is the voters who have no party and have . . . nobody knows how the hell that they are going to vote, and so they are called ni-ni. We are conducting research but we are also working on youth political culture—the succeeding generations from the Revolution are tuned out on youth—to see how it's changing and obviously on communication, on media, research on media, on how the market and technology is changing everything. We have an observatory on media and an observatory on governance and democracy to oversee the political process. After we went out of the paper, we started building this Center and we, besides the program on research, we have developed two television programs, one radio program, and now we have a digital paper, which is called *Confidencial.* And we also publish a bulletin, monthly bulletin, on political analysis and the situation in Nicaragua. That's my professional work, and I'm an activist and leader in the Women's Movement—Movimiento Autónomo de Mujeres—and that has been like that since 1995 up to this morning.

What are some of the current issues you're working on as an activist in the movement?

Well, how to make women go back to big politics again, to construct resistance against the new dictatorship that is developing and is attacking the Women's Movement. This office was raided in 2008—and the Women's Movement was raided by the will of the First Lady of this country, Daniel Ortega's wife because they wanted to shut us out.

What were they looking for when they raided?

They accused us of laundering money. We have an agreement with the Women's Movement because they have no legal status to receive donations. So, we have an alliance between the Women's Movement and journalists here to fund the Women's agenda. These are funds we were offered by international cooperation in which you can apply with a project. This funding, which was from the Europeans—eh, Sweden, whatever—all

European countries have this funding for promoting the rights of citizens and civilian society. So, the Women's Movement applied to this funding, to further advance the struggle to regain the right of therapeutic abortion and for demanding political participation and they got the grant. But since they have no formal organization, they had to make an alliance with someone who has an account to administer the money, so that's what we did. So that, which is perfectly legal in this country, they used that to accuse us, me in particular, of laundering money like it was, eh, *narcos*,[33] drug money. They were saying that we were passing on this money as a third party to these women who are basically, these horrible, feminist women, *abortistas*.[34] They tried to invent a case to penalize us and close the center and close the media but at the same time shut down the Women's Movement. Why the grudge? For old times' sake,[35] but for new times' sake—the Women's Movement gave its support and defended when Zoilamérica Narvaez, the daughter of the First Lady of Nicaragua, made a denunciation of the rape by the president of Nicaragua, her stepfather, and nobody was there to back her up. But, this Women's Movement did and took the risk to back her up, defying the power. And the whole feminist movement in Latin America backed her up, so whatever she's[36] doing now against me, against Carlos, against the Women's Movement, is just an act of revenge. When they came to power,[37] they decided that they would destroy the Women's Movement.

You just referenced this larger movement of Latin American feminists. Can you talk a little bit about that? Do you work across borders with women from other countries to share strategies and work on feminist issues?

Absolutely.

Can you talk a little—just briefly—about that?

Since the Revolution, we have been steadily getting acquainted and involved in the different debates, organizations, regional—not only Central America, but in the whole Latin America—through the feminist meetings which are every 3 years, which is like a big congress of feminists in Latin America: *Encuentro Feminista Latinoamericano*.[38] I think this time it's in Colombia, Cartagena de India. We have been developing networks on health, on violence, against rape, against—you name it, and obviously we have been involved in all that. We keep a close contact through the networking, and I think that in this last time, if it hadn't been by the mobilization of the whole feminist movement in Latin America, they would have destroyed the Movement. Because they [feminists in Latin America] mobilized and have almost impeded that Daniel Ortega visit any country. Every time that he announces he is going to visit a country, there is picketing of feminist women waiting for him in the airport. It's a big scandal because this is the rapist president, coming from Nicaragua, you know? So now he has a fear of going out. This is the reason why he fell, because it was a big, big scandal, as it should be. But the moment they[39] got into power, they came back to power, we knew that we were in trouble and we still are in trouble, and if he stays and he makes a fraud of the elections, and stays against the people's will, we have to prepare. In the Movimiento Autónomo, we are preparing for the worst. We have been preparing for the worst since 2006 and what's coming doesn't look better. It can only get worse if these elections don't give the possibility for the people of Nicaragua to get rid of Daniel Ortega in a pacified, civilized manner, through elections. If that doesn't happen, well, probably we will have a new period of violence and turmoil in Nicaragua until we get rid of him like we got rid of Somoza. So, we have come full circle.[40]

I'd like to also ask you to talk a little bit about neoliberalism and the effect that neoliberalism has on women in particular in Nicaragua.

Well, it was very brutal because in the case of Nicaragua there were no small doses. You must remember that in the case of Nicaragua we passed from a state economy to a market economy, from a country that was at war, at peace, from a closed, controlled, militarized country to liberalization, and the transition was very short. From one day to the other, the State, who was a sort of protective, father-like State, authoritarian father, but father nevertheless, was dismantled.[41] So, it was the most brutal transition from state to open-market economy, and it had no netting in which you could fall when the net of the state was pulled out.[42] So, everybody had a very hard hit. You have inflation that had to be controlled, the dismantling of civil services, whatever.

And how did that impact women in particular?

Big unemployment. Women, in particular, because everything became privatized, you know ... the electricity. The only thing they didn't dare to privatize was water, but after that, the state was sold by peanuts and into pieces. So a counteragrarian reform started, reconcentration of property and goods, and it was hell, it was hell. I mean people recognized that we needed the role of the market, but not an unleashed market. It's a market with some democratic regulations is what we need. Capital is a producer of unevenness, inequities, while democracy tends to equalize everybody. That's a contradiction of terms, to have capitalism on one side and democracy on the other because they are always fighting each other, and usually when you unleash the market, democracy is the one that loses. This is the reason that politics must run the economy; I'm convinced, absolutely convinced of that, obviously a democratic regulation.

Can you talk about the role of what you call NGO-ization in this process you're discussing right now?

It was part of the model. In fact, I have written about it. To have this model of big market, little State. In order to have that you have to adjust, not only the economy and the state, you have to adjust civilian society, and so enters the NGOs because the NGOs have been more efficient operating at the small scale and tend to be cheaper in the sense of an investment, than investing in a welfare state. I would say that NGOs became, during neoliberalism, the sort of Mother Theresa of neoliberalism because it was the NGOs who have to pick up the poor, feed the hungry. And the State? *Muy bien, gracias.*[43] It left the citizens, *desamparados*,[44] without protection at all. So, the only protection that was more or less offered was through NGOs, which permitted the neoliberals to become quote-on-quote efficient, very cheap. I mean they don't have expenditures on social things and try to contain things through what NGOs give to society or citizens. But it had a perverse effect because instead of financing the organizations of movements and citizens' fight for the rights—that is, for more equality— they gave it to the NGOs who administer inequality. You see?

And this move created a tendency that groups of organized citizens became institutions to administer foreign aid. And this is the perverse side of NGO-ization. It weakened the social movement, whose task is to create collective identity, either for women or for youth, or for anyone who is excluded and is fighting for their lives or for their rights. The institutions are executing some programs to attend development or the poor or the sick or whatever. But, they are not trying to fight powers, the powers that be of change. Movements do; that's the role of movements. And obviously they could be in a strategic alliance between institutions—that is NGOs for development, feminist institutions, and movements—because power and the change of power is always through a correlation of forces. If civil society is weak and citizens are weak and the women's collective is unorganized and weak, you cannot win the battle. And you don't have to be Vo Nguyen Giap to realize if you go to war unarmed by knowledge, by thinking, and without organization, you are a dead woman.

This is my last question, I promise. You've referenced—you've referred to intellectuals before and the role of intellectuals. Do you think there's a relationship or a connection between scholarship and feminist activism?

Absolutely, absolutely. The only way you can—and this is my personal conviction—but it has been so all over the history of humanity: It's the minority that organizes ideas. No big idea has been won through big assemblies, and you may think that I am an elitist; absolutely, feminism started as an elitist movement and still is because you have to get out of the box of thinking, of common thinking, in order to rethink the world, and women are at such a disadvantage. As I told once to someone, women are too busy fighting for their own life and on top of that you want the poor to think how they are going to change the whole structure of power of patriarchy and economics and big politics? And that's what you need your intellectuals for. That's what you need your academy for. That's the alliance between the poor women, rich women, middle-class women, intellectual and workers. That's the way it works; this is the only way it can work and establish this unity within diversity for common projects that women can have all over the world. What we want is democracy, freedom, and justice. That's what women want all over the world and that's what we want. So, you need all the forces you can get and all your thinkers, each one of them, all your scientists, all the allies you can find, and all the brightness and intelligence of women all over the world to change this. And obviously you need troops and perhaps generals, like me [laughter].

Sofía's social location at the intersections of patriarchy and capitalism is distinct from other women who were involved in the Movimiento and who are included in this book. As a daughter raised in the ruling class, Sofía's elite upbringing was afforded in part by the fact that her father and brother held high ranks in an army that served a dictator who had for years been supported by the United States. As members of the elite ruling party, Sofía's parents, in the midst of a war-torn country, were able to afford sending her to school in the United States so that she would be shielded from the very war in which male members of her family were fighting and dying. In her pursuit to learn English while in Florida, Sofía read feminist and Marxist literature, some of which had been banned in her own country by the dictatorship that her parents were supporting. Because Sofía did not confront economic inequities in an experiential manner, as did most of her *compañeras*,[45] the ways in which patriarchy and capitalism influenced her activism played out differently for her than they do for many others in the Movimiento.

Unlike many of the other women included in this book, who began their *testimonios* with memories that illustrate a confrontation with and questioning of economic inequity, Sofía started her interview with memories that reflected a critical consciousness that questioned the unfairness of *gender* inequity. As a child, she keenly problematized the observation that the privileges afforded to her brothers, but not to her, were not based on merit when she noted that, as a girl, despite having the hardest work in the house, she had more rules applied to her than did her brothers. In contextualizing how gender limited and restricted her experience, Sofía quickly shifted her story to the context of the growing war that was unfolding in her youth. Given that the stress of war was undeniable, Sofía's problematizing of gender roles led her to question why she was excluded from participating in the political conversations that were occurring among men in her household simply because talking about politics was not "ladies' business." Sofía's rejection of this exclusion informed an oppositional ideology that centered on the importance of inclusive participation and the dissemination of diverse perspectives in the democratization of a society.

Sofía attributed the growth in her critical thinking, in part, to knowledge obtained by reading feminist literature that was relevant to her lived experience and, at the same time, connected that experience to political structures (e.g., gender, class). Women's contribution to political thinking through writing would prove to leave an impressionable mark on Sofía. Although her reading of these perspectives touched her deeply and validated her own experience, it also exposed how intellectual women can be at the forefront of a political conversation. For example, Sofía was introduced to influential Marxist (male) thinkers and writers through the voices of *women* writing feminist text. The knowledge gained from these readings positioned her to participate in impassioned political conversations in art school when she returned to Nicaragua.

However, Sofía was not satisfied with simply folding understandings of inequity into intellectual conversations; she wanted to become active in lessening, rather than simply discussing, inequities in her country. Her first step toward action was to find a route whereby, as a woman, she would have a seat at the table to participate in the political conversations that were determining the landscape of Nicaragua during the Revolution, but from which she was excluded as a daughter in a Somoza-supporting family. As a woman, her "heroism" will have to take a different form than the combat male heroes sought. The tools most readily available to Sofía for this task were her words and intelligence—tools she acquired, in part, precisely because she *was* a girl, one from an elite family that, in excluding her participation, sent her to boarding school in the United States.

The first action Sofía took as a student of journalism—making underground copies of the Marxist text that was censored during the dictatorship—reflect how she problematized the exclusion of certain voices from the larger dialogue. Sofía actively resisted this exclusion by finding an alternate route by which to have those voices influence political thinking. In rejecting the dominant ideologies that aimed to censor knowledge and narratives that ran counter to the interests of the dictatorship, she actively disseminated text with the interest of promoting thinking that would lead to inclusive political participation among the people of Nicaragua. When the Revolution triumphed in 1979, Sofía employed her newly honed skills as a journalist in the Revolution's official newspaper, the *Barricada*. This positioned her to be in control of one of the resources she had found most valuable in her life—that is, critical writing—and to put it forward to the masses through a news outlet. This experience, in many ways, elevated her voice and positioned her, rather than at the margins or the hallways of her girlhood home, as central to a political conversation that was taking place globally as the Sandinistas took power, and fought to maintain it during the Iran-Contra affair, as the entire world watched. In rejecting the social norms of her youth that dictated that politics were not ladies' business, Sofía used journalism to gain access and mobility to political conversations that were unfolding in a country torn by war.

Over time, Sofía became increasingly disillusioned with the project of revolutionary journalism when she began to see the *Barricada* as a tool of propaganda rather than the means by which to make a broader political conversation more accessible to the masses. In effect, she began waging another battle surrounding censorship—this time within her own party because the party excluded women's voices in the political agenda. Sofía felt pushed to the margins politically by this exclusion and began to recognize that although she was able to use her voice through her role at the newspaper, she had been able to do so, in part, because she was having the conversation that her male compañeros were having—and those were conversations about economic inequity and the war. This meant that although Sofia had a seat at the table, it was still *men* who were driving and controlling the substance of what was being discussed and written about. Sofía rejected the limits that the party, and by extension, the newspaper, put on women and did so in a manner that harkened back to her rejection of the traditional gender roles that her mother taught her when she said that women were not "the servants of the Revolution."

Rather than viewing women as voiceless members whose role was to serve the vertical or top-down interests of a male-dominated authority, Sofía used the feminist perspective offered in *A Room of One's Own*, in which Virginia Woolf argued for both a literal and a figural space for women writers within traditions dominated by patriarchy, to produce *Gente*. Sofía developed *Gente* as a newspaper supplement that elevated women's voices by generating a conversation regarding the concerns being raised by women. Through this publication, Sofía overtly challenged the dominant ideologies surrounding gender that have served to exclude women and their issues from the broader societal conversation. In particular, in resisting the restrictive nature of analysis and information rooted solely in class-based politics, Sofía created a space for what she called a "feminist perspective." Sofía's praxis, whereby this perspective is implemented in action, involves diversifying the nature of women's concerns by having women participate from their respective social locations, whether they are from a proletariat, peasant, or Black background. Therefore, Sofía's ideological commitment to inclusivity strategically informed her praxis when she used her "words and intelligence" to take to the people conversations that had, to date, not entered mass print circulation before in Nicaragua (e.g., about sexuality).

When Sofía attempted various means to democratize women's voices by lobbying for a women-centered space that would allow for the inclusion of diverse perspectives, her education and training in journalism were used by her compañeros to marginalize and attempt to silence her—in effect, to take away her seat at the table when her voice became perceived as a threat to the party agenda. Thus, although being raised in a family that supported the ruling class brought Sofía privileges that she would not otherwise have been afforded, she was later accused of being an imperialist by identifying as a feminist who was educated in the United States. This was meant to silence her and redirect her loyalties to the (male) party members' priorities. Her compañeros suggested that the revolutionary struggle was about the peasants, not the elite, and there was no space for urban, intellectual women to assert themselves in the political agenda.

Therefore, rather than being a venue to facilitate political thinking, like the literature that she copied and disseminated underground during the start of the Revolution, Sofía described the newspaper as "a straightjacket for thinking, for acting, because no one could write anything. This was killing any possibility of doing good journalism." Sofía resisted the restrictions being drawn by the compañeros, who suggested an intellectual, urban, and educated woman could not participate by articulating her belief in a pluralism of feminism. In doing so, she deideologized the universalizing of women and argued that women from various backgrounds have different demands and therefore distinct contributions to make toward change. Therefore, in opposing the exclusionary male leadership, Sofía articulated an intersectional ideology whereby contributions from all women—whether peasant workers or liberally educated—are imperative to enact liberatory change. The ideology that she offered in opposition to the vertical abuses of patriarchal power reflect a strategy that would later serve as the backbone of the Movimiento's initial meeting, "Diverse but United," in 1992.

Although Sofía began as a revolutionary under a dictatorship that censored material that would educate the masses about grave injustice suffered at the hands of those in power, she, ironically, lost her position as a journalist at the *Barricada* for the very same reasons. From this socially marginalized position, Sofía began working to bring words and knowledge to the people, free of the limits imposed by the leaders of the Revolution. As an act of resistance and a commitment to a political project, Sofía directed her opposition by starting a center for research and communication, a center that focuses on investigative journalism and brings information about culture and politics to the people. This action reflected the aims that Sofía developed as a young adult to "change the world" by bringing information to the masses. Moreover, by continuing to seek a strategic place from which to work as a writer, she was trying to change her own circumstances at the same time she was working to change the social structures that marginalized women's voices from the greater conversation (Martín-Baró, 1994). As someone both trained in journalism and yet still marginalized from participating for her democratic tendencies, Sofía developed a plethora of venues in which people in Nicaragua could contribute their voices and perspectives to democratic and political processes through her center—via research, television, radio, Internet, monthly bulletins, all reflecting a commitment to democratizing political analysis of the situation in Nicaragua and working in solidarity across diverse lines. Although working from the margins, the collective efforts in which she was participating with other women in the Movimiento resulted in continued aggressive attempts from the government to silence her.

The very rights Sofía has fought her life for—for women to be included in political conversations—were further threatened when the State dismantled its social programs and invited dependence on NGOs after the fall of the Revolution. Sofía described the market as being "unleashed" when Nicaragua transitioned from a socialist state economy to a market economy driven by global neoliberal policies and values. Sofía's oppositional ideology surrounding resistance to exclusion is evident in her analysis of the neoliberal (free-market capitalism) policies that were being supported by the new Ortega administration and that further exacerbated the inequities that excluded the marginalized from political conversations.

Because Sofía's activism had been driven by collective mobilization to transform the structures that excluded women's participation, she opposed the neoliberal policies that weakened the collective by suggesting that NGOs, to the extent that they were not inclusive of democratic voices engaged in rethinking the world, became another agent that silenced and marginalized the people. For example, Sofía described NGOs as the "Mother Theresa" of neoliberalism because she problematized the very nature by which they excluded the agendas of citizens fighting for transformative change through social movements and instead privileged outside (i.e., foreign) agendas that put short-term band-aids on consequences related to neoliberalism. The problem she sees with the current situation is evidenced when she stated that "politics must run the economy" instead of the other way around. Sofia resisted the notion that the economy, which operates through a capitalist model that inherently produces inequities, drives society and proposed instead that political values, such as democracy and citizen rights, should be influencing political decision-making. Sofía's ideology surrounding inclusion—or that democracy tends to equalize everybody—culminated in the current focus of her work, which is to "make women go back to big politics."

Throughout her life's work, we observe Sofía enacting her thesis that knowledge and organizing in social movements is power. In her words, "if you go to war unarmed by knowledge, by thinking, and without organization, you are a dead woman." Throughout her life, she resisted being a subject for a revolutionary project that would not legitimize the truths of those who were marginalized and instead enacted an alternative subjectivity that allowed her to challenge prevailing power. Although she articulated that women are at a disadvantage when it comes to being able to "rethink the world," she provides an extraordinary example of a citizen subject resisting the structures of domination through the creation of "rooms of their own" in which she speaks truth to power.

Notes

1. As one of the most prominent feminist leaders in Nicaragua, Sofía has given countless interviews to numerous political scientists, nonprofit social justice organizations, and news organizations (e.g., Adam Jones, Karen Kampwirth, Margaret Randall; the North American Congress on Latin America, the Working Capital for Community Needs [formerly the Wisconsin Coordinating Council on Nicaragua]; and news outlets such as NPR, the *New York Times*, and the BBC). She was also extensively interviewed for her role in the Sandinista newspaper to inform the book *Beyond the Barricades* by Adam Jones (Athens: Ohio University Press, 2002).

2. At least 10 articles in the 1987 Constitution reference women's rights as a result of political pressure applied by mobilized women.

3. Margaret Randall published the books *Sandino's Daughters* (1981) and *Sandino's Daughters Revisited* (1994), which are heavily cited in the Introduction of this book and are among the most widely read books on the Sandinista Revolution.

4. On January 22, 1967, the National Opposition Union (*Unión Nacional Opositora*, UNO) staged a demonstration in the capital city of Managua in support of their candidate, Fernando Agüero. Somoza ordered the National Guard to attack the march, killing over 500 people.

5. Sofía's interview was conducted in English.

6. Caroline Bird's *Born Female: The High Cost of Keeping Women Down* was published in 1968 by David McKay (New York, NY).

7. Kate Millet's *Sexual Politics* (New York, NY: Doubleday, 1970).

8. Shulamith Firestone is a Jewish, Canadian-born author, artist, and feminist. She published *The Dialectic of Sex: The Case for Feminist Revolution* (New York, NY: Morrow, 1970).

9. Eisenstein is a feminist activist, author, and professor. She edited the book *Capitalist Patriarchy and the Case for Socialist Feminism* (New York, NY: Monthly Review Press, 1978) and wrote *The Radical Future of Liberal Feminism* (New York, NY: Longman, 1981), which made a strong case for Marxist feminism.

10. The actual name of the school is the *Escuela Nacional de Bellas Artes* (National School of Fine Arts).

11. Many reference the Sandinista National Front Liberation (*Frente Sandinista de Liberación Nacional*, FSLN) as simply the Front, in English.

12. Marx, K. (1867). *Capital: A critique of political economy: The process of capitalist production* (Hamburg: Verlag von Otto Meissner).

13. Ludwig Andreas von Feuerbach was a German philosopher (1804–1872).

14. Võ Nguyên Giáp is a retired officer in the Vietnamese People's Army and a politician.

15. The university's autonomy meant that the grounds were off limits to Somoza's army, so it was the only space dissidents had where they were not in danger.

16. Sofía laughed at this history because, despite being a loyal Sandinista, she suffered extreme political persecution at the hands of Daniel Ortega in 2008. She was noting that even then, she and Daniel worked from different perspectives.

17. The term relates to the followers of "Il Duce," Benito Mussolini, the Italian fascist leader. Sofía was making the point that Ortega and his followers were authoritarian.

18. The term *sublevate* is from the Spanish *sublevar*, meaning to "incite," "stir up," or "revolt."

19. Sofía was making a feminist reference to Virginia Woolf's book, *A Room of One's Own* (London, UK: Hogarth Press, 1929), in which Woolf made the argument for both a literal and a figural space for women writers within a literary tradition dominated by patriarchy.

20. A French term commonly used in Latin America, particularly in the 1980s, *petit bourgeois* refers to the middle class who, in theory, support Marxism and the Revolution but who live by subjugating the proletariat and peasant classes.

21. In 2014, Ortega rewrote the Constitution to eliminate term limits to allow for a third term. This, among many other acts of accused political corruption, led many Nicaraguans to view him as operating a dictatorship, despite that he was the former leader of the Revolution.

22. The AMNLAE is the FSLN's exclusively women-centered organization, the Luisa Amanda Espinoza Association of Nicaraguan Women (*Associación de Mujeres Nicaragüenses Luisa Espinoza*).

23. *Fuerzas motrices de la Revolución* means "motor forces of the Revolution." Rural and peasant women were considered the forces that would move the Revolution forward.

24. "To get themselves proletariatized" means for them to become proletariat.

25. The "mass organizations" indicate the women's offices inside governmental organizations, such as labor unions, farm workers' associations, and so on. Those offices played an important role in the development of the Nicaraguan women's movement by creating spaces for women inside male-dominated institutions.

26. The word *claustro* means "cloister," as in the cloistered or secluded life of some religious orders.

27. Carlos Fernando Chamorro worked with Sofía as editor of FSLN's newspaper. He is a son of Violeta Chamorro and Pedro Joaquín Chamorro. His father was editor of the only anti-Somoza newspaper in the country until his assassination in 1978. His mother became president of Nicaragua in 1990 during the fall of the Revolution.

28. Sofía was referring to the campaign against CINCO in 2008 that she explains further in her story.

29. [commanders]

30. Defenestration (noun), 1: Throwing a person or thing out the window. 2: a usually swift expulsion (as from a political party or office source http://www.merriam-webster.com/dictionary/defenestration).

31. [nongovernmental organization]

32. *Ni-ni* loosely translates to "neither-neither" or "neither-nor."

33. Drug traffickers are termed *narcos*.

34. *Abortistas* are supporters of abortion.

35. Sofía was referring to the grudge Daniel Ortega had against her because of the disagreement at the newspaper.

36. Sofía was referring to Rosario Murillo. During Zoilamérica's trial, Rosario stood by Ortega. The administration is largely viewed as a presidential couple, "Ortega-Murillo," and has a documented history of coercion of feminist activity (Jubb, 2014).

37. The Ortega-Murillo administration began in 2007.

38. Feminist Encoutners of Latin America. It is one of these feminist gatherings in Latin America (Peru, 2014) that inspired the cover artist Favianna Rodriguez to create the image used for this book.

39. She was referring again to the Ortega-Murillo administration.

40. Ortega was reelected shortly after this interview in November 2011.

41. This transition occurred in 1990 when the Revolution fell.

42. This expression means there was no safety net.

43. This translates to "Very well, thank you," a statement meant to imply that the State knows what its responsibilities are but is avoiding them because others are dealing with them.

44. *Desamparados* indicates "helpless" or "forsaken."

45. *Compañero* is used to reflect political solidarity with someone who is a partner, colleague, or classmate. *Compañera* is the feminine form of *compañero*.

Yamileth Mejía

3

The Role of Education and Knowledge
in the Building of Citizen Subjectivity

As long as you keep people in the dark, not knowing anything,
of course you will be able to do what you wish with them and
manipulate them. Ignorance is the best friend of abusive people's
manipulation.

—*TESTIMONIO* FROM YAMILETH MEJÍA

The previous two chapters detailed how problematizing the lack of access to information and opportunity contributed to the creation of available spaces and the inclusion of women's voices in a manner that led to wider democratization and political participation among women in Nicaragua. Although there are several routes by which information and knowledge can be obtained, formal education is certainly one of the most obvious. Yamileth Mejía served as a teacher during the Revolution and has since committed a lifetime to using education and knowledge to contribute to addressing problems caused by social inequities. In the late 1990s, Mejía became involved in the Network of Women Against Violence (*Red de Mujeres Contra la Violencia*) as a psychologist working on the 1998 devastation of Hurricane Mitch. In 2006, Mejía would become involved with eight other women in the *Movimiento Autónomo de Mujeres* (Women's Autonomous Movement) in defense of the 9-year-old girl "Rosita," who received a legal abortion after having been raped. Along with Juanita Jiménez (Chapter 1), Mejía was subject to political persecution for her involvement in this case and received support from an Amnesty International campaign in the United States to have the charges dropped. Mejía has held a number of positions at different nongovernmental organizations (NGOs) throughout Nicaragua, all aimed at using her education to address problems caused by social inequities.

Mejía was born in 1967 in the town of El Viejo, in the Department of Chinandega, a western department of Nicaragua that shares a border with Honduras. She spent her childhood years, beginning at 12, as a youth volunteer with the Sandinista National Literacy Crusade. In the 1980s, she went to Cuba to be trained as a teacher. On returning to Nicaragua, she spent years teaching in the Nicaraguan countryside before studying psychology at the *Universidad Nacional Autónoma de Nicaragua* in Managua. The role of education plays a prominent aspect in the development of subjectivity in Yamileth's testimonio. For example, in being positioned very differently from Juanita and Sofía, Mejía described the consequences experienced within her family as result of her parents not being educated. As her story unfolded, she described a lack of knowledge—or ignorance—as something that functions to serve the dominant ideology, which, in effect, subjugates women's full and equal participation as citizen subjects. Many aspects of Mejía's testimonio reflect the ways in which she benefited from the creation of spaces of inclusion for women that were pioneered by women, like Juanita and Sofía, who came before her. The following testimonio by Yamileth Mejía demonstrates the role of education and critical knowledge in lifting people out of the "dark" and becoming "superrevolutionary" in their expression of citizenship:

> *Yamileth, we will talk for about an hour, and I'll start by asking you first about yourself, about your personal history, your family, your childhood.*

I want to thank you very much for choosing me from the many women who are the feminists of Nicaragua. In my country, there are many valuable women with very interesting stories, worth retelling, strong women who were pioneers in feminism.

I was born in a town called El Viejo in the Department of Chinandega. I was born in a small, semirural, semiurban town into a very humble, poor family that lived on the outskirts of town. My mother worked in the banana plantations that were developed in the '60s and '70s; those were the years in which the banana and cotton industries were developed. They cut down all the trees in Chinandega and began to plant bananas and cotton for export. So, my mother worked in the plantations, and she was also a seamstress. She finished the second grade. I am the daughter of a man who didn't finish even the first grade, but nevertheless knew how to read and write and during some time in his life was a political leader, during the Revolution, and always ready to give his support for the Revolution's cause. I come from those two honest, hard-working persons.

We are two sisters from my mother and father, and my father had another three children outside the marriage. My father was a Don Juan,[1] a man who, if he saw a pretty girl, he would try to seduce her, and well, sometimes the pretty girls would be interested in him, too, because he was a very handsome man in his youth. Anyhow, this is the type of psychological violence and discrimination that my mother lived, because he always had many girlfriends, many other women, and my mother was his wife.

Currently, they are together, *juntos pero no revueltos.*[2] My mother will kill me the day I tell her I said this to the camera, but she decided about 25 years ago to separate from him because she no longer loved him the way she used to. She wanted to end a relationship that no longer satisfied her and decided to be alone. He decided to stay there, as company, which is what happens with many couples, right? And well, they continue to live in the same house. She lives her life, and he lives his.

Within our family, she broke with those norms, by separating, even though she didn't do it legally. In the family, it is not permitted to leave your husband no matter what, even if he is psychologically violent or even if he beats his wife. We were a traditional family. So, I was able to see what a relationship like theirs was; it was not the most adequate because they were always fighting, always in an argument. I grew up listening and watching how they fought. And she would tell me, "You have to study, so that no man can boss you around; you have to study because you have to be independent, you have to earn your own money." Those were like the first signs of autonomy, and I would have to say of feminism, at some level. I began to understand that not everything was like that, like they had lived. Another thing, which my grandmother used to say: "Love does not take away knowledge," which meant that no matter how much in love you are with a man, it does not mean that you have to put up with everything all your life. That is, the knowledge that you have, you have to protect yourself and you have to love yourself. Those were the two lessons that I took from those two women who are the fundamental pillars of my own internal power.

Within my own family, there were many violent men, many, many violent men: my uncles, cousins, we knew that sexual abuses were being committed. Like I said, we were an average family, like any other in this country where many sexual abuses take place, as well as violence against women, battering, and where the norm you must follow—regardless of what my mother and grandmother had told me—is "you have to suck it up because he is your husband" and also that "you don't air your dirty laundry in public." But I kept thinking we can't just keep on being quiet about it; we can't be silenced, and one day I decided to talk about the abuse I lived and the abuse my nieces lived.

How old where you when you decided that?

I was 17 years old. When I was 15 years old, I decided to start a relationship with the man with whom I still am today. So this person, just as young as I, both of us very young, we would talk a lot. Now he talks less, it's terrible; he used to talk so much more! [Laughter.] We talked a lot about life, the situation,[3] what went on in our homes—in his home and in my home—anyhow, all the things that supposedly you don't talk about with your boyfriend, because the norm is that you're always kissing and hugging and touching. But we talked about more than just that, and we decided, later, to get married. This was when I was 17. It was my personal decision at that age. Besides, the Revolution had triumphed, and I had participated in the National Crusade for Literacy.

How old were you when you participated in the literacy crusade?

I was 12 years old; I was still a child, but I felt older, I felt mature. So, I decided to become involved, and my mother would say, "And with whose permission are you going?" I would say, "But it's fun, we're going to go teach," and somehow I would find a way to convince her to let me go to the training workshops to learn how to teach people to read and write.

How does a girl so young learn about doing that without her parents' consent?

Because, well you see, they were very socially conscious, so although they complained about it, my own father was involved in the Revolutionary process; he was involved with the unions. So, I would tell myself, "My father is involved, I also want to be involved." They would have cultural events, and one way I could participate was singing Revolutionary songs with my father, who played the guitar. He still plays the guitar. So I would sing with him during cultural events in my town and outside my town. On the other hand, my mother, who was a seamstress and a plantation worker, well, she would tell me about the discrimination and injustices within her group. They were treated like prostitutes; people would say that the women who worked at the plantations were prostitutes. She would complain, but she also would refuse to feel like a prostitute, because they weren't. She would say, "We are field workers, why do they have to call us that?" So, in a way they did agree with my involvement; it's just that they were very scared because the war was going on. Even when the Revolution had just triumphed, there were still people who would show up dead around town, or we would hear about people who would show up dead throughout the country. So, there was a lot of tension; fathers and mothers were very scared. She would say, "Okay, you can participate in the cultural events, but not other activities, something could happen to you." So, I would go to the cultural events, sometimes 200 kilometers from my town; we would leave one day and come back the next.

During that time, I was in a group called Association of Amateur Artists [laughter], and it was awesome to be a part of that group because we would do theatre, we sang, we danced, and we expressed ourselves as youth. Later, when I was 13, I was also the president of the Federation of Secondary School Students. During that time, they also sent us to cut cotton to defend the Revolution's crop. So, I joined a production battalion, along with over 200 students, to go to Puntañata and Cosiguina[4] to cut cotton, when those areas were still war zones. Then, I went to study to become a teacher and returned 7 months later. I went to Cuba to study with a brigade called 50 Anniversaries—the 50th anniversary of Sandino's birth.[5] I was part of that brigade and was placed in Guantanamo. That's where I learned to be a primary school teacher, and then I was sent back. The members of this group, we were 16 by then; we had been together from 12 to 16. At the age of 16, I decided to go to Somoto, also a war zone: Estelí, Somoto, Ocotal, all the Segovias were war zones; that's where the Contras were.

How old were you when you went to Cuba?

Sixteen, and at that age, I went to teach in the countryside. I was in charge of a classroom with two grades, second grade and fourth grade in Somoto, in an area called El Rodeo #2. It was dangerous because it was on the other side of the Coco River, and on the other side of the Coco River was the Lancite Hill, which was occupied by the Contras. Every night, if we opened our windows, we couldn't see the stars; what we saw were the tracers,[6] the red bullets, the tracers from one side to the other. My teaching partner, we roomed together with a family that was assigned to us, the Alfaro family—very lovely people. "Fran, Fran," I would say to her, her name was Francisca; I would say, "Look, there goes another tracer." And she would say, "Yes, let's go to bed so we don't see them." "But you can hear the gunshots, you can hear them," I replied.

At that moment I wasn't even, I didn't have any idea of fear. What I wanted was to develop myself as a teacher, what I wanted was to help the Revolution. I wanted to teach them like Carlos Fonseca[7] had told us: "Also teach them to write." I was a faithful believer of that Revolution, of that life project for an entire nation. I am still a faithful believer that it is in education, that education is the principle base on which a nation can develop. As long as you keep people in the dark, not knowing anything, of course you will be able to do what you wish with them and manipulate them. Ignorance is the best friend of abusive people's manipulation.

So there, I grew up that way, from the time I was 12 to when I was 16, in a Revolution that moved my senses, my feelings, my emotions, and mixed in with all that, my relationship with my boyfriend. For me, this was a life lesson and also a lesson for that future couple, that future family. Because in those times there was a lot of talk about equality, and I believed it. I believed it. When my boyfriend came to visit me, instead of kisses and hugs and all that, what I would do was to take out a magazine that was called *Los Muchachos*, which talked a lot about sexuality and provided a lot of orientation, I think in a very advanced way. In those days, it had plenty of information on the equality between men and women, about equality during courtship. Now I know that Sofía Montenegro[8] was behind that magazine, because it was part of the ideological framework, of the instrument that there was to be able to give information to the youth. Well, I was part of the youth that read that information.

So, I would read this with him, and then he used to say, "When we get married, we're going to have six kids," and I would think to myself, this guy is crazy! [Laughter.] I don't know who will bear him six kids, but not me. [Laughter.] Me? Never! One or two, tops! And really, I have two children, a daughter and a son. But it was a good coming of age for me, a good coming of age within everything that the Revolution represented, within all the sacrifices that many of us youth made, both men and women—the people who joined the military service; the people who went and did other things. For example, the 50th Anniversary Brigade group, we left our homes and lived in the countryside for 2 years, out there in the bush, and taught.

Later, the Ministry of Education incorporated the bunch of us who had studied to become teachers. When I was in Somoto, the person who monitored our Revolutionary activities as much as our educational activities—and I had no idea that I would meet her again, later in life—was Martha Munguia,[9] who was part of the Ministry of Education and the Association of Nicaraguan Women (AMNLAE).[10] So, there you can see how chance later brings you into contact with those same people, you see? So, in my life: a Sofia Montenegro, through paper, through concrete information, and also a Martha Munguia, through her follow-up and monitoring work that she did back then. But to see yourself as part of that network, of that Revolution, well, it's nice. If you stick to the objective of honesty, the objective of equality for all, for women and for men, not just equality for men—for those four men who today are the owners of a made-up Revolution—but of a whole revolution for a whole country. To be a part of that . . . you felt like a piece of sand and suddenly you see yourself with all these monumental women, because of their thoughts, because of their actions, because of their honesty, because they are part of what is now that great women's movement. In addition to the seed that my mother and grandmother had already planted in me and of my need to do something social, which I saw in my father, with the work I had with all the organized men and women in Monterrosa,[11] which is a sugar-processing plant, well, I slowly formed myself in that way and that concern of searching for something that represented the women, searching for something that resignified what it is to be a woman.

When I turned 17, I said, "All right, we'll get married," bowing to my mother's pressure, but still I said to myself, I am getting married because

I want to be free. This is contrary to the norm. My mother calls that "dog's enrollment." She says, "You are the one who enrolls yourself and then the man owns you." But I said to myself, why? No, for me getting married was my ticket to freedom, so I would not have to live under my father's orders, nor my mother's. I had it easy with my boyfriend, very easy [laughter]. So I told myself, "No, this is my ticket to freedom." And it really was.

What year was it that you got married?

I was 17 and now I'm forty-three; it was '86, I think, '87. I was a baby, I was just a baby, but with a critical mind. I don't know where I got it, too early. I think that we are a generation matured with carbide; carbide is the thing they put on bananas to make them mature faster. We were a generation that matured very quickly, very fast, with a lot of responsibilities. For example, I became responsible for my sister when I was 6 years old. My grandmother took care of both of us, but when my mother would go to work, and my father worked out of town and only came home every 2 weeks, I would stay under my grandmother's supervision, and my sister under my supervision, a 6-year old girl! I was like her mom when I was 6. My mother would tell me before leaving for work—she went to work at 3 in the morning and would come home at 11 at night from working in the plantations—so she would say, "Yami, I'm leaving two córdobas[12]; take them and buy the milk, the firewood for the beans and the tortillas." This was something normal for me, to take on responsibilities. I was 6 years old, so at 17, well, I think I had done a lot. So then, it was time for me to win some freedom; I wanted to be free [laughter], and that's what it meant for me.

What kind of work did you focus on after you were married?

Well, I continued to teach at night, and I went to college. I finished high school at night and taught during the day. Then, I moved to Managua to go to college, for 5 or 6 years, and I continued working in the afternoon. I studied in the morning and worked in the afternoon. I was studying psychology when I learned of the existence of the Network of Women Against Violence, in '92. I went, when they founded the Network, to see what was going on. Then, about 2 years later I showed up again when they introduced Violeta Delgado.[13] She was the new executive coordinator for the Network, and I was at that meeting. I even remember how she was dressed; she had on light blue pants and a white shirt. I told myself, "I want to be part of this, I like how these women think, I want to be like them."

So, I began to learn about how to be part of this Network of Women. At this point, I'm talking about when I was 20 or 21 years old. There's a time where all I did was study and work. But, I wanted to be part of something else, so I become involved with the Network and continued doing other jobs, I continued working, and I continued going again and again to the Network's meetings. After I finished my degree, psychology, because it's what I liked best, I think it was what meshed better with what I did and with what I had lived. And maybe I also chose it to find myself and take care of myself, of my mental health, because as I've told you, I had had a pretty full life, and so I had to find a way out. But, I also studied it because I wanted to contribute through this career, I wanted to contribute to other women. For a long time, while I was still studying, for about 2 years, I worked at *La Verde Sonrisa*,[14] an NGO that worked with children. So there I learned to do community work, how to relate to young boys and girls who are glue sniffers, the children who inhale fumes from glue, who are addicts, who have been led to such savagery by poverty, to forget who they are or to forget the violence they have suffered. I also saw that they had been abused, boys and girls. Everything I had learned during the Revolution was turning out to be very useful; this was about when Doña Violeta won the elections. I joined the Network and started doing political work. This is because this organization promoted development and education, but it also included ideas from the Sandinista Front, and I was also part of that. I worked there for 2 years.

After finishing college, I went to work at *Dos Generaciones*.[15] This is where I learned to work around issues of sexual abuse, because Dos Generaciones's focus was the prevention of sexual abuse in boys, girls, and adolescents, as well as treatment for the victims. So, I learned more and continued to be part of the Network of Women. I continued hearing a lot about feminism, continued seeing Violeta Delgado, and started to meet with Juanita Jiménez[16] and with Martha in their sphere of influence. And, I would say, "Wow, these women know so much, they know a lot, they produce ideas and promote Act 230. How are we going to get laws like this passed?"[17] So, they brought in a bunch of women lawyers at that time, Juanita was one of them, also Azahálea,[18] Angela Rosa Acevedo, who is now on the Supreme Court and is part of the FSLN,[19] she is still part of the FSLN but she has to—it's horrible to have to use "but"—well, she is still also a feminist woman; it's just she does her work within the FSLN. Not us; none of us do.

I want to ask you to tell me a little about the work you focused on when you were at the Network of Women Against Violence? What kind of issues did you work on and what kind of strategies did you use?

When I started, I was responsible for a commission that we called the Commission on Psychosocial Development, which began after Hurricane Mitch.[20] A large group of psychologists, social workers, health workers, and mental health workers got together, and we began to organize ourselves in a way that we could contribute our skills to the aftermath of such a large natural disaster and contribute the feminist focus, which each one of us had already embraced. So, we began to organize processes of emotional healing, but with a different focus, not the traditional clinical focus, but a feminist focus and a focus on human rights as well. Because if a woman comes to you and tells you, "I feel bad because my husband died and I am happy," and you ask her why she is happy, and she tells you, "Well, he used to beat me and so now I am happy that he is dead; I'm happy that the mudslide took him with it." So then, which is the only explanation that can justify the pain, the guilt, and the happiness of that woman? It's the feminist focus and the human rights focus, because the traditional focus would have blamed her more, the traditional focus would have told her she has a disorder, while our focus was telling her, "Your feeling is valid. His time was up, and he died. Now what? What are we going to do now so that from now on you don't go on carrying the guilt of feeling happy?" You see? So, you get this from a different angle, a different focus, a different look at psychology. It is not the traditional psychology. I am a psychologist who can work with a woman who is living with domestic violence, but I work with her with a different focus, a different viewpoint; I see her as a human being, in charge of herself just as any other human being, with rights, with opportunities just like everyone else. I do not see her as a mentally deranged being, without values, just because she decided to feel happy about her husband's death. That liberated her! That is the opportunity that feminism gives me, that the Network of Women, with its focus on human rights, and also that Dos Generaciones gives me.

So, how to connect those strategies? That is the main strategy we introduced in the Network of Women. After that, I became a member of the executive board, professionally. So, there we were, Rosa Maria, Juanita, and I trying to push the national processes. I was no longer part of a commission, in that large national umbrella organization, but rather part of the umbrella. But, I also felt like a member because of my own personal responsibility. So, to train women as leaders? They are the leaders. Someone once asked me, "And you are going to teach me to be a leader?" To which I replied, "No, you are already a leader; you will teach me in the process." What we wanted was for other women, who were also leaders in their own communities, to share their knowledge, so that the other women, all the female leaders, can have the possibility, the opportunity to hear about the different theories that other valuable women have built—to learn about how women in other countries had written about feminism, to discover other women, from the French Revolution, I mean the beginning. Many of the participants came to me and said, "How is it possible that so many women participated in the French Revolution and they didn't even include them in history?" Women were also erased from the history of this

Sandinista Revolution. So, then, how to awaken, unveil, break ground, and also how to identify feminist books? For example, to know about Carmen Alborch,[21] who talks about the rivalries among women, how the machismo forces us to become rivals and see them as the trophy. How sexism or the way we are socialized to be women domesticates us; we are domesticated like animals. We are told what things women should and should not do and what things men will do freely. We are taught the right way to perform our domestic duties, that's why they call them domestic duties, and women perform them because they have been domesticated to do so. It's as if they can just turn on a switch when placed before a stove. I do not like to cook; I do it because otherwise I go hungry, but I learned to dislike it. But, you know, men and women should learn to cook, men and women should know how to clean a house. But, no, because that is a woman's work, because it is domestic, it is what domesticates them and forces them to stay inside the house. So, we learned all that in the processes of feminist formation in the Network, of which I, fortunately, was part of.

And how did you make that decision to leave?

Well, within the Network, as it was growing, our process was that every 3 years there would be one Coordinating Commission and three Network executives; our term was coming to an end, it ended in 2007. The possibility of a second term with the Network existed, but this transition period coincided with the presidential elections, and there was a rupture within the women's movement. Some women who were members of the Network decided to become involved in the Autonomous Women's Movement and decided we wanted to do things a different way. Another group decided they wanted to do things differently. Really there were two groups, which led to a rift.[22] This all coincided with the Executive Commission's transition period. They decided there would be a new Coordinating Commission to steer the Network, and that our term was over, period. And it was a great learning experience because they tell you that, well, what the assembly wanted, and the democracy we are promoting, we promote it from within, and this can work for or against an organization. We could have decided that half the previous members of the Coordinating Commission could stay, so there would be some continuity, but no, they were more radical. They said, "No, we are going to have a new Coordinating Commission." But, the thing is they also said we were very partisan because we dared to voice our preference for X or Y party because it was more in line with our ideas. Yet, during a different moment in history, when the Network was just starting, many women were also members of the FSLN and decided to run for a seat in the Assembly and the Network supported them. So, I dare to say that even within those women's organizations that there are still many ideas that convene with those of the old FSLN. My friends and colleagues in the Women's Movement may not agree with me, but I do see it that way because there are still many authoritarian attitudes, attitudes that tell you, "This is what we are going to do, and it's what we are going to do." But, we tried, I think we at least tried very very hard, to democratize that space. And I think that was one of the legacies that both our Coordinating Commission, as well as the one prior to ours, left: to attempt to have democratic processes within that organization, and well, they are still there.

So, where did you start working after that?

Afterwards, I worked as a consultant, voluntary work, activism, voluntary work with the Autonomous Women's Movement and the Women's Network Against Violence. I consulted for Xochilt Acalt,[23] for the Women's Movement of Chinandega. In León, in Matagalpa, I lent my support to different places in Nicaragua.

Until you started with your current organization?

Yes. Well, after that what I did was apply for a job that appeared in the Spanish Agency for International Development Cooperation's[24] website. I liked it because it sought to support and strengthen that critical route that we had talked about for so long in the Women's Network and how to strengthen it so that the institutions would finally, once and for all, start providing services to women. We wanted a concrete project that would support the Women's Police Station, the Public Prosecutor's Office, the Institute for Legal Medicine, women's organizations, and shelters. Shelters are necessary so that fewer women become fatal victims of violence, so that women, although they have lived through violence, know where they can go to place a complaint and know that they will be well received at those places where they place the demand, and be treated respectfully. We didn't want just words, but for women to be taken, in a timely manner—not 2 or 3 months later—to the Institute for Legal Medicine. We wanted this woman not to have to return home, not to become a victim again. So, that is basically what this project is trying to do, and I felt that I was a perfect match for it because of all the work I had done in the Network.

So now, I am doing the same things I was trying to do in the Women's Network, but now it's based out of this project—called the Comprehensive Services to Victims of Gender-Based Violence Project,[25] within the Spanish Agency for International Development Cooperation. I feel that we are introducing the same feminist focus in all these processes with the state institutions; they don't walk the talk, they have refused to—and still refuse to—work with women's organizations, even though women's organizations have been providing services for women victims of violence. These women's organizations have even provided treatment models for them to follow! So, simply stated, Daniel Ortega said, "No more work with women's organizations; now you must work with the ETC," and they broke away with the coordinating network they had built.

So, with this project we have been able to rebuild some of that network of interinstitutional coordination, as well as coordination with the women's organizations, at least at the local level, at least in Puerto Cabeza, a little bit in District 6 and some of the other districts in Managua. Proof of this is that the Police Station, for example, sends women who are victims of violence and in danger of death, well they send them to Acción Ya, to Acción Ya's shelter; but, they don't include them in the National Budget. So, the women who are coordinating shelters, at this point, they are the ones who have to scramble to keep and support the women victims of violence and also those women whom they have at their shelters.

I have two more short questions; you've used this term feminism. *Can you tell me what it means to you? How do you define it?*

A better way of living life, a way of finding balance, the equality between men and women, between men and men, and between women and women. It does not only mean to find equality between men and women, but to find it between all human beings. For me, it is a philosophy of life that I apply to my life every day, and it's hard to undertake sometimes because it's also about principles. It's among the most revolutionary philosophies of life. It's superrevolutionary because it goes against injustice, not just injustice towards women, but towards men and women; it is in favor of full citizenship, a citizenship without any type of discrimination. That's what feminism is for me.

Are you a feminist?

Yes, [laughter] until the day I die [more laughter].

And I also want to ask you, how have the consequences you've received politically affected your life?

It does affect you because whether you like it or not, your family becomes involved. When they brought charges against us, against the nine feminists, at the end of the year—it was 2007—my son was getting ready to graduate from high school, and he comes up to me and tells me, "Mom, you know, I was thinking, I had a dream and I've been thinking a lot about it." "About what?" I said. "Well, you know, the moment that you take me by the arm to receive my diploma, if the police show up I will call my friends and we will surround you so that the police can't take you." I laugh about it now, because it didn't happen. A friend told me once, "That story you shared about your son, well, it really got to one of our members, tears were running down her face." And you know, it wasn't until that moment that I really realized how much it affected my son and daughter. They would also say, "Mom, don't go to the marches, Mom, they're going to hurt you, don't go." I'd try to calm them down, "No, don't worry, nothing is going to happen to me, don't worry." As they got older and the marches became more violent—we were attacked with stones, they would insult us, they wanted to beat us with sticks, all of that—well, they started to see things were much more serious. They lived that harassment very close to home.

I lived that harassment, too, but I was incredibly angry; I mean, how dare they say that we had engaged in unlawful association to commit a crime? We are not criminals; we are defenders of human rights. They would say we were in favor of abortion; yes, so what? What is the problem with that? They are our bodies, right? They would accuse us of being accomplices to sexual abuses, when the biggest accomplice was the president's wife![26] And the criminal was the president, not us. So, because we were in favor of human rights they were making slanderous and defamatory allegations about us, accusing us of being criminals; we weren't criminals. We were not criminals. Oh, I would get so angry, so very angry.

I also was not able to get a couple of jobs that I applied to. They would say, "The thing is, while you have this unresolved matter, we just can't hire you." Same thing happened to Martha; they told Martha, "We can't hire you because you have an unresolved matter with the courts." And this affects our survival, it affects our children's survival and our right to employment, right? Until, well, the Spanish Agency for Cooperation ventured to hire me, although I still had that unresolved matter—after that, I just pressed forward.

The extent to which education and knowledge played a prominent role in Yamileth's formative years can be explained, in part, by the social positioning of her youth. Chinandega, where Yamileth was raised, is in the northwestern region of Nicaragua, where banana plantations represented the first major U.S. agricultural investment in the 1880s and the industry in which her mother was employed. Although the banana industry has thrived, it has done so at the expense of its labor force. For example, starting during the Somoza dictatorship, unregulated use of pesticides by multinational corporations in an effort to boost export of bananas. Despite that the chemicals were banned in the United States by the Environmental Protection Agency in 1977, corporations like Dole, Del Monte, and United Fruit continued to administer the banned pesticides in Nicaragua until the Nicaraguan government intervened in 1985. Thus, although export agriculture was a booming business for the U.S. companies, health problems reported by banana workers included atrophy of the testes; sterility; skin and breast cancer, liver, pancreas, and kidney problems; nervous disorders; mis-carriages; and genetic malformations. By the end of 2005, over 1,000 former banana workers had reportedly died from pesticide-related diseases (Foundation for Sustainable Development [FSD], 2015). The devastation that came to work-ers, families, and communities suffering from poverty and sicknesses related to pesticides has led to several lawsuits against companies headquartered in the United States (e.g., Dole). The multinational banana companies therefore had sig-nificant influence on the economic, political, and social lives of people living in this region and influenced the social location from which Yamileth would work.

Yamileth began her testimonio by describing how the context of poverty in which her family lived prohibited either of her parents from receiving an education. Her mother, despite working long hours on one of the banana plan-tations, did not make enough money to support the family. She would leave Yamileth with the equivalent of 8 cents a day to buy milk, firewood, beans, and tortillas for the household. It was in this context that Yamileth learned at an early age that education was a pipeline out of poverty. As a poor daughter of a mother ensnared in the feminization of poverty at the global intersections of gender and class, Yamileth problematized the lack of choice or agency she observed in her mother's life. For example, both the exploited labor in which her mother was engaged and the relationship she had with Yamileth's father reflected a lack of power and control that Yamileth rejected.

Very early in her story, Yamileth described the manner in which she began to problematize traditional gender norms when she identified that her father's philandering served as a source of her mother's suffering and was a form, in Yamileth's view, of psychological violence. Yamileth deide-ologized the gendered norms that allowed for this behavior and pointedly contended that, despite the cultural normality of her parents' interactions, a relationship like theirs was not desirable. Yamileth attributed her oppo-sitional ideology not only to observing her mother's experience but also to receiving the explicit messages her mother and grandmother communicated about the freedoms they wanted for Yamileth but were not able to bring to fruition in their own lives. For example, the seeds by which Yamileth prob-lematized a lack of access to education were planted early by the women in her life—women whose lack of opportunity was partly determined by global economic policies. At the outset of Yamileth's story, she shared more about her parents than herself, in particular noting that her parents did not study beyond the second grade. Moreover, her mother experienced discrimina-tion and injustice both from her father and as a result of her employment in the banana plantations. Yamileth's mother and grandmother both sent her messages rooted in a deideologization of gendered norms by invoking the importance of education. Yamileth internalized these messages from her mother ("you have to study because you have to be independent") and grandmother ("Love does not take away knowledge") into what she called the "fundamental pillars of my own internal power." In this way, her fore-mothers served as exemplars of women who rejected the dominant ideology, yet lived in situations limited by power and cultural norms situated in a global context that prohibited their own rejection from translating into resistance and action.

The Revolution provided an opportunity for Yamileth, at the young age of 12, to actualize the potential of her education, not only for her own gain, but also for the betterment of others. In particular, because Yamileth had internalized messages of resistance couched in education and knowledge from her foremothers, these values guided her collective engagements and activist work in the national literacy brigades of the 1980s. This would prove to be the first opportunity to begin addressing the gender asymmetries her mother and grandmother spoke of through the use of education.

Although Yamileth did not begin her efforts with explicitly gendered aims, her decision to become a literacy teacher as a young girl put her on a decidedly different educational path from that of her foremothers. This experience, whereby she volunteered to teach peasants how to read and write, would prove foundational to informing her later activism. By the age of 13, she became a leader within an education-based organization, and at the young age of 16 she received teacher training when joining a brigade to Cuba.

Yamileth was able to receive this postsecondary education, in part, because of the nature of the conflict in which her country was embroiled. Yamileth was volunteering in a Revolution that was being strangulated by the Iran-Contra affair, in which the Contras were both financially and militarily supported by the U.S. government. In a context of solidarity and shared recognition for the value of literacy and education, the Cuban government provided educational and vocational training to Nicaraguans in return for Nicaragua providing food supplies to help overcome the effects of the U.S. embargo on Cuba.

It is in the context of these global relations in the 1980s that Yamileth received her training as a teacher. Yamileth's social position as a child helped shape her opportunity to become involved in education, but the experience of education itself helped facilitate the ideological value that "education is the principle base on which a *nation* can develop" (emphasis added). Yamileth illustrated her belief regarding the role of knowledge in bringing awareness to the masses when she stated that the consequence of *not* doing so included ignorance, which she defined as the "best friend of abusive people's manipulation." In this way, Yamileth shared an oppositional ideology with Sofía Montenegro (Chapter 2), who believes that access to knowledge is a right.

In Yamileth's first step toward bringing education to the masses, she took a teaching post in a rural area occupied by the Contras. Although she was positioned as a teacher, she was not quite an adult; therefore, many events during the Revolution occurred during her formative years. Thus, Yamileth was inevitably shaped by what was occurring in the context of the community in which she was engaged. In one example, although adolescents all over the world may relate to stargazing from any given location, Yamileth's experience in the middle of a war-torn country took on a greatly different reality. Instead of gazing at stars, Yamileth fell asleep to the illumination of tracer bullets fired by Contra weapons that were funded by the U.S. government. Despite the potentially traumatic nature of these experiences, as an adolescent girl who had committed her youth to educating the impoverished and marginalized, Yamileth stated, "At that moment . . . I didn't have any idea of fear. What I wanted was to develop myself as a teacher, what I wanted was to help the Revolution."

Although making a contribution to education as a teacher, as a Sandinista youth Yamileth was also a direct beneficiary of knowledge that had been popularized by women involved in the Movimiento (e.g., Sofía Montenegro). In particular, the writing that was produced to educate Nicaraguan people about gender and sexuality played a critical role in shifting Yamileth's ideology and action as a youth. For example, in setting out to break the silence imposed on women in her family, Yamileth was determined to bring her deideologization of gender into her budding relationship with her boyfriend by strategically laying a groundwork informed by feminist knowledge. Thus, in many ways not permitted by her mother and grandmother, Yamileth's resistance moved forward to a deepened subjectivity. Yamileth even described her marriage, although at a young age, as an act of opposition. She rejected the precocious domestic role assigned in her family by suggesting she had to mature too fast, something she attributed, in part jokingly, to the carbide pesticides used on the banana plantations. She therefore viewed marriage as her "ticket to freedom." Her efforts in developing an "oppositional" relationship reflect important steps in *conscientización*—Yamileth was working to change her own circumstances; at the same time, she was working to change the social structures that disadvantaged others. This is consistent with Freire's (1970) understanding of liberation. Yamileth's decision to marry was, in effect, an act of resistance that allowed her to focus further on her life goals surrounding education by honing skills that could contribute to developing the knowledge and tools that could help others out of the "darkness."

As part of her continued development into a citizen subject, the role of learning about inequity played a central role in Yamileth's story and her desire to be like the women who "know so much." Although her affiliation with the FSLN came to an end when many others' did as well, after the 1990 electoral loss, Yamileth maintained her belief in education and knowledge. When enrolled in university, Yamileth found meaning in psychology, the study of individuals in context, because it allowed her to both address experiences of her past and find a way to contribute to other women's lives. She would use this experience to become directly involved in promoting education and awareness among the solidarity of others who shared a similar oppositional ideology, first through the Network of Women Against

Violence. Over time, Yamileth's involvement in various NGOs led to an educational praxis aimed at promoting an alternative way of knowing and teaching. For example, rather than use her education to establish herself as the "knower," at the cost of silencing others' voices, Yamileth deconstructed traditional ways of understanding teaching and learning by recognizing the subjectivity among the women with whom she was working. She refused an invitation to teach a woman to be a leader and opted instead to focus on the woman's subjectivity by recognizing that she was *already* a leader in her community with invaluable knowledge. In effect, Yamileth deflected the opportunity to control the flow of knowledge—directly underscoring her belief in the links between knowledge and power.

Although Yamileth's experience of inequality and revolutionary activity as a youth led to the creation of a political subject who sought change throughout the course of her life, she did so within the constraints of powerful economic, political, and social relations operating on local and global levels. For example, at the time of her interview, Yamileth was employed by the Spanish Agency for International Development, largely because she was viewed as unemployable by the Nicaraguan government due to the political persecution she received at the hands of Daniel Ortega. Therefore, the dismantling of social services and privileging of neoliberalism have led not only to the dependence of social services on unstable international funding, but also, more indirectly, to Yamileth's dependence for a livelihood.

Like Juanita Jiménez (Chapter 1) and Sofía Montenegro (Chapter 2), Yamileth was a Sandinista youth who problematized how a lack of access to education disenfranchised the masses. Yamileth's experience as a beneficiary of knowledge, however, more directly demonstrated *how* access to education and knowledge created ideological change that had an impact on individual citizen subjectivity. Before even beginning her story, for example, Yamileth entered into her testimonio by paying homage to the women who had blazed a trail before her, in effect having paved the way for her to use her voice to contribute to a growing knowledge about inequities within the country. In honoring these women, Yamileth identified feminism as a local construct. When prompted to define feminism, Yamileth reflected an intersectional perspective held by many active women in the Movimiento, which is that feminism is not simply about the inequities between women and men that can be explained by a power dichotomy reflected in one aspect of social location (e.g., gender), but rather it is an ideological framework through which to understand any form of discrimination that violates the rights of all human beings. She explained this intersectional ideology as "superrevolutionary" because it is an inclusive framework for deideologizing all forms of power, in favor of full citizenship. Although she continued throughout her life to identify lack of knowledge and access to education as the structures through which the dominant are able to sustain the subordination and marginalization of the people, in the end her work demonstrated that without the rethinking and resisting that come with feminist knowledge, in particular, the dominant will do with women what they wish and that in doing so women will be kept in the dark and "domesticated like animals."

Notes

1. Don Juan is a legendary Spanish character famous for his obsessive skills in seduction and philandering.

2. This is a saying used to describe a relationship in which two people may be together, but there is no obligation between them. They may decide to be with each other because it is better than being alone, as opposed to being with each other because they cannot stand being apart.

3. Yamileth was referring to the Revolution.

4. Puntañata and Cosiguina are on the western coast of the country on a small peninsula.

5. Augusto Sandino was a Nicaraguan revolutionary leader in the early 1900s who fought against U.S. occupation and was assassinated by Anastasio Somoza in 1934. He is considered a national hero in Nicaragua. Sandino was born in 1895 and died in 1934. It is more likely that the brigade was commemorating the 50th anniversary of Sandino's death.

6. Tracers, which were used by the U.S. Army's M16 assault rifle, were small pyrotechnic charges that allowed a phosphorous tail to burn brightly, making projectiles visible to the naked eye.

7. Carlos Fonseca was a Nicaraguan teacher and librarian who founded the Sandinista National Liberation Front. He was assassinated in 1976, which was 3 years before the FSLN took power.

8. Sofia Montenegro's testimonio is included in Chapter 2.

9. Yamileth and Martha Munguia were two of the nine women who were caught in a legal battle concerning their support of Rosita.

10. *Asociación de Mujeres Nicaragüenses Luisa Amanda Espinoza* (AMNLAE; Luisa Amanda Espinoza Association of Nicaraguan Women) was the FLSN-organized women's organization started in 1979.

11. Ingenio Monterrosa, located in the Department of Chinandega, was one of four sugar-processing plants that were confiscated and given to the workers as a result of the Sandinista triumph of July 19, 1979. Years later, during President Violeta Chamorro's government, they were privatized.

12. The córdoba is the Nicaraguan currency. One córdoba is equivalent to approximately 4 cents in the United States.

13. Yamileth and Violeta Delgado were two of the nine women caught in the legal battle concerning Rosita. A testimonio from Violeta is included in Chapter 5.

14. This translates as the Green Smile.

15. The meaning here is Two Generations.

16. Juanita Jimenez was also one of the nine women caught in the legal battle concerning their support of the 9-year-old girl. Juanita's testimonio is included in Chapter 1.

17. Act 230 was a law making domestic violence illegal and punishable by jail time. The law was passed in August 1996.

18. Azahálea Solís was a member of the Network at the time and is currently an active member of the Movimiento.

19. Frente Sandinista de Liberación Nacional or Sandinista National Liberation Front.

20. Hurricane Mitch was a hurricane that hit Central America in October 1998. Between 9,000 and 11,000 people were killed, largely due to flooding, and roughly 2.7 million people lost their homes.

21. Carmen Alborch is a Spanish politician and author.

22. Through the mid-2000s, the Network of Women Against Violence served as the organizational space for the Movimiento, mobilizing a membership until the movement founded an official organization with the name *Movimiento Autónomo de Mujeres* in 2008. Yamileth referenced another group of women representing 18 organizations that chose a different strategic route to addressing women's rights that uses the name the Nicaraguan Feminist Movement (Lacombe, 2014).

23. Xochilt Acalt is a rural women's center located in Malpaisillo in the Department of León.

24. The Spanish Agency for International Development Cooperation (La Agencia Española de Cooperación Internacional para el Desarrollo AECID) is a public entity within the Ministry of Foreign Affairs and Cooperation; it is responsible to the secretary of state for international cooperation. Its fundamental aim is to promote, manage, and implement public policies with particular emphasis on reducing poverty and achieving sustainable human development.

25. The project aims to support public institutions that provide services to victims of gender-based violence, as well as to influence civil society to reduce impunity and eradicate violence toward women. It is currently being implemented in two cities: Managua and Puerto Cabezas.

26. Rosario Murillo, wife of three-time (and current) President Daniel Ortega, disavowed her daughter, Zoilamérica Narváez, and the accusations of sexual abuse Narváez brought against him.

Matilde Lindo

4

Elevating Voices by Resisting Universalism

If we could just reach where we could have really strong women,
strong character and enough knowledge, because knowledge is
important to start doing things, you know, from a women's point of
view, from our cultures.

—*TESTIMONIO* FROM MATILDE LINDO

As one of the only Black members of the *Movimiento Autónomo de Mujeres*
(Women's Autonomous Movement) who was raised in the North Atlantic
Region in Nicaragua, Matilde Lindo brings a different perspective to the
ways in which democratic spaces need to be opened up for women. Lindo
was one of the most prominent activists representing women from the *Región
Autónoma del Atlántico Norte* (RAAN; North Atlantic Autonomous Region).
The RAAN has a history distinctive from the rest of Nicaragua. For example,
the territory of the Atlantic Coast is markedly geographically isolated and
suffered British rather than Spanish colonization. The British began coloniz-
ing the Atlantic Coast in the mid-1600s, resulting in the forceful relocation
of African slaves from Jamaica to work on the cultivation of sugar cane and
indigo near Bluefields, the current capital of the South Atlantic Autonomous
Region (*Región Autónoma del Atlántico Sur*, RAAS). Descendants of these
Africans in Nicaragua often refer to themselves as English-speaking Creoles.
The region has also experienced extensive resource exploitation and is pop-
ulated by indigenous peoples and multiple ethnic communities (Miskitus,
Creoles, Mayangnas, Ramas, and Garifunas).[1] In 1987, the Sandinista government sought to redress the injustices created by centuries of foreign and internal colonialism by implementing an Autonomy Law that legitimized those
from the Atlantic region to reclaim their historic right to the natural resources
of the region as well as the right to defend, preserve, and promote their identity, history, culture, and traditions.

In the early 1990s, Lindo helped form the Afro-Latin American and Afro-
Caribbean Women's Network. She attended the U.N. World Conference on
Women in Beijing in 1995. She later moved from the North Atlantic Region
to direct the Network of Women Against Violence in Managua when she was

in her 50s. At the time of the interview, Lindo was a leader at the Network of Women Against Violence; however, the Movimiento suffered an unexpected loss when Lindo passed away from a heart attack on January 20, 2013.

Lindo was born in 1954 in Puerto Cabezas, the capital of the North Atlantic Region of Nicaragua. Unlike many others involved in the Movimiento, and included in this book, Lindo did not begin her political career at an early age. However, she did develop a passion for learning and teaching at a very young age that would eventually serve her interests as an activist. Yet, it is not until Lindo was in her mid-30s, when she was alerted to the marginalization of women from democratic spaces, that she developed an oppositional consciousness that would drive her interests in enhancing the capacity of women as political subjects.

In finding her political voice, Lindo problematized women's lack of learning how to deal with public affairs at the same time that she cautioned using a universal approach to understanding women's diverse experiences and perspectives. In particular, Lindo resisted downplaying her racial and ethnic identity to privilege gender and called on others to respect an "autonomous consciousness" that upholds an intersectional perspective on power while trying to elevate women's voices in democratic participation. The following testimonio by Matilde Lindo demonstrates the role of knowledge and awareness in processes that lead to political participation among women:

> *I'd like to start by asking you a little bit about your personal history, about your childhood, the kind of family you grew up in, or your earliest memories.*
>
> I will start by saying that my ethnicity is, ah, I'm a Black person. You know in Nicaragua, some of the Black people prefer us to be called Creole, and some of us say, "No, we're just plain Black." Well, I'm just plain Black. My father and my mother were people who speak English. My first language is Creole English. That's the language that I knew in my childhood, that we speak in our homes.
>
> *And where were you born?*
>
> I was born in Puerto Cabezas, but I actually grew up in Rosita Mines. In Rosita there was a gold mining company; that's where we grew up, me and my brother and my sisters. And there was everything that we needed, you know like encampments or the satellite towns that are made by these companies.
>
> I grew up as a Moravian.[2] From when I was very small, I don't remember myself not being in a church. And I am a teacher; that's what I actually studied to be, a teacher. In my working experience, I have taught in a primary school, and I have been a secondary teacher also. I have three children—three girls. I didn't have any boys. My children have their children, so, from these, my children's children, I have eight grandchildren.

Oh, congratulations!

[Laughter.] Thank you. Five granddaughters and three grandsons. Then it was like 1989, I actually started getting involved in the women's movement, and all that has to do with women, human rights.

Were there experiences you remember from your childhood that helped you get involved in those things?

I come from a home where it was a general practice that whatever my mother decided, I mean my father couldn't come and change that decision. I didn't grow knowing that the women didn't have voice. I mean, that in my family, women always have voice, and that voice was heard and had to be obeyed, you know, just as much as the men in the family. So, I come from that sort of family. I come from a family where everybody had rights, really; that's what we would say today.

Were there experiences from your childhood that made you interested in getting involved in political work?

Ahm, no, not really. Not, directly because, in my childhood I was interested in learning language, imagine? Yeah! I remember a girl, Connie Francis,[3] and she was sort of famous around the time, and people said, "She sings in seven languages." "Oooohhhhh!" That is what I'd like to do—speak seven languages! But, I had my first child when I was just 16 years old, and it reminds me that at that time when you had a child, that really changed your whole status. So then I had to learn to be a mother.

In what way? What things changed for you?

If you had a baby, you couldn't go back to school. I was in fourth year at the time.[4] So, it was like my life had ended there. You know, according to society. But, I had such a loving family that my dad said, "No way, your life is not ended here; you're going to finish high school, and you're going to learn whatever we could afford." At the time, we didn't know what was a university. What was our option? Go to nursing school. Or, go to teaching school. And then you would go and learn to be a secretary. That was it. Since my family kept on supporting me, I decided to go to teaching school there. I would really rather do something else, but it was impossible at the time. So, I went to Waspán, which is in the northern part of Nicaragua, very near Honduras on the Rio Coco side. I took out my teaching degree, and I started working and then things started changing in the country. We had a Revolution, and when the Revolution started here, I got a job. I was working with the INSS—Instituto de Seguridad Social.[5] I worked with them for a year, and then I was working the MIDINRA[6] that has to do with the *derechos agrarios*.[7] Since I was a teacher, I had to see about the training courses with the farmers and courses that had to do with forest fires and those kinds of things. That was in Puerto Cabezas.

What made you interested in working for the organizations that were working on agrarian rights?

Since I was working for the government, it wasn't an option if I wanted or not. They, said, "Since you're a teacher and you have these capabilities, well, we need you here," and I went there. But, I really liked it, because anything that has to do with methodology, that has to do with teaching, I really like that.

So, in the end, did you go to university to become a teacher?

No, I did not. What I did is got a course to go to Cuba. And then I studied social investigation.

Is that like sociology?

Yes, yes. We went like in depth sociology, working at how to deal with people, how to understand this and that and the next. I really enjoyed that and that really gave me a lot more of understanding people.

Why did you do that in Cuba?

Because that was in 1976, and from Nicaragua, most of us, most people have an option to go to Cuba to study, and since I was working with these agrarian things, well, they sent to me an invitation, and I applied since it was a thing of getting more education.

And what was your first job?

When I came back, I had a big fight where I was working, and then I decided to go back to teaching. I went to teach at the Moravian High School.

And how did you make the decision to go back to teaching?

I had walked off my job [laughter] because they didn't want to give me a raise of pay, and they wanted me to do much more work, and they said, "No, you have much more skills, so you're going to do much more work." So, I said, "That's great and what about my salary?" And they said, "Noooo, we need to see if you can really do it," and I said, "No, I don't need to show you people anything." And I decided that I didn't need to make some political issue with my job, I was like clear on that. I'm working for the Nicaraguan government but I am not part of the Sandinistas' party. But I put limits and fully negotiate me being here, and if this work is not good enough, well, I'm out of here.

So you were out of there and went back to teaching?

Mm hmm. I went back to teaching for a year and a half, and then they looked for me and they said I was going to work at what they called the *Casa de Gobierno* at that time. They hired me as an analista,[8] and it was to see about the social issues that were happening in the RAAN.

And where were you living at the time?

I accepted that job and it was okay seeing what, all the social issues, education, healthcare, social security, and things like that. I got that experience, and after 1990 when the Sandinistas lost the election, I kept working. And then, I have a friend, her name is Raquel Dixon[9]—right now actually she is a deputy in the National Assembly—and she was looking for women and she said, "Strong women, we need strong women here because we're about to lose our space." Because the men from the Sandinistas party wanted to take over the House. So then we got together with like six women, and we would meet every Wednesday, religiously. I don't remember why this meeting was so important, but the thing was that, as women, we need to make our voice be heard, we need to know and to understand and to defend ways that we have human rights because we are human people. And I was like, "Oohhhh, I've never heard that said. I like it! I like it!" [Laughter.] And I continue on with the group and eventually things started to be a little tough and you were politically attacked. They were like, it's not important for women to be together, for a woman to have a better raise, to be organized and those kinds of things.

Because of this, I joined the Women's Movement, and I left my job to dedicate full time to this. Because I found out that there are so many things that have to be done around women's rights and I learned about violence against women and one of the first big things that we did in those days was we started a radio program. We would get on the radio show and just start telling people, "Women should not be living violence. There is a possibility of another kind of relationship." And of course, people were laughing at us and saying, "Oohhh, oh my gracious; you want to change the world. Don't they know that this is the world?" And, I remember I had some men friends, and they would say things like, "Matilde, you sound real good, you have a nice voice. What are you going to do; are you going to tell everyone, or what?" Besides the radio show, we started having workshops. We were in a learning process and teaching other women about this. And we kept growing, and then we had the support of Oxfam[10] from England, and they really supported us in the first years in 1990, 1992, those years; they supported us so that we could be strengthened, institutionally strengthened, and we worked a lot with women in the communities, in the indigenous communities.

What strategies did you use at that time to work with women?

At that time, what was our strategy? We didn't even know the word *strategy*! [Laughter.] But, the first thing we learned was that we had to become brave people. Because if we weren't brave, we wasn't going to reach anyone. The next strategy was alliance. We really met women from this other part of the country, and we worked a lot in alliance with women who are here [Managua], and at that time, in the early '90's—at that time, there was a big revolution among women here, because the women were breaking off from AMNLAE[11] We were in the right pattern at the right time in the right place, so we really worked in alliance, and that made us strong. Yet, we learned that we needed to keep our autonomous conscience[12] active because we're just so different, we're naturally from a different culture, we see the world through different eyes, and so we had to learn to hear what our colleagues were saying, try to understand it. To work with that, in our grassroots labor, where we would change things around and actually put it in our context. So, that was the main strategy; learning about things and saying, "Okay, we could do that here," and there were things that we said, "Look, definitely, we're out; I mean, this doesn't fit in the way of our lifestyle."

Okay. I know you're one of the most well-known spokespeople for issues on the Atlantic Coast. Can you talk a little bit about what some of the issues were for women on the Atlantic Coast and why they might be different than what women in Managua were working on?

One of things that we were working on and continue working on is that we need to strengthen, we need to get strengthened as people. When I says people, I am meaning that we are different historically, you know, the Atlantic Coast, it wasn't even Nicaragua, I mean, until 1894. We continue being very different, and we got our Autonomy Law.

We believe that our Autonomy Law has to do with our life, men and women. So then, things that we do from the women's movement, we consider men also. Meanwhile, our colleagues[13] are, their main thing is, you know, I—I don't want to say working against men because it's not really like that, but I mean, men are like a target, you know, that men must learn how to relate, men must change their violent way and things like that. Meanwhile, we have much more because we need our men to understand that we could grow together, you know, because we all live discrimination, and that's a point that we have, that we, *geopoliticamente*,[14] I mean because of where we are from, who we are—Spanish is not our first language and things like that. So, these are issues that we consider also when we're talking about empowerment and development and those kinds of things.

Mm hmm. And how did you make the decision to move from the organizing that you were doing on the Atlantic Coast and move to Managua?

Well, of course that has to do with personalities, right? There was a time when I needed to grow and I felt the need of sharing things from a different point of view. Because when I was on the Atlantic Coast, I would mainly do grassroots-level issues. I really wanted to go on to the political issues. For example, right now what work we're doing here in the Network Against Violence is, we're dealing with the National Assembly because there is a law that is about violence against women.[15] We're right down in that, and I am one of the main persons from the National Network who is right there and looking at the lines. Just last week we were reviewing again what the deputies are saying, and we're finding out that some of the main things being left out, like they've stopped saying in the law "violence against women." They're saying, "we're against violence." Then, what they are putting in is like, "violence against children," "violence against youth," and this and that, and of course they are trying to say that women are violent. We caught them. We have to get really smart and say, "Okay, politically, how should we go around this? What are the words? Where do we put these words, and how do we go and do lobbying?" I'm really interested in doing this kind of thing at this point of my life, and there aren't a lot of opportunities on the Atlantic Coast to do these kinds of things. When I was there, I tried to do these things and I was very lonely at it. In fact, there weren't much women saying, "Oh, yes, that's true, and here I come along with you." No, I started feeling lonely in that point.

And when was that? Do you remember what years those were?

Yes! I remember it was from 1995 when we had the World Conference of Women in Beijing.[16] I was involved in everything that had to do with Beijing.

Yeah?

Yep! I was in the local organization, the local commission, the national commission, the Central American commission, and then the regional commission that had to do with all of Latin America and Caribbean, and I really loved the experience.

Can you tell us about that experience?

At that point, as Black women, we realized that we needed to have our things, too, you know, and we formed what is called the Afro-Latin American and Afro-Caribbean Women's Network.[17] That didn't go so good, but, well, we did it, and it's somewhere there resting, but it might wake up sometime.

But, the thing is that at this point we had to be studying the documents. We had to really learn what was happening, and, I remember, we were getting these bulletins. From the UN, from the women from South America, from all over, and we would get a bulletin that would say, "Religious men, they're trying to take this and this rights away from women." And I would say, "Oops, that can't be. I know about that, and I know about religion, come, let's see what this is about," and we would make some kind of proposal. The proposal was going back and forth and even with the UN, and we would meet in one of the countries, most of the time it was Guatemala.

Did any women get chosen to attend the Beijing conference?

Nicaragua had one of the biggest delegations from Latin America.

Yeah!

It was more than 60 women that went from here. Yeah, we were there. [Laughter.] And, we even made friends with the government at the time. Because you know before Beijing, it was El Cairo[18]—that's work about the reproductive rights and what not. And there it was horrible what the government did. The government said, from Nicaragua, that we would not have sexual education, because that would be transgressing cultural rights, because we have this different kind of culture. No. The government never really cared about the word *culture*. 'Til all of a sudden when it came to women rights, and especially over sexual and reproductive rights—ooooh!— it was like, "Noooo! That can't be!" Nicaragua met with the *Vaticano*[19] and did their things in Cairo, so we learned a lesson there. And we said, "No, no. We gotta prepare ourselves." So we went to work, here in Nicaragua, and we made sure that whoever went to Beijing first, that it could not be a man. Because who was going to Cairo was the minister of education. Then we decided that we would tell her what to do and say, so we started having meetings here and there, actually like sat here in the country and said, "Okay, what things are not negotiable?" And then we had our points, and the government naturally said, "Look, these definitely we are not going to touch because we are not going to reach any agreement with you people because our point of view and so, so." So, we went with an agenda.

We did that here in the country, and then we did it in other countries also. We did it in Honduras, and we did the same thing in Costa Rica. Of course, it was Central America, and then we were kind of touching the government and saying, "You know, women in our countries, and maybe you don't know about this, but, we'd like to tell you that women are dying because they are getting pregnant too young." Those kind of things. "Are we accepting that women continue dying in the name of being mothers?"

So, it went better. It went well, really, in Beijing. What we finally had happen in Beijing was that somebody from the women's movement went along with the official delegation. So, it wasn't only like we were saying—we got somebody there. So, it was good. That experience is there. My dream is that we, on the Atlantic Coast of Nicaragua and in the rest of Central American countries also, we could reach there as women, you know, empower women. Not just women who will get a place in the government and, you know, she got a place, and she's obedient. If we could just reach where we could have really strong women, strong character and enough knowledge, because knowledge is important to start doing things, you know, from a women's point of view, from our cultures.

You've worked with a lot of organizations and a lot of issues throughout your career. Is there something that stands out for you that is the thing that you're most proud of in your career?

Well, one of my accomplishments in the Women's Movement is that we recognize that women's issues have a lot of different manifestations, culturally I mean. It is important to understand what is going on, so it is not a thing that is black and white or red and blue, you know. It is an issue that is much more profound because it has to do with women's daily lives, and that means it has to do with the way I see my life, the way I live my life and things like that, which doesn't mean that there is an excuse for women to live violence. There is no excuse, absolutely none, that women should be living violence. How could we go around eradicating, struggling against violence and really being successful in it? That's a challenge. That's a big, big challenge because we need to understand women much more.

How did that come to be an important topic for you? You said you were from a family where women's voices were really respected.

When I was working with agrarian people, one of the women that was around, she's a sociologist, a Mexican, and somehow we got talking, and I say, "You know, I'm so surprised at this." She said, "No, you are the one that is very different from everybody else!" And she was like, "You know you are from a Protestant church and your mind is so open." I said, "No, but I think everybody is like that." She said, "Well, guess what? No! It's not like that." I kept learning that the world wasn't the way it was in my life, in my small world. Then, when I learned about violence of women and I start seeing it in the society it was shocking.

And once you started working with these organizations, what was your experience like as a woman? Did you feel you experienced discrimination? Were there difficulties for you?

Of course! I remember because I used to like fighting. In Creole language, we used to fight us some. And, I remember I would always present myself and say, "I am Black and then woman!" Hhheee! They wanted to drop dead. Ooohh, they wanted, they wanted to just die, and said, "That's not possible. You have to be a woman and then Black," and I said, "Uh uh. *Es más* I am Black, Christian, then woman!" [She slams her hand down on the table.] That was for years, years. And I kept saying it because I really made it a hobby. You know? More than a political thing. Because like a hobby, I really liked to see that people get mad. My colleagues, my feminist colleagues, eventually came around to actually dealing with the subject.

I was just invited in the month of March to give a talk, on a big assembly that a group of women had, and they wanted me to talk about discrimination. One of the things that I spoke about was my experience and of course my experience I had lived with a lot of the women that were there. And I said you don't have most Black women that are feminists in this country. We are very, very, very, very few, I mean. I said that is one of the reasons, because you girls haven't been able to actually look to us, look at our culture and respect it. I mean, not even understand it, you just need to respect and say this is something different from what I've learned and the way I have been and you need to accept and respect the difference. I'm not saying that you need to understand it because I don't need to come here and start explaining my difference, because that's a lack of respect. Everybody was like, "Hahh! Really?" Because I'm Black, they look at me bad. And I said, "You know, no, we need to change. We really need to go for a change, we need to really have a different insight of this thing so we need to grow, and if we need to grow, we need to sit around the same table and say, you know what? This and this and this and that." So, we have to learn to make our voice be heard.

Now to reach to the point where they are actually inviting me to say these things, it's like, "Ooohh! I've come a long way, baby!" [Laughter.] Yeah! I was all excited, to tell you the truth. I was very, very excited.

You've used this term feminism. *Can you tell me what that means to you or how you understand or define feminism?*

Well, to me feminism means *corriente de pensamiento*—a way of thinking—it gives you different kind of criteria to face the world. And I actually see feminism very close to Christianism. Because I take feminism, not as a dogma, I will never take it as a dogma. And I don't take Christianism as a dogma either. So, it's like taking the best things and saying, "You know, this helps me to create a way of living."

What are some of those criteria that you would use to define them?

Some of those criteria that I use to define feminism is, in first place, a relationship of respect among people. You know, between men and women and between women also. So, that's the first very powerful thing for me. The next thing is that you could learn to be this way. It's not a natural and normal thing. It just doesn't come. It's like, it has to do with your lifestyle, it has to do with your life. And it's something that could be used basically with anybody. I don't think that feminist criteria are only for women. Since for me, it is a way of living—it is for men also. So, we could use the same criteria to deal with whoever.

So, you consider yourself a feminist?

Yup, because of those things.

Do you see a relationship between scholarship or academic work that might come out of the university and the work that women's organizations are doing in Nicaragua? Do you see any connection between those two things?

Yes, I do! I do see the connection because our lives have to do with a way of thinking, and our lives have to do with sharing these ways of thinking. And, it's not a common person, you know, like an everyday woman like me who could really go in depth and interpret certain things. Because even if I am thinking something, a lot of time I don't have the capability of interpreting what I am thinking and the way I am acting. So it is just like, well, we need, we need a doctor! Because if I'm feeling sick and my heart is not going well, I mean, the cardiologist is the person to say. So, in this case, it would be like, the scholars who would say what's not really going well between men and women, or from a woman's point of view. So these works that they do, especially things that have to do with research and investigation, those kinds of things, are, I think they're real necessary, they are really needed, for us to really understand the matter. I mean, it's an ongoing thing, and it's an in-depth thing. So, we really need to have the grassroots and scholars. Yeah, I'm convinced of that.

And with the other organizations, can you talk a little bit about how you are working with other organizations in Nicaragua, through the Network of Violence Against Women?

Maybe I should briefly explain to you how the Network works. The Network, we're like a space where we get together, and we're like about 90 organizations and women who are there individually. For example, like me, for years I've been here, but I don't represent an organization. I'm here on my own. So, we get together, and we make national assemblies, and there we kind of like take out the *lineas gruesas*,[20] you know the big things, what we're going to do, we're going to dedicate this year to the law—that is the new law that has been passed, and then we come in the office, and we kind of like plan everything. That means that we, that the group have to be in the National Assembly. Okay, who in the room could be in this group? Well, we need a lawyer and we need sociologists, okay? And then, we make a list, send it out, you know, then they say, okay, this is approved. Or, I propose that I can be on the list.

What are some of the current issues that women are working on right now, and are you working on issues that women from the Atlantic Coast are working on, or are you working on issues now more central to Managua?

We're working on mostly more general issues. What I have committed myself to has to be happening on the Atlantic Coast also. We have *derechos consuetudinarios*[21] that has to do with the indigenous way of claiming justice. They have their own judges in their community, and I made sure that this was, that this was being respected by the law. I got together with our deputy, and I said, "Look here now, you know, that this law that you people are handling, ta, ta, ta." And then I went to the Atlantic Coast. I sat with a group of women, and we discussed this and they say, "Look, to make this work, this is our proposal, ta, ta, ta, ta."

I am going to Bluefields day after tomorrow, precisely, to work with a 2-day workshop. One that is just for Latin America, so I'm going to work with them with that. And what they are saying here at the office is: "No, no, Matilde, we need you here," and I say, "Yes, and I need me there, and that's enough work all around." Well, I know it's going to become an issue. I know. But, I know they are really sensitive to the issue now than they were a year before, so I have alliance.

And what are some of the issues that women on the Atlantic Coast are orga- nizing around right, right now? What are the current problems that women are addressing?

I wouldn't know; I—I don't think it is like real specific issue because before one of the specific issue was around the Autonomy Law. But the whole autonomy system is not working, so that dropped back. One of the main reasons why it is not working is because the national parties who are ruling there. What is the difference with the rest of the country? It's the same way that they deal with politics everywhere. And, it's not easy for the women on the Atlantic Coast to get together.

Why?

I don't know. I really need to deal with that. When my mother got sick, and when she died, I wasn't anywhere. And when I came back, I found so much change, you know? One of the things that I have observed is that since the organization needs to get economic help, the financial support every day is less, it's not leaving space for women to actually say, you know, really the issue, are political issues, or it has to do with violence or women's economic situation, whatever. What really happened, leaders that were there are not there anymore either.

Are there specific things that the movement or that the organizations have done that create changes for women's health?

I'm working here with the National Network Against Violence. We have decided that what we do from here has to do with political incidence. I told you about the law,[22] and we're like trying to be updated in other things that are happening in the public world, in the political world. Then, the next thing is that we should not get contaminated, you know? Contaminated by what is happening in this social and political world because we are in an electoral campaign. In the past, that has really divided us, because of the different parties. And so this year, what we have done is in May we got together, 75 of us and started to say, okay, what will be the rules for us to go by this year and that we could stick together and pass this wave?

If the law was passed, would that be sufficient for women to address health?

Ooo, no!

What's the role of the women's organizations then?

The role of the women's organization is to keep the violence subject on board. To keep saying things that we have already learned—that this is not natural and all of the causes to women, and to their family, and in their environment. Because we are learning that violence against women really has to do a lot with the production in the country, has to do a lot with the economy in the country, and it has to do so much with her health! Oooff! I mean, her mental health, her physical health. We're updated on all these investigations. Some of them are like worldwide, so then we bring it and we make it an issue of our learning process. This year, for example, we have gotten funding from a Swedish organization. We're going to go work in the different territories. When we talk about the territories, the two territories on the Atlantic Coast. And we're going to go by León and Chinandega. We have seven territories in the country. We are going to work around strengthening women's leadership so that women from their local environment could start talking out. Our thing is that the leaders will become strong leaders and that they could actually approach the subject wherever and whenever in their own environment. That's one of the things that we're doing right now. All of our process is towards that, the strengthening women leadership, that we may be able to really deal with struggling against violence.

You've brought up economic situations a couple of times, and I know you've been outspoken about globalization and neoliberal policies and how they affect people on the Atlantic Coast. Could you talk a little bit about how those neoliberal policies impact women in particular?

Look, as long as women doesn't learn, as long as we don't learn how to deal with public affairs, we'll continue being domestic workers. If they are living in the farm, there are the women who know how to do the planting and the reaping and whatever. They are not there discussing, and therefore, they are not handling the resources. When we get started talking about these macroeconomic things, we doesn't even have a market, a local market in Puerto Cabezas where we produce enough locally to maintain that market, but yet they are talking about exportations. This is a problem that really affect the whole society, but particularly it effects women because, especially in the indigenous community, women are there doing in the farming. So, if women doesn't learn about these issues, we just continue seeing it like part of our domestic work, and there isn't any growth for us. Of course, this has to do with the whole global policy, but women are even being drawn farther from really becoming a subject, a political subject, and not being a political object.

Can you talk about the role of working with international groups, and addressing women's issues in Nicaragua?

I have years of not doing that because after Beijing, and Beijing Plus 5,[23] I'm just fed up of so much words, and there's so much less deeds comes out of those words. But, working with these international groups is like being able to share things. And, remember when you spoke about the scholars and academic things that strengthen the grassroots level and grassroots level strengthen also these investigations. Well, I think that working with international organizations is like that, because it's like learning globally how to deal with what you have locally. And, in terms of women rights, you know, it's not like everybody going to reach to the UN or to the commission[24] or to the *Interamericano de Derechos Humanos*.[25]

We work with these groups in a way that we could strengthen each other. Now, we're working with an international mission, that's their name, International Mission, and they are working around the death of women, that is growing just so fast, and at a very alarming rate—femicide or *femicidio*. We have linked up as the National Network Against Violence with international organizations. They keep us posted with what is happening in the world, and this research has shown us that this, and this, or whatever. One of the frightening things about this, for example, the femicide, is that a lot of women are being killed because they have decided to leave a violent relationship. How are we going to deal with that? We can't stop saying "Say no to violence." But does saying "No" to violence mean your life? So we're stuck there. It would be much more fruitful to deal with other organizations who are not here.

I remember coming in 1995 when I went to the United States after I came back from China that was one of the things that women were saying. I was in Burlington and Washington, and when I sat with the women they were like, "You know, women are dying here because they are saying 'no.'" And I'm like, "But, how?" Well, they are dying here also, so I understand it better. Then, we were talking about when these men goes to jail, they will pass through a public relation process and this and that, but it's not really working. It's not really working. Maybe one out of a thousand comes out and say, "You know, I actually did wrong." We really need to work together, with anybody and everybody who is working on that subject. It's not like we have a relationship where it's like anything and everything. The international relationships are specific things that we deal with.

Were you one of the 60 women from Nicaragua that went to the Beijing conference?

Yes! I was at the Beijing conference. And, then I went to your country and then I spoke about the Beijing conference.

You've used this language about human rights. Is that something that the movement uses a lot when—

Oh, yes, yes! What happen is we deal with violence against women as a lack of human rights. That is, that's the way we deal with it from our Network.

Why not a public health problem?

Because public health is a problem of human rights. When we talk about human rights, we're talking about economic problems, because now we're dealing with violence, like physical violence, psychological violence, economic violence, patrimonial violence. We are kind of like seeing that violence is a thing that is like a cancer. It's spreading. And it's not even true really that if you have a high academic level, you doesn't live violence. That's even more frightening because it's like, nobody could really escape this thing. So, we need to get together, you know.

The fact that Matilde began her story sharing that she was raised in a gold-mining town is not insignificant. For over two centuries, the Atlantic Coast of Nicaragua was subject to different forms of foreign control, one of which involved the U.S.-owned gold-mining companies in northeastern Nicaragua. The gold mines represented a focal point for resistance to the continually shifting patterns of economic development on the Atlantic Coast. For example,

Augusto César Sandino, the namesake of the Sandinista Revolution, seized two U.S.-owned gold mines in the 1920s. The U.S. Marines fought this local insurrection. Prior to this, the region was a British protectorate, with colonization of the coast resulting in the forceful relocation of African slaves. Moreover, during the time of British colonization, German Moravian missionaries began working in Bluefields, the capital of the South Atlantic Region, establishing churches, schools, and clinics. When Britain eventually withdrew from the Atlantic Coast in 1905, the territory was ceded to U.S-based companies, which economically dominated the area until they were gradually replaced by the Somoza family and its allies.

Although Nicaragua's Caribbean population is similar to other Latin American peoples who experienced multiple colonization processes, the Atlantic Coast of Nicaragua is exceptional in that it was granted political autonomy in 1987, which afforded the opportunity to construct a society that harmonized very diverse racial, political, and cultural interests. The autonomous regions of Nicaragua—the RAAN and the RAAS—were created in 1987 and elected their first regional governments in 1990. As described in Law 28, the Autonomy Statute proposes a nation that is effectively "multiethnic, multicultural and multilingual, based on democracy, pluralism, anti-imperialism and the elimination of social exploitation and oppression in all its forms" (Grigsby, 2003). The massive influences of colonization, slavery, economic occupation, and religion in the area have resulted in distinct intersections of global and local power that position Matilde's experience differently from her *compañeras*[26] in other parts of the Movimiento, the majority of whom are not from the Atlantic Coast.

Although Matilde ultimately shared an ideology with others in the Movimiento that links education and knowledge to diverse democratic participation among women, she did not connect her initial interest in education to revolutionary ideals as the others did. In fact, Matilde described much of her upbringing in nonpoliticized ways. If not prompted to do otherwise, Matilde may have jumped from a brief description of her childhood, to her mid-30s when she became involved in the women's movement in the early 1990s. Although Matilde did not credit childhood experiences with developing a yearning for social change, she did credit them with developing a yearning to learn and obtain knowledge. This is reflected in who she chose to name as an early role model, a woman who was not a grandmother, mother, or revolutionary, but rather a U.S.-based multilingual singer because she represented Matilde's desire to learn additional languages.

When describing her youth, Matilde suggested that she was not exposed to traditional gender norms in her family, yet she also explained that having a baby at the age of 16 created obstacles because societal norms for girls often prohibited them from continuing education when they became mothers. Matilde problematized the social norms surrounding gender when she stated that not being able to go back to school would have been "like my life had

ended there." Although this problematization demonstrated a budding awareness of how inequitable access to education may limit women's potential, it was
her father who demonstrated resistance to these norms to ensure that Matilde
would complete her schooling. As she advanced in her education, Matilde
again problematized the structures surrounding gender when she critiqued
that the only routes available to women (e.g., teaching, nursing) were not ones
she would have otherwise chosen.

Despite not becoming involved in education based on a shared ideology with the Revolution, the revolutionary context was, in fact, how Matilde
received her own advanced education. Like Yamileth Mejía (Chapter 3),
Matilde received advanced education in Cuba as a result of Revolutionary
efforts to train more teachers and was assigned a post in a governmental
office when she returned. However, unlike Yamileth, whose interest was in
supporting the Revolutionary aims, Matilde left a government job after the
Revolution when she problematized the fact that she was asked to work for
less pay than she felt she deserved. Perhaps because the Revolutionary aims
did not take into account the geographically and politically distinct experience of those on the Atlantic Coast, Matilde did not demonstrate loyalty to
the party and instead rejected unsatisfactory conditions to go teach at the
Moravian school.

At a major turning point in Matilde's testimonio, she shared a story of
a friend who sounded an alarm in the early 1990s regarding democratic
spaces for women when she said that, "We need strong women here because
we're about to lose our space." Although Matilde reported not understanding at the time why women gathering together was so important, she
remembered the message that was being delivered clearly: "As women, we
need to make our voice be heard, we need to know and to understand and
to defend ways that we have human rights because we are human people."
That the friend Matilde referred to in this part of her story was not just a
random friend may help to explain why this belief became what guided
Matilde's life's work.

As a result of the establishment of the autonomous governments in 1987,
some members of the Atlantic Coast's Creole population rose to positions of
political prominence. Loria Raquel Dixon Brautigam, Matilde's friend, became
involved in early democratic processes and would in 2006 be the first person of African ancestry elected to the Nicaraguan National Assembly. At the
time that Raquel called the meeting of women, the country was going through
a political transition whereby the fall of the FSLN was creating space for a
collective and diverse mobilization of women and their interests. Although
Matilde's political involvement at these meetings began at the bequest of her
friend, Matilde came to believe so strongly that knowledge and learning were
central to the ability of women to represent themselves as citizens in their society that she quit her job to work collectively with others who shared the aim of

arming women with knowledge so they could best represent their standpoints in democratic spaces.

Matilde's first action was driven by the need on the Atlantic Coast to "get strengthened as people" and resulted, in part, in the development of the Afro-Latin American and Afro-Caribbean Women's Network. Being involved in this network positioned Matilde on an international landscape where the concept of "women's rights as human rights" was gaining increasing ground in the early 1990s, with many organizations throughout the world focusing on women's empowerment and the recognition of women's rights violations (United Nations, 2014). Matilde's experience as an activist working on women's rights led her to participate in one of the most historically important U.N. meetings focused on women's issues, which occurred in 1995 in Beijing, China—a rather huge step for someone who only years earlier had not been politically involved in areas related to social justice for women. At the U.N. meeting held prior to Beijing (e.g., Cairo), Nicaragua had sent male representatives to speak on women's behalf regarding issues related to reproductive health and invoked notions of "culture" in an effort to prohibit the actualization of women's rights. Despite Matilde's commitment to the recognition of culture, she viewed this use as a misappropriation and problematized the very nature of men representing women's interests in this manner. Matilde's solution pulled on her friend Raquel's call that women needed to become knowledgeable in order to represent themselves in these political spaces. She swiftly turned awareness into direct action when she, herself, became prepared and knowledgeable so that she could attend the Beijing conference to represent Nicaraguan women.

This experience underscored for Matilde that women in these positions need real political agency, which means serving the interests of women rather than conforming to the patriarchal establishment by being "obedient." In opposition to token representation, Matilde's point was that we need to "reach where we could have really strong women, strong character and enough knowledge, because knowledge is important to start doing things, you know, from a women's point of view, from our cultures." This oppositional ideology whereby women become informed to represent their own interests, and do so from particular standpoints, is the position from which Matilde engaged her life's work.

The intersectional position from which Matilde worked shapes her resistance to universalizing women's experiences by maintaining the imperative to work from an autonomous consciousness because, as Matilde pointed out, women from the Atlantic Coast are "from a different culture, we see the world through different eyes." The autonomous consciousness that Matilde referred to is the distinct and separate experience of Nicaraguans on the Atlantic Coast, rather than the desired autonomy from political parties that many of the other women in the Movimiento referenced. By problematizing the universalism of women's issues, Matilde deideologized the idea that feminism is a one-size-fits-all philosophy and instead put forward that women's interests as equal participants in democracy will be expressed differently based on their social locations. For example, in resisting the universalism that may stem from holding patriarchy as the primary institution against which to offer resistance, Matilde explained that the multiple oppressions experienced on the Atlantic Coast extended beyond gendered oppression and were therefore shared by both men and women in the region.

Although Matilde initially met resistance from others in the Movimiento to an intersectional ideology that emphasized race, she shared an evolution whereby her ideas eventually became widely received, and she was regularly invited to speak publicly on the topics. In fact, the extent to which many of the women included in this book offer intersectional definitions of feminism has likely been influenced by ongoing conversations within the Movimiento that were in part driven by Matilde. Yet, Matilde is the only one included in this book who noted in her definition of feminism that respect "between women" is important, underscoring that there are multiple dimensions in which women can participate in the collusion of power that oppresses other women. Matilde's holding of an autonomous consciousness that does not conform to dominant power allowed her to constitute a political subjectivity that was directed toward change rather than conformity.

For example, throughout her activism, Matilde's actions were driven by the value of having multiple perspectives inform a multiprong praxis for addressing women's rights. Within the Movimiento, this value is reflected when she described how difference can be a functional tool used toward change. Thus, rather than internalizing a responsibility to explain cultural differences to her colleagues, Matilde suggested that with acceptance and respect for difference women can learn from each other's perspectives and determine how to place new knowledge in their respective contexts.

Matilde expressed a similar value for synergy between grassroots activists and scholars when she described the manner in which she and others in the Movimiento used findings from research in the effort to strengthen the knowledge base necessary to represent themselves politically. She also described working with international organizations similarly when she said that, "It's like learning globally how to deal with what you have locally" and was candid that despite working from an autonomous consciousness from the outset, she did so in partnership with Oxfam in England. In this manner, the multiple institutions of power that had come together to construct Matilde's worldview and experience likely also informed the extent to which she valued multiple collaborative vantage points in working toward change.

Although Matilde spent the majority of her life on the North Atlantic Coast, her commitment to social justice issues for women led to a deeply rooted desire for solidarity that could not be sustained in the region. Therefore, in her later years she took a position with the Network of Violence Against Women in Managua to work on both legislation and increasing women's democratic participation. In her capacity as director of the Network, she demonstrated a form of praxis that enacts citizen subjectivity by using research on violence against women to educate herself in order to represent women's perspectives in the National Assembly as well as work on "strengthening women's leadership so that women from their local environment could start talking out." Although Matilde began as a youth who valued education and knowledge in apolitical ways, the activism she engaged in over her life course reflects the imperative role of knowledge in women's ability to engage in their own political representation. In reflecting on the increasing threats that neoliberalism poses to women's experience, Matilde was explicit that women need to learn about politics because through the exploitation of their labor they "are even being drawn farther from really being a subject, a political subject."

Matilde's testimonio reflects the iterative nature of *conscientización*— how awareness and action develop together over the life course. For example, Matilde had a clearly defined consciousness-raising moment where her newfound awareness sparked a desire to begin taking necessary action to politically represent women's interests in an informed manner. She was able to connect her childhood passion for learning to act in the service of others by using knowledge to better politically represent women's standpoints. In resisting and rethinking the social structures that disadvantaged women from holding influential political positions, Matilde demonstrated how those with less structural power began to take action to transform the social structures that maintain gender inequity. In doing so, Matilde modeled that by operating from an autonomous consciousness, women can advocate for themselves as citizen subjects by working toward change from their respective social locations to transform the conditions by which they would ordinarily serve as laborers in someone else's struggle.

Notes

1. This is distinct from most of Nicaragua, with 96% of the population being of mixed indigenous and Spanish ancestry, almost 100% Spanish speaking, and predominantly Roman Catholic.

2. German Moravian missionaries started work in Bluefields, the capital of the RAAS in 1847.

3. A pop singer in the United States, Francis became famous in the 1950s and 1960s with an album called *Connie Francis en Español*. She recorded in many languages, but she was actually only fluent in Italian and Spanish.

4. Through most of Latin America, primary school is first to sixth year, and secondary school is first to fifth year. The fourth year of secondary school is roughly equivalent to tenth grade in the United States.

5. The full name is *Instituto Nicaraguense de Seguridad Social* (Nicaraguan Social Security Institute).

6. MIDINRA stands for *Ministerio de Desarrollo Agropecuario y Reforma Agraria* (Ministry of Agricultural Development and Agrarian Reform).

7. The Spanish *derechos agrarios* translates to "agrarian rights."

8. This translates to "analyst."

9. Dixon was the first Afro-Nicaraguan to be elected to Nicaragua's National Assembly.

10. Oxfam is an international organization seeking and working toward solutions to poverty and injustice throughout the world.

11. [Asociación de Mujeres Nicaragüenses (Luisa Amanda Espinoza Association of Nicaraguan Women)].

12. Matilde was referring here to Atlantic region autonomy, not the autonomy that many others speak of regarding the women's movement, underscoring that there are large regional differences in experiences and perspectives.

13. "Our colleagues" indicates women in the Movimiento who are mobilized outside the Atlantic Region.

14. *Geopoliticamente* translates to "geopolitically."

15. The Comprehensive Law Against Violence Toward Women (Law 779) was being reviewed by the National Assembly in 2012. It passed, but pressures from conservatives led to its amendment in 2013.

16. The Fourth World Conference on Women was held in Beijing in 1995. The Beijing Platform for Action was created at this conference to promote women's empowerment worldwide.

17. This network was formed in 1992 to promote the interests of African descendent women in Latin America and the Caribbean.

18. The 1994 International Conference on Population and Development met in Cairo and created four goals: universal education, reduction of child and infant mortality, reduction of maternal mortality, and access to reproductive and sexual health services, including family planning.

19. *Vaticano* translates to "Vatican."

20. "Broad strokes" is the translation for *lineas gruesas*.

21. "Customary rights" are indicated by *derechos consuetudinarios*.

22. She was referring to the law addressing violence against women that she was helping to lobby in the National Assembly.

23. The Beijing Plus 5 was a review done 5 years after the Beijing conference to evaluate progress.

24. "Commission" here means the Inter-American Commission for Human Rights, part of the Organization of American States.

25. The *Interamericano de Derechos Humanos* (Inter-American Institute of Human Rights) was created in 1980 through an agreement signed between the Inter-American Court of Human Rights and Costa Rica. It uses a multidisciplinary approach to research and teach about human rights.

26. *Compañero* is used to reflect political solidarity with someone who is a partner, colleague, or classmate. *Compañera* is the feminine form of *compañero*.

SECTION ONE

Summary: Citizen Democracy and Knowledge

LEVELING THE PLAYING FIELD BY CREATING
PARTICIPATORY SPACES

Taken together, the *testimonios* from Juanita Jiménez, Sofía Montenegro, Yamileth Mejía, and Matilde Lindo all demonstrate how problematizing the control of political participation and knowledge in a society can lead to effective action that enhances women's citizen democracy. Although their stories evidence the production of outcomes that make possible women's political participation in the context of extremely limited conditions in Nicaragua, it is only through understanding the *psychology* behind the women's resistance that we can understand how these outcomes were possible. For example, despite working from very different social locations in the country, all four women made clear that it is critical to problematize the *ideologies* behind abuses of power, rather than focus on the consequences. For each woman, this problematization led to collective mobilization for transformative change, or change that altered the structural conditions in which women live their lives, as opposed to providing services or band-aids that cover the consequences of being marginalized.

In this manner, the women in this section demonstrated evidence for the famous quotation by Audre Lorde that "the master's tools will never dismantle the master's house" by rejecting the structural conditions created by a male-dominated leadership (Lorde, 1984). This quotation by Lorde is taken from a talk she delivered in the early 1980s at a conference when she elaborated on the importance of intersectional identities among women and the imperative for these identities to lay the groundwork for alternative political action:

> As women, we have been taught either to ignore our differences, or to
> view them as causes for separation and suspicion rather than as forces
> for change. Without community there is no liberation, only the most

vulnerable and temporary armistice between an individual and her oppression. But community must not mean a shedding of our differences, nor the pathetic pretense that these differences do not exist. Those of us who stand outside the circle of this society's definition of acceptable women; those of us who have been forged in the crucibles of difference—those of us who are poor, who are lesbians, who are Black, who are older know that survival is not an academic skill. It is learning how to take our differences and make them strengths. *For the master's tools will never dismantle the master's house.* They may allow us temporarily to beat him at his own game, but they will never enable us to bring about genuine change. And this fact is only threatening to those women who still define the master's house as their only source of support." (Lorde, 1984, p. 2, Italics added)

Although Lorde called for feminists in the early 1980s to include lesbian, women of Color, and majority world women's perspectives in the development of feminist theory, these perspectives remain largely absent in feminist theorizing in psychology (Kurtiş & Adams, 2015). The *testimonios* in this section underscored that understanding resistance among women who experience marginalization based on multiple intersections of global power, and for whom support does not come from the "master's house," is crucial to understanding transformative change.

For example, Juanita's story illustrates that abuses of power that restrict political spaces for women's participation need to be challenged, and that the real project is in creating a different society that can institutionalize freedom. Similarly, Sofía's testimonio reflects that an outright rejection of the dominant ideology regarding political participation is necessary because she learned that simply using one's voice *within* the existing structure cannot contribute to change. Yamileth's testimonio demonstrates, in part, how the pathways paved by Juanita and Sofía become actualized and create possibilities for citizen democracy among other women. And, finally, Matilde's testimonio underscores that strategies within feminist action need also be problematized to avoid universalizing women's experience and that value for different standpoints is one of the more critical tools for enhancing the collective mobilization aimed at women's political participation.

It is clear in all of these stories that a system in which one was not involved in making the rules is not a system that facilitates autonomous and free subjectivity among those at the margins of the system. Rather, what each woman demonstrates is that the rules within the current system need to be problematized for an alternative subjectivity—one poised to challenge and change the rules—to develop.

The women included in this section demonstrated that in developing their own subjectivity they also opened spaces that promoted the citizen subjectivity of other women. None of these women did so, however, in a vacuum;

they all demonstrated resistance from the "between" spaces of local, national, and global influences. These four members of the *Movimiento Autónomo de Mujeres*, each from notably different social positions in the context of globalization, struggled to level the playing field of democratic participation, in part because they knew that without a democratization of political spaces it would be impossible to defend women's human rights in Nicaragua. In many ways, the actions undertaken by women involved in the Movimiento Autónomo de Mujeres as a result of this democratization have been among the most promising changes in Nicaragua in the past couple of decades. One area of focus in which this has been particularly true, the legislation of women's human rights, is the focus of the next section.

SECTION TWO

Intersectional Ideology

LEGISLATION AND WOMEN'S HUMAN RIGHTS

In many countries, social justice movements have shifted their orientations away from the revolutionary goal of state takeover and, instead, make transnational claims based on human rights by appealing not only to the state but also to global institutions. The international women's movement, building on the 1985 and 1995 U.N. World Conferences in Nairobi and Beijing, respectively, created arenas in which women began to take advantage of legislative and policymaking opportunities to advance women's human rights in Nicaragua. Although an internationally accepted discourse of women's rights as human rights emerged in the early 1990s (Bunch, 1990), feminists of the majority world have cautioned that using dominant human rights discourse can ignore the diverse perspectives of women's oppression by universalizing women's experiences (Alexander & Mohanty, 2010). In Nicaragua, activists recognize that violations of women's rights are an intersectional problem that reflects abuses of patriarchal, economic, and global powers. Because human rights everywhere are actualized through multiple social locations that involve power (e.g., gender, one's position in a neoliberal state), examining the psychology of resistance in Nicaragua can help to understand how transnationally intersectional experiences are important to advancing women's human rights everywhere. This section explores how the psychology of resistance led members of the *Movimiento Autónomo de Mujeres* (Women's Autonomous Movement) to appropriate globalized discourses on women's human rights to strategically influence legislation that was critical to the recognition of women's human rights.

In Nicaragua, after the fall of the Revolution, women in the Movimiento were no longer willing to conform to the ideology and agenda of the Sandinistas and were committed, instead, to making a bold assertion that women's rights in Nicaragua needed to be upheld and not dismissed to the margins. Although the *Frente Sandinista de Liberación Nacional* (FSLN; Sandinista National Liberation Front) party that was denying women's interests was no longer in power, the new neoliberal administration elected in 1990 only served to further exacerbate or ignore threats to women's rights. Therefore, in addition to patriarchal abuses of power, women experienced further marginalization in the context of global economic policies. Feminist activists therefore explored the applicability of international human rights guarantees in advancing women's rights, while remaining attentive to their particular local context in Nicaragua.

For example, in one of the first actions in this effort, many women in the Movimiento mobilized around the ratification in 1994 of the Inter-American Convention on the Prevention, Punishment, and Eradication of Violence Against Women (also known as the Convention of Belém do Pará for the place in Brazil where it was signed) in 1994. As a result of the emerging oppositional ideology that prioritized women's rights through transnational collective action, Nicaragua, along with 32 of the other 34 inter-American countries involved, ratified the convention in 1995.[1] Immediately following this effort, women involved in the Movimiento capitalized on the international recognition of violence against women as a violation of human rights to present a bill to the National Assembly that would penalize domestic violence in Nicaragua.

To gather National Assembly support for this bill, members of the Movimiento combined a growing oppositional ideology that valued women's experience with innovative transnational strategies by partnering with researchers from both local (University of León) and foreign (University of Umea, Sweden) universities to document, for the first time, the incidence of violence against women in Nicaragua (Ellsberg, Peña, Herrera, Liljestrand, & Winkvist, 2000). The result of this multiprong approach led the National Assembly to pass Law 230 in 1996, the Law of Reforms and Additions to the Penal Code to Prevent and Punish Domestic Violence. In many ways, the agenda-setting U.N. conferences gave women's rights advocates in Nicaragua an opportunity to resist dominant ideologies and advance feminist agendas with tangible gains. Moreover, as processes of *conscientización* among the women in the following section will reveal, these bottom-up strategies were connected to the ideological analysis and action that was being developed in the Movimiento at large.

Women's human rights advocated in Nicaragua, however, experienced a series of setbacks beginning in 2006 that demonstrate how human rights in Nicaragua have been shaped by patriarchy through a predominantly male judiciary, as well as legacies of colonialism and the pervasive influence of the Catholic church. For example, in 2006 the National Assembly passed a bill that outlawed abortion in all circumstances, making Nicaragua only the sixth country in the world to do so.[2] The FSLN strongly endorsed this law, in part because of Daniel Ortega's strong alliance with the Catholic Church. In 2007, Ortega added criminal penalties to the law, thereby implementing reforms that sanctioned violations of women's human rights into law.

Although the women's movement has played a crucial role in promoting the discourse and legislation of women's rights at the national level, it has also been imperative to establishing organizations that bridge human rights discourses with lived experience that is compromised at the intersections of patriarchal, neoliberal, and religious power (Alvarez, 2000; Ewig, 1999). For example, when the defeat of the Revolution led to the closure of state-owned textile factories, a once-unionized female workforce was dislocated and unemployed. With the neoliberal policies of the Chamorro administration, transnational factories were able set up production in free trade zones (FTZs),[3] tapping into a desperate labor force that was willing to work for poverty-level wages (Renzi & Arguto, 1993). The failure of the administration to oppose legislation that established the FTZs was viewed by many in the Movimiento as a betrayal stemming from the self-interests of male leaders (Mendez, 2002).

A nongovernmental organization, the *María Elena Cuadra* (MEC) was founded to redefine rights and citizenship for women in the FTZs by focusing on gender, labor, and human rights in Nicaragua (MEC's cofounder Sandra Ramos's *testimonio* is included in Chapter 6 of this section). Similarly, in anticipation of the Revolution's fall from power in 1990, three organizations emerged from AMNLAE (*Asociación de Mujeres Nicaragüenes Luisa Amanda Espinoza*, [Luisa Amanda Espinoza Association of Nicaraguan Women]) to focus directly on rape and violence against women as human rights violations: *Colectivo Xochilt, Colectivo de Mujeres Itza,* and *Ocho de Marzo*. A testimonio from the cofounder and director of Colectivo de Mujeres Itza, Bertha Inés Cabrales, is included in Chapter 7 of this section.

Because continued rights violations against women will maintain a system whereby men will retain political power over women in Nicaragua, women in the Movimiento have continued to push for legislative change that will undermine the dominant ideology and could be a conduit for the actualization of women's rights. Most recently, activists within the Movimiento (including members of María Elena Cuadra and Colectivo Itza) came together to enact more comprehensive legislation surrounding violence against women. Members of the Movimiento were concerned that Law 230, passed in 1996, did not adequately attend to imbalanced gendered power relations that put women at risk for violence both inside and outside the home because it did not recognize the misogynist context in which women were being murdered. Activists within the Movimiento recognized that to accelerate progress toward gender equality, the development of a critical consciousness and new vocabularies that reflected their oppositional ideology were necessary to improve strategies for women's rights. For example, women working on a new comprehensive law began using the term *feminicide* because, unlike femicide, which is broadly defined as the killing of women for being women, feminicide recognizes "[1] murders of women are founded on a gender power structure and [2] systemic violence rooted in social, political, economic, and cultural inequalities . . . is based . . . on the intersection of gender dynamics with the cruelties of . . . economic injustices in local as well as global contexts" (Fregoso & Bejarano, 2010, p. 5).

As a result of a mobilized commitment behind an oppositional ideology that recognized how gendered power imbalances heightened women's risk and threatened their lives, the Comprehensive Law Against Violence Toward Women (Law 779) that the Movimiento was working on was passed unanimously by the National Assembly in 2012. The first article of the new law states the following:

> The object of this law is to act against the violence exercised against women with the purpose of protecting women's human rights and guaranteeing them a life free of violence that favors their development and wellbeing in accordance with the principles of equality and nondiscrimination; and establish comprehensive protection measures to prevent, punish and eradicate violence and provide assistance to women victims of violence, promoting changes in the sociocultural and patriarchal patterns that underpin the relations of power.

Because the law embedded a concept of oppression in its definition of violence against women and prescribed severe punishment for crimes that heightened women's oppression, its passing was considered an enormous victory for women's rights advocates everywhere and served, in many ways, as a revolutionary model for change. In particular, although many countries and organizations (e.g., the United States, the World Health Organization) tend to cloak violence against women in the language of public health and focus on the consequences, feminist activists in Nicaragua were satisfied with nothing less than identifying violence as a human rights violation and one that existed predominantly because of abuses of power and structured injustice.[4]

Because systems of oppression involving multiple institutions (e.g., patriarchy, capitalism) have continued to aggressively limit the situations in which women live their lives in Nicaragua, efforts toward liberatory change cannot be understood outside this context. It is important to examine how the psychology of resistance develops among political actors in the spaces between local, national, and transnational processes that contribute to reconfiguring women's human rights. Many women within the Movimiento have developed an oppositional ideology that reflects the rightful claims of half of humanity— that is, women—to have their rights recognized and upheld by the State. In moving ideology to action, all of the women in this section believe in the need for the rule of law to enact and uphold legislation in protecting the rights of women. The *testimonios* of the women in the following section focus predominantly on how processes of concientización among women in Nicaragua led to an oppositional ideology that was used to build laws that responded to their situations.

Notes

1. Canada and the United States were the only two nonsignatories.

2. The others were the Philippines, Chile, El Salvador, Malta, and Vatican City in 2006.

3. Free trade zones function as enclaves set apart from the rest of the national economy and are referred to as "free" because foreign-owned factories can import raw materials and export factory products with a range of tax exceptions.

4. Because the interviews in this book were conducted in 2011, the women did not discuss the passage of this law. However, 1 year and 3 months after the passage, the Catholic Church argued that the law was an attack on familial and religious values by threatening to break up the "family unit" and encouraged the FSLN to vote for an unconstitutional reform. The law was reformed in 2013 to include mediation, whereby women are now required to attempt conflict resolution with their assailants.

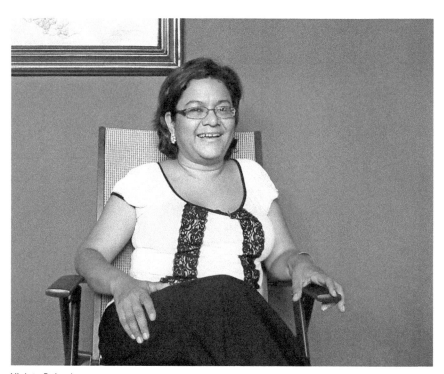
Violeta Delgado

5

Linking Lived Experience of Violence and Transformative Feminist Action

We had a feminist vision and we were a very politicized social movement. . . . We demanded changes in legislation. . . . We don't just take care of victims.

—*TESTIMONIO* FROM VIOLETA DELGADO

Although there are different strategic spaces from which to push oppositional ideologies into legislation, the one most pivotal in the 1990s in Nicaragua was the Network of Women Against Violence. Violeta Delgado began working for the network as a coordinator of the national campaign to ratify the Inter-American Convention of the Prevention, Punishment, and Eradication of Violence Against Women when she was only 25 years old. Delgado served as the executive secretary of the Network from 1994 to 2003. She traveled extensively in the 1990s, forming transnational feminist alliances, starting with attendance at the U.N. Fourth World Conference on Women in Beijing, China. At this conference, the Beijing Platform for Action was enacted that determined to remove "all the obstacles to women's active participation in all spheres of public and private life through a full and equal share in economic, social, cultural and political decision-making" (United Nations, 1995, p. 7). Delgado attended U.N. conferences every 5 years afterward to remain active in revising the platform.

In 2003, after 9 years of coordinating the Network, Delgado accepted a position as one of Nicaragua's civil coordinators, a position charged with overseeing over 450 social organizations and nongovernmental organizations (NGOs) active in civil society. In recognition of her denunciation of the state of women's human rights in Nicaragua, Delgado was among a group of 1,000 women who were nominated for the Nobel Peace Prize in 2004. In 2006, after running for a seat in the National Assembly as an affiliate of the *Movimiento de Renovación Sandinista* (MRS; Sandinista Renewal Movement); Delgado accepted a job at the Center for Communication Research (*Centro de Investigación de la Comunicación*; CINCO), where she currently works and is able to combine her university training with her commitment to political activism.

Delgado was born in 1969 in the small town of Diriomo, in the Department of Granada in western Nicaragua. As a child, Delgado became active in the Revolution by volunteering for the National Literacy Campaign when she was 11 years old. As a youth, she dedicated the remainder of her high school years to receiving political training and was active in organizing youth battalions in the war zones. After graduating from high school, Delgado took a recess from political activity and attended the *Universidad Nacional Autónoma de Nicaragua* (UNAN; National Autonomous University of Nicaragua) in Managua to study math. Throughout her story, Delgado weaves back and forth between personal experiences of trauma, seeking refuge, and engaging in political action. Through her political activism to defend other women's human rights, she developed a framework for understanding her own experiences of abuse as rights violations. In doing so, she established an oppositional ideology that underscores not only that women's lived experiences are valid sources of knowledge but also that women have the right to experience integrity and dignity that will be protected by law. The parallel nature with which Delgado told personal and political stories of violence in the following testimonio unveils a context of patriarchal and neoliberal oppression that warrants a transnational feminist approach to liberation:

> *Violeta, I'd like to start by asking you to tell me a little bit about your personal history, some of your earliest memories, what your childhood was like, what kind of family you grew up in, those kinds of things.*

> I'm from a very small town called Diriomo in the municipality of Granada. I'm the daughter of a Nicaraguan father, a Honduran mother. I'm the second of four brothers and sisters. When the Revolution was won, I was 10 years old.

> During that time, just like many other Nicaraguan children, I knew what was going on politically, and I took a political position. I lived the war. I was in the refugee area with the rest of my family. I celebrated the victory of the Revolution. And in November of 1979 when I was 10 years old, I began to organize in the Sandinista group. Since that time I've been active in organizations; for the last 32 years, I've been part of the political project and collective that tries to transform lives.

> *What was your experience like as a 10-year-old becoming organized?*

> I think that I could recognize some sense of liberty in this, because at that time, there weren't any obstacles to my participation. I think Nicaraguan society in general lived like a tsunami of freedom. Everything was being rebuilt. I went to teach people how to read and write.[1] I was 11 years old. It

was an essential experience in my life in all the sense of the word because I went to live outside my home for 4 months in a rural community. And we lived in a big hut with walls made of sugar cane stalks, dirt floors, and without a bathroom. So, very different from the comforts that I had in my house in Diriomo.

It obviously impacted my life; it inspired in me a commitment to change. I think it shaped my character to survive in different conditions. And I think it obviously developed in me a stronger commitment to the Revolution. When I came back from teaching how to read and write, I went back to school, but I knew that there was something in me that had changed. I knew that I had this history and experience that was very different from my other friends. So I continued being a member of the Sandinista Youth.

This became more difficult about 2 or 3 years later because my father distanced himself from the Revolution, and the rest of the family didn't. My brothers, my mother, and I continued to be very committed. This implied violent situations at home, my dad exercising power over us, a lot of control, and it was very hard. I think it was a very sad adolescence. In the end, I decided to leave home when I was 15 years old. I couldn't return to my home. It was a very difficult time with a lot of aggression, many clashes. I think that the Revolution was going through a difficult time as well. The war was getting worse. There were a lot of friends and *compañeros*[2] who were being killed in the front lines. The work that we were doing in the communities was very difficult because we were recruiting youth. It included political work as well, so the people understood why the country was going through the present economic limitations. It was a very hard period, but also very hopeful. But very difficult for me, personally and politically.

What were you doing after you moved out of the house?

I stayed in high school, and I dedicated the rest of my time to political work. And I lived for a pretty good deal of time with my grandma. I was involved organizing production battalions, harvesting coffee or cotton with student brigades or receiving political training. It was a very intense period, very intense.

I think it was a peculiar adolescence. [Laughs.] I don't think it was very different from many of my compañeras, some of the women whom you're going to interview. And a lot of the women whom I am now friends with, I met during that time, like Juanita Jimenez.[3] It was hard because during that time, my mom was diagnosed with breast cancer and that led me to go back home. The relationship with my dad started to calm down a bit. My mother decided to separate from my father and go back to Honduras.

I decided to stay and enroll in the university. And it's kind of a funny story because after having had an extremely politicized childhood and adolescence, I decided to study something that didn't have anything to do with humanities or political sciences, and I studied math. [Laughs.]

Why?

I decided to separate from this environment of humanities and political science. I wanted to study something I had always liked, math. If I stayed in humanities, I ran the risk of going back to getting involved and that would make my college very irregular, too.

What influenced your decision to step back from that focus and turn to math?

I think that some things are transitional in your life. I was finishing school and going to live outside of my town. I came to live in Managua to attend the university, and for me it was an opportunity for a fresh start, and that included that crazy idea to study math and to try to have a more stable higher education experience.

But I was not successful in this endeavor [laughs] because 3 years after starting college I went back to organizing. [Laughs.] During my third year of college, someone found out that I had been a student leader in high school and asked me, why don't you join UNEN, the National Student Union of Nicaragua. We need someone to be in charge of the cultural affairs within the department. And I decided to do it. After that I became president-elect of the Science Department, which housed the mathematicians, the physicists, the statisticians. And then I was president of the student body, and when that happened I was totally involved again.

What kind of things were you involved in?

There was a political clash at that time because the Sandinista Front lost the elections. So, the student movement became a force of resistance to fight so that they didn't reduce the budget for the universities. This historic struggle in defense of the 6% for the universities happened in the '90s, the struggle for the student transportation subsidy,[4] to keep education free of charge, to have need-based scholarships. This obviously required a lot of work and a lot of organization.

There were a lot of student strikes, and we were out in the streets for many months showing there was support for budgets to be allocated according to what the law prescribed so that the universities didn't become privatized. We were out in the streets, on strikes; we were doing a lot of work in the *barrios*,[5] too. We also had the first confrontations with the police. I experienced a tear gas bomb for the first time.

How did you move from being a student organizer to being an organizer pivotal in the women's movement?

Well, about the middle of 1990, through my leadership in the university, I was part of a project that was called the Constitution of the Youth Council of Nicaragua. There were representatives from almost all of the youth organizations in the country on that council.

It was a very beautiful project because for the first time, in the early '90s, youth that had been on one side of the trenches met with youth that had been on the other side. We were Sandinista youth along with Contra youth. And, we all came with our bandanas to show our alliances so there would be no doubt that either side was ceding. But little by little, we started to share things, and we began to identify problems we had in common. We began to see that we were the same, we were all youth. And a group of women that was there, we decided to make a group of women youth leaders.

What made you decide that?

Because we felt that the way the youth organizations were organized weren't recognizing the leadership nor the contribution of women. Some of us needed to have our own space to reflect upon things. We came out of the youth movement, but some of us started to make connections with the Women's Movement.

It was the boom of the Women's Movement in Nicaragua. And we were like, here we come, here come the youth, right? In the coed youth organizations, there was resistance to incorporate the demands of women, and in the Women's Movement there was resistance to recognize the needs of the young. So, we were sort of stuck there, kind of battling within both groups.

And there was a point when I broke away from the Sandinista Youth. I was finishing my studies at the university during that time, and the Women's Movement called me and told me that they wanted me to join them. I was already heavily involved with the Women's Movement. I had already participated in the Latin American Feminist Encounter.[6] I had had the opportunity to go to a meeting of young women leaders in Chile, a women's political meeting, and that bond with the young Chilean feminists was very important for me.

And during that time, at the end of '94, I was 25 years old. I was finishing my studies; the Network of Women Against Violence chose me to coordinate a national campaign against violence.

Wow, so young!

Yes, it was a job that I was going to do for 3 months, and I stayed for 9 years.

Why? Why did you stay so long?

I stayed for 9 years because, to organize this national campaign was a marvelous exercise. It taught me so, so, so much. We started to work on the idea to organize a campaign that everyone could be a part of. We started to use a badge as a way to be part of the campaign. And that helped show that you didn't have to go to a march, or a meeting, that women could participate even if they weren't necessarily politically active in the women's movement. It meant that a secretary could participate, a bank teller, housewife, student, just by wearing the badge on your clothes or on your backpack or purse.

Can you tell us very briefly what this campaign was about?

The campaign was to demand that the Nicaraguan government ratify the Inter-American Convention Against Violence Against Women.[7] I think that a lot of people didn't necessarily understand the name, Inter-American Convention. It sounds so grandiose; basically, it was about the people signing a paper and wearing a badge that said "I'm in favor of the government getting involved" and for the government to legislate in favor of women's right to live without violence. All this led a lot of people to say I want to be a part of this, I want to organize, how do I do it? And it went from being an initiative where there were approximately 18 organizations, to a network of more than 150 organizations, in addition to having many women participate individually.

We organized national meetings, and we worked very hard so that the National Assembly would pass a law for the first time in history recognizing and punishing domestic violence, and that was very intense work. We collected more than 40,000 signatures from citizens. We did a lobbying campaign, we went to each of the representatives' homes, we talked with the representatives' wives. We were at the National Assembly every day. We made alliances with the representatives' secretaries. We asked people to send a fax, to really jam the representatives' fax machines so they would pass that law. The women in the National Assembly, the secretaries, the cafeteria workers gave us lunch so we could be there all day. I mean, we were persistent, persistent until they finally passed this law in 1996.[8] I think that this law, which has since had many reforms, definitely contributed to saving many women's lives. We were also part of this project that is called Family Services Division, specialized police stations that focus on domestic violence. It's a pilot project in Latin America, it probably only exists in Peru, Nicaragua, I think in Ecuador, too. And we were part of this project that aimed to open more stations in more places and have the centers that were part of the network, have them commit to serving women who reported violence. Well, I stayed for 9 years and as the network's executive secretary until 2003.

I lived through many intense events during this period, like Zoilamérica Narváez's lawsuit against Daniel Ortega. That was very intense at both the political and personal levels because although I hadn't been active within the Sandinista Front for a long time, I still had had a very strong history. This lawsuit helped me realize that during the time I spent teaching people how to read and write, I had lived through a situation of sexual abuse from another adolescent in the community. At the time I had not recognized it as such. I think that it had been traumatic for me. And I had never—well, I had pretty much erased that part of my past. But through Zoilamérica's lawsuit, I was able to recognize that what happened, that teenager's sexual aggressions towards me, had been sexual violence, and it had impacted my life during this period. I had succeeded in getting over it because I returned to my house and I found my classmates—I went back to being a girl.

But it had been sexual violence, just like Zoilamérica, but in a different context. I had never talked about it. I didn't even talk about it in that moment; I have never even talked about it, not with my mom, who was there, not with the teachers. I didn't talk to absolutely anyone. So I think that was obviously a very difficult thing because a lot of women decided to talk, to put the topic of sexual violence in Nicaragua on the table. They questioned us a lot, and the Sandinista Front made a very harsh move by creating a protective wall against Ortega. The decision to protect him at all costs had meant a change in the political structure of the country because this created the conditions for the pact between Daniel Ortega and Arnoldo Alemán.[9] So that was very tough for us because we felt betrayed because Ortega was an important figure in all our lives.

And my departure from the network—I finally made the decision to leave the coordination of it in 2003. This year the network accompanied Rosita, the 9-year old girl who was pregnant and had been sexually abused, and we supported her demand to terminate the pregnancy. It was very, very, very, very, very hard politically, and personally, too, because we faced the clerics, the Church, with all its power. And we knew that that was a political fight and a right but it was also a matter of life. We couldn't wait for the Church and the state to make a decision 2 years later because the girl's life was in danger and we had to make decisions. That was very hard for many of us, too.

That year I decided to leave the network because I had to put some distance. My job was political, but I also had to deal with and confront and listen to personal stories. And I think that, like for many women who worked in the issue of violence against women, there's a moment when you have to make a break. I left the Network to work in the leadership of a much broader coalition of NGOs, that the Network was a part of, too, that was called the Civil Coordinator.

Violeta, did you experience any personal consequences from your support surrounding Zoila or Rosita?

Yes. Having backed Zoilamérica, they described a lot of us as people that we aren't. I mean, as enemies of the Sandinista Party. This meant that we were no longer recognized as leaders of a political movement, that public organizations were not allowed to establish any type of relationship with us. And obviously we cannot work in the government.

And was there also a governmental response to your support of Rosita?

In Rosita's case, there was pressure coming from the Church; they excommunicated us. I have been a Catholic all my life. At some point, I was scared that there would be a break with my community. I had stopped living in Diriomo a long time ago, but for me it has always been a vital space. But the community was supportive of me, the old ladies, my grandmothers, and they were telling me, "No, that priest is crazy." [Laughs.]

But later, after that pressure, which was more emotional, when the Sandinista Front came to power[10]—it made use of the law, and there was criminal accusation. That had a much stronger impact on us because we were investigated, and we were called to testify. This had an impact on my family because obviously my mom, who was still alive, always worried about me because of what could happen to me in this country. I had a son who had been born in 2004, and obviously I worried that if I was arrested, what was going to happen to my baby? It obviously impacted my job, too, because I had to invest a lot of time attending the judicial and political defense and a lot of time, a lot of meetings, a lot of debates to try to understand what was happening and what the best strategy was. And a lot of time was invested to not fall prey to the government's strategy to divide us. And that lasted 3 years.

So it was all of these pressures that led you to decide to take a step back. You started to tell me a little bit about what you did next. You started to work on issues more in civil society?

As the civil coordinator, yes, very interesting because I went back to a coed space after 9 years. I liked it because I went back to dealing with numbers. I got to lead and monitor issues of economic policies and to work with economists. And I followed the IMF's[11] policies, and it was very interesting because the economists looked at me and thought, "What are we going to do with this *woman*?" A lot of them didn't know that I was a mathematician, and it ended up working very well. We did amazing research on the subject of political economics. We discovered sums of money that the government collected and did not enter in the budget, and we demanded that it be used for social programs and that there be better transparency. It was very good for me.

Working there I met a man that I had a relationship with and became pregnant. And I think that it could only happen that way, going back to a coed environment [a lot of laughter] because I spent the previous 9 years exclusively dealing with my female friends and peers. And my son Diego was born. I was there for 3 years and decided to leave to become involved in the electoral campaign of the Sandinista Renewal Movement[12] and the 2006 elections. I ran for Congress.

It seems like there are some key transitional times in my life. I think that the first time of transition was the Literacy Crusade—teaching people how to read and write—the triumph of the Revolution and the Crusade. After that I think it was the decision to study math [laughs] and go to college. And then it was the clash with the Sandinistas and the beginning of my work in the network. And then it was the decision to resign from my work at the Civil Coordinator to go to the electoral campaign because I went back to being part of a partisan political project. It had been 12 years—since '94.

To go back to an electoral campaign was to go back to the communities, to "Good morning, I'm Violeta Delgado, and I'm a candidate for Congress, and I want you to vote for me because I'm a woman committed to women's rights." It was going back to looking people directly in the eyes, those personal ties, without intermediaries. So, I went all over the country for 6 months together with Azahalea,[13] my running mate.

How did you end up at the Center for Media and Democracy [Center for Communication Research] where you are now?

I came to work at CINCO because after the electoral campaign—which ended with a victory for Ortega for president—I wasn't elected. This little party [the MRS] had five candidates, but we didn't get enough votes for me to be elected. So, the moment came where I decided to separate my active participation in the Women's Movement from my work life. I decided to use my mathematical education, to dig into the closet and refresh my academic training. And suddenly many of my friends said, "You're good at doing numbers." So, Sofía[14] told me, you know the majority—many of the employees from CINCO are humanists, journalists, communications specialists, sociologists—but when it comes to numbers and matrices and those things, they just don't want to have anything to do with it. So, I said okay, and Sofía offered me a job as project manager to deal with all the numbers and to continue my active involvement with the Women's Movement on the side. I'm part of its political coordination but I'm not a paid staff member. To be able to separate my work life from my—although we have to put that in quotes, right? Because at CINCO we do engage in a lot of political debate, a lot of debate about what's happening. It's an organization that takes a political position. I like that part of this project a lot. And I'm also very happy, satisfied with my involvement in the Women's Autonomous Movement. And that's where I am right now.

I'd like to switch gears and ask you, throughout your work, how have you made sense of or how do you define feminism?

One time I heard Marcela Lagarde,[15] this feminist—fabulous, fabulous Mexican feminist anthropologist and she said a phrase and it made me think, "That's it, that's where I want to be"—she said, "Feminism is a proposal for humanity." That is, it is a proposal from women for humanity and when we say for humanity, for all of us. I then understood why feminists had a vision; we proposed the idea of fair and equal relationships with respect to men. For me, feminism obviously transcends my participation in a women's organization—that's where I advocate for it. I think that for me feminism is a proposal that comes from women but it's a proposal for change in men and in humanity; it's all connected.

And do you see a relationship between feminist activism and scholarship or work from the university?

I was able to be part of a very interesting case where the results from one investigation were used as material to create an impact, by women, on the issue of violence against women. I was part of a formative process where female academics engaged in many debates with women in the community. I think that in Nicaragua, like in no other country, there is recognition for these women's wisdom, community leaders who have never been to college but whose life experiences are of vital importance. I think that theorists feed a lot from these vital life experiences. Even myself, I am not a quote-unquote intellectual, but I think that I have learned techniques to do political synthesis and identify lessons learned. I think that Nicaraguan feminists, even though so many of them haven't set foot in a university, they have developed the ability for political abstraction, an ability to synthesize their life history and their experiences in order to gain knowledge. I think that what we've lacked are the resources to write it.

You've also talked about your experience working with women's organizations from other countries. Can you tell me about some of your international experience working on women's issues?

Yes, well, it's been in a variety of ways. I have been part of the process to form feminist regional alliances, and this has been, super, super, super great. I think that if it weren't for this a lot of us would have been in a situation of greater risk, for example, all of the supportive campaigns organized by feminists from Central America and Latin America to support Nicaraguan feminists. During 2008 and 2009, when Ortega's policy was very aggressive towards us, many feminists organized outside the entrance to the [Nicaraguan] embassies and also at the airports, visibly showing their opposition to Ortega's visit to their country.

I have been involved in creating projects and very strong alliances between us in Mesoamerica[16] and in Latin America. During the period when I was in the leadership of the Women's Network Against Violence, I could also identify the differences in what we were doing with what other organizations were developing, particularly in the North. I mean I was able to visit homeless shelters in the United States—in Wisconsin—and in Europe. The difference is that we had a feminist vision, and we were a very politicized social movement, nonpartisan but very much politicized. What I mean is that we took in the victims, we supported them in the process of transforming their lives, but in addition, we were a political organization with certain demands. We demanded changes in legislation; we monitored public policies, and later on we had an official position on what we thought of the course the country was taking. When we found out about how women's access to justice was being impacted by the government structure becoming partisan—for example, if women were going to a Sandinista judge, and the judge and the aggressor were both Sandinistas, there was no possibility that he would go to jail. This happened after the pact between Ortega and Alemán in '98; this forced us to take a political position. When we made trips abroad, we would say, "We have a position about what goes on in the country. And we are a political movement that demands changes. We don't just take care of victims."

Violeta, in addition to your regional organizing, have you made use of international treaties or meetings like the United Nations, for example?

Yes; I was at the conference in Beijing. And then I participated in subsequent meetings every 5 years where we revised the platform.[17] Like many of my peers, I got to face off with the delegates from the government of Nicaragua: look for them in the hallways, pressure them so they didn't sign with the Vatican, lobby the delegates from other countries. And in recent years, I have been able to go to the U.N. Human Rights courts[18] and the Inter-American Human Rights Courts of the OAS,[19] to denounce the state of human rights for the women in Nicaragua. I don't tell this very often—in 2004 I was selected, along with five other Nicaraguan women, to be part of this group called 1,000 Peace Women.[20] In 2004, a Swiss organization nominated 1,000 women from all over the world to be candidates for the Nobel Peace Prize.

What an honor to be nominated!

Yes, I was nominated along with Vilma Núñez[21] and four other Nicaraguan women. I just came back from Argentina last week, from a meeting with other women who were also nominated from Ecuador and Mexico, because we try to communicate amongst ourselves and keep in touch.

Some of the strategizing that you're doing across these regional networks, has part of that involved using this international discourse on human rights?

Definitely; in the first place, it's been very difficult to get recognition for this work. It's work that I think has a precedent in Vienna, from the Vienna Conference of 1994,[22] for women's rights to be acknowledged as human rights. In Nicaragua, the ways in which one can press charges are very limited for various reasons. Because the government has bought almost all of the mass media outlets—you know that it has bought almost all of the television channels and radio stations? There is very little possibility of engaging in public demonstrations because groups that are close to the government come and hit you, they follow you.

So, obviously, the international sphere is one of the few places we still have to condemn what is happening. The human rights forums are the spaces that we've used the most. One of our friends, Azahalea, worked on a document that is going to contribute greatly to support human rights because she made a report to the Committee of the Rights of the Child[23] regarding the penalization of abortion in Nicaragua as a violation of children's rights. Many pregnant teenagers who cannot terminate a pregnancy, many of them of them are minors—they're still girls.

Violeta, can you talk a little bit about how—give me some concrete examples of how the women's movement has made advances in women's health?

I think that there are two main contributions: one, all the work that the women's organizations have done to have violence against women recognized as a major health problem. There is a government survey from 1995 that says that out of every 10 Nicaraguan women who live with violence, only 3 talk about their situation. This was the 1995 survey. The last survey, I think that it's from 2007, says that 6 out of every 10 talk about it.

How did the women's movement contribute to that change?

The first people who started to bring this up, building on all the other things that I told you—about the badge campaign, the law, the signatures, right—were the women's organizations. When I was a girl, I never realized that my dad's aggressions, his emotional aggressions towards my mom, were violent and that they were a crime. I never realized it. Never. I knew that it hurt me, that it made me very sad, and my mom never even considered reporting it. Never. Because it wasn't recognized as a crime either, you know, not in my family, not in my community. No one was going to report an incident of domestic violence. It was just something that happened. It happened. Period.

Many years later, it's recognized as something that isn't right and that is an offense. I also think that to bring up abortion—when, before the whole debate surrounding Rosita's pregnancy and the termination of that pregnancy, nobody was even talking about abortion in Nicaragua. Now, many years later, this subject has been put up for debate. And now people talk about it, either in favor or against it. They talk and debate the issue of abortion, and that, I think, is an extremely important contribution. If this subject isn't brought up and it continues being taboo, the life stories of women who secretly terminate their pregnancies and die from it are going to remain hidden.

And, there's the painstaking task from hundreds of women's organizations that have a clinic, provide healthcare services, hand out fliers, do trainings, and put together communication campaigns about sexual and reproductive rights that no one else does in the country. That the government doesn't do, that the churches don't do, that no one else does. I think that, yes, there's been a transcendental contribution.

Violeta, you've also talked about some international issues. I'm interested in your opinion of whether or not you think neoliberal policies or this idea of globalization has any unique consequences for women in Nicaragua.

Obviously, the model in itself had awful consequences. I mean that from the late '80s, when the Sandinista Front was still in power, we started to see a reduction of the government. And a lot of people took to the street; there was unemployment. And from '90 and on, with Violeta Chamorro's victory, the model settled in aggressively: the privatization of social services, the reduction of the state, the decrease of social spending, and the Nicaraguan government got rid of the majority of the social programs. So, all the children's programs had to be taken on by the hundreds of NGOs that were created at that time. Sexual and reproductive health services for women stopped being the responsibility of the State and were basically taken on mostly by the women's organizations. Besides, keep in mind that [Chamorro's] government was greatly influenced by the top-level hierarchy of the Catholic Church. So, politics got in the way—the refusal to have a policy designed to provide comprehensive sexual and reproductive health programs. We ended up doing all of that ourselves.

At the moment, almost 100% of all services for victims of violence are still in the hands of women's organizations. The government of Nicaragua doesn't even have a shelter, not even a protection center, not even a center to serve female victims. And all the rest was privatized, including everything that is related to the protection of rights, particularly of women's rights. So, obviously, yes, the neoliberal policies that Ortega's government continues to implement continue falling on the shoulders of women.

You've been so busy in your life organizing around so many political issues, what do you think about your upcoming election?[24]

Perhaps because of Sofía's influence, we always have an apocalyptic discourse. We Nicaraguans always have an apocalyptic discourse. You know, these are things that happen, that are going to mark a dramatic change in the country.

What do you want to see happen?

One, that people participate because I believe that the biggest adversary of democracy is that skepticism and incredulity prevail in the community and that people don't participate.

In the past, a high percentage of Nicaraguans used to vote, and that's changed. What happened?

Well, there isn't much confidence that your vote is going to be respected, because the Supreme Election Council is in the hands of the Sandinista Front. Ortega has total control. The president of the Supreme Election Council has a house in Costa Rica, and Ortega's children who study in Costa Rica live in his house. So, there is a relationship, a very strong personal and political alliance. I think that a lot of people feel they don't want to be duped by going to vote and for their decision not to be respected.

Why does Ortega send his kids to study in Costa Rica?

As I understand it, he sent them to study film and television. So now those children that used to live there, they are the directors of the television channels that Ortega has bought. Ortega has four channels.

How many channels are there?

There are nine channels.

There are nine and he owns four?

Of those nine, four are Ortega's. Excuse me, five, because channel 10 isn't his, but he owns half and the other half belongs to Carlos Slim, the Mexican millionaire. Of 10, five belong to Ortega.

And which stations are the major news programs on?

These five channels are propaganda channels for Ortega, and each channel—Chanel 8 is directed by Ortega's son, and Channel 13 is directed by a daughter—so his children are directing the television channels. I think that only Channel 12 is doing some type of independent journalism. The rest that Ortega hasn't bought try not to talk about politics for fear that they might pull the publicity funding and suffer retaliations. I think that at this time the population isn't completely aware of the risks that this country is going through. This is a family; it's Ortega, his wife, and his children who make the decisions. It's a dynasty, and we run the risk of not even having elections in a few years.

Throughout Violeta's testimonio she weaved back and forth between personal experiences with violence and trauma and political action engaged from the margins aimed at transforming the structural and ideological context of violence against women. Like others in the Movimiento and included in this book, Violeta became involved in the Sandinista Revolution that was mobilizing to address human rights when she was just a child. In fact, she began her story by astutely describing her childhood through the expression, "I lived the war." Because the Revolution was fighting an international counterinsurgency, Violeta experienced a war that would otherwise not have provided the backdrop for her childhood had it not been for the fact that Nicaragua was of interest to an economic superpower that had a vested stake in suppressing social change.

The experience of "living the war" in the literacy brigades as a child inspired in Violeta "a commitment to change." Living among the marginalized poor of Nicaragua broadened Violeta's framework for understanding inequity. This experience was so formative that it shaped major decisions Violeta would make regarding her involvement in political change while she was still an adolescent. For example, when her commitment to the Revolution appeared to anger a violent father who abused his position of power, Violeta drew parallels to the clashes and aggression that were occurring in her home and those that were occurring in the Revolution. At the age of 15, she chose to weather the aggressions of the Revolution over her father's and left home to commit the remainder of her youth to political work. Although her experience of violence in the home shaped her decision to engage in the political project of the Sandinistas, she described her political activity as similarly traumatic when discussing her involvements in the student battalions and the loss of friends who were being killed on the front lines of a war that was being waged, in part, to keep Nicaragua in an economically subservient global position. The tension between the personal and political nature of violence that characterized Violeta's youth began to take a toll in high school and shaped a strong desire for stability and the absence of trauma.

Violeta made a break from the violence and turmoil of her youth to seek refuge at the university by intentionally choosing an area of study that would free her from the battlegrounds she experienced when she was young. She hoped that studying to be a mathematician could give her a "fresh start" and provide the security that had been lacking in her personal and political experiences. Despite being able to effectively hide out in the mathematics department, the oppositional ideology Violeta developed as a youth was reignited when she became a leader defending student subsidies in the university's budget. Therefore, her interest in refuge and stability only allowed a short reprieve from political action. In the position Violeta held as a student leader, she deideologized male-led spaces when she observed that the student organizations "weren't recognizing the leadership nor the contribution of women." Rather than accept that the male leaders would be the primary decision-makers who drove an agenda that affected everyone else, Violeta demonstrated resistance to the imposed dominant ideology by collaborating with other women to seek a "space of their own." Similar to others in the Movimiento (e.g., Sofía Montenegro; see Chapter 2) who have made feminist reference to Virginia Woolf's thesis that women need to have a "room of one's own," Violeta expressed a shared desire for space in which the demands and needs of women could be met. Violeta's testimonio demonstrates that her political interest in having a space of one's own to *make decisions* about one's interests freely and securely as a woman ran parallel to her personal desire to have space of her own to *live* freely and securely as a woman.

In her return to political work, Violeta began to form alliances with others working collectively on women's human rights violations. Her first action in this collective was based on demands that the Nicaraguan government ratify the Inter-American Convention on Violence Against Women. Violeta's role in this campaign allowed her to enact an oppositional ideology for which the demands and needs of women were no longer marginalized, but rather were moved front and center, in part through the use of internationally recognized agreements. Violeta recognized that although the terminology of the international convention may not have been immediately accessible, the use of it generated citizen participation by raising awareness that the government could legislate in favor of women's right to live without violence. Strategically using the International Convention proved to be useful in mobilizing 150 women's groups, thereby contributing to the successful passage of Nicaragua's first law criminalizing domestic violence in 1996. Violeta's iterative process involving the deideologization of male-dominated decision-making contributed to the creation of women's spaces that were imperative for mobilizing a large enough groundswell to affect legislation.

Although Violeta's experiences of violence in the home undoubtedly shaped her interest in engaging in political action related to violence against women, her experiences as a social activist also helped shape her understandings of her own experiences from the past. For example, because her political commitments placed in her solidarity with women who were taking risks to defend others' experiences of sexual violence, Violeta became involved in a highly publicized lawsuit whereby Zoilamérica, the stepdaughter of Ortega, accused him of over a decade of sexual abuse. Violeta's support of Zoilamérica, and the national conversation surrounding sexual violence that ensued, served as a catalytic event whereby Violeta could no longer deny her own experience of sexual abuse that occurred during adolescence, but for which she had remained silent.

Similarly, Violeta described a reciprocal process whereby political progress made through legislation that had enabled other women to come forward with their personal stories of violence allowed her a deepened awareness of experiences in her family when she said: "When I was a girl, I never realized that my Dad's aggressions, his emotional aggressions towards my mom, were violent and that they were a crime. I never realized it. Never." The intensity of these revelations, coupled with the political persecution and betrayal she experienced from President Ortega, led Violeta to try, once again, to depoliticize, and therefore depersonalize, her work. She described this period of her life as personally intense and indicated that, even in political work, there comes a "moment when you have to make a break." She resigned from the Network of Women Against Violence and accepted the civil coordinator position in Nicaragua in an attempt to find the stability she was seeking when she chose to study math at the university.

Nevertheless, because these iterative steps Violeta took in connecting the personal and political are part of the process of *concientización,* or the process by which those working to create bottom-up change participate in analysis and action, Violeta found herself involved in the political project again in a short amount of time. Her exit strategy did not last long because she fundamentally resisted the blind eye the government turned on women's human rights and recognized that social actors needed to uphold women's rights because it was the work that "no one else does in this country." As it was becoming increasingly clear that continued rights violations against women would maintain a system whereby men would retain political power over women, the Movimiento entered in an electoral alliance with the Sandinista Renewal Movement (MRS) to disrupt the political hegemony with the Supreme Court and the National Assembly in 2006 (Lacomb, 2014). This decision was part of a strategic effort to build representation of women in the National Assembly, which would facilitate the defense of women's human rights. Violeta was one of the MRS candidates. Although not elected to a position that may have more directly influenced legislation, Violeta continued to engage her citizen subjectivity in the advancement of women's rights from the margins.

Violeta's methodology was informed by the collective value among feminist activists in Nicaragua for recognizing women's wisdom and experience as vital sources of knowledge. For example, despite that Violeta demonstrated resistance to the violation of women's rights in Nicaragua through the strategic use of transnational alliances and international treaties, she sharply discerned this strategy from the mere adoption of international practice. Therefore, despite strong transnational alliances, Violeta articulated that the knowledge that spurred action in Nicaragua was not imported as part of an international agenda, but rather was built based on the experiences of real women, "community leaders who have never been to college but whose life experiences are of vital importance." Precisely due to her transnational collaborations, Violeta was positioned to understand how social movement actors in Nicaragua took an approach that she defined as uniquely transformative. In particular, despite drawing on international *discourse*, Violeta distinguished the political action engaged among members of the Movimiento from international *practice* she observed elsewhere. More specifically, she underscored that unlike social actors in Europe and the United States that attend to the consequences of inequity, the Movimiento was committed to collective action that reflected ideological aims that required the transformation of the structures that maintained inequity. She articulated how the praxis involved in the Movimiento did not distinguish between the "personal and political" when she said, "We are a political movement that demands changes. We don't just take care of victims. . . . We demanded changes in legislation; we monitored public policies, and later on we had an official position on what we thought of the course the country was taking." Violeta was astutely clear that part of the success among activists in Nicaragua came from operating from a feminist standpoint—or the idea that women's status as a subordinate group enhanced the production of knowledge (Hesse-Biber, 2007).

Throughout her life course, Violeta built a citizen subjectivity that reflected an understanding that women's experience in Nicaragua, and the emerging knowledge from that experience, was inextricably linked to systemic inequities of global power. This became most evident when she suggested that the threats to liberty and justice that women in Nicaragua experience are not simply a result of the local context, but also larger global processes that alter the priority and responsibility of the Nicaraguan government.

For example, Violeta discussed how an aggressive privatization of resources has led the government to absolve responsibility of the health and safety of the citizenry when she stated that, "the neoliberal policies that Ortega's government continues to implement continue falling on the shoulders of women." Because of the collusion of patriarchal control and neoliberalism, women's movement activists became charged with upholding women's rights because the State halted its responsibility. The understanding that the intersection of patriarchal power and neoliberal interests put women in Nicaragua at heightened risk of human rights violations led Violeta to resist these structures and strategize alliances that crossed borders.

In deideologizing the prioritization of capital over people, Violeta made strategic use of U.N. conferences and their resulting calls to action, like the Beijing Platform, to apply strategic pressure on the Nicaraguan government to recognize women's human rights. Given an increasingly hostile political environment for women in Nicaragua, coupled with setbacks in national legislation, Violeta suggested that "obviously, the international sphere is one of the few places we still have to condemn what is happening." Therefore, the role of solidarity within Nicaragua is imperative for influencing the legislation of women's rights, but the role of solidarity through transnational regional alliances proves to be an imperative part of upholding of them.

Violeta's *testimonio* demonstrates how an alternative form of citizen subjectivity can emerge from the margins when an unwavering commitment to recognize the personal as political is rooted in an oppositional ideology that refuses to see women as victims. Rather than action aimed at gaining services for women who have been marginalized through violence, Violeta used the experiences and standpoint of women in Nicaragua to demand changes that will transform their experiences through legislation and international human rights treaties that serve as one mechanism in a guided pursuit of making women's personal injustice a matter of law and human rights in Nicaragua.

Notes

1. She did this in the Sandinista National Literacy Crusade.

2. *Compañero* is used to reflect political solidarity with someone who is a partner, colleague, or classmate. *Compañera* is the feminine form of *compañero*.

3. Jiménez's *testimonio* is included in Chapter 1.

4. The Nicaraguan Constitution, approved in 1987, allocated 6% of the national budget to public universities.

5. *Barrio* can technically be translated to English as "neighborhood"; however, the word *barrio* carries a connotation more specific to a working-class neighborhood.

6. The Seventh Latin American and Caribbean Feminist Encounter took place in Chile in 1996. The encounters are a series of conferences that have been held periodically since 1981. The first was held in Bogotá, Colombia. Attendance at the one held in Peru inspired the cover artist, Favianna Rodriguez to create the image used for this book.

7. This is the Inter-American Convention on the Prevention, Punishment, and Eradication of Violence Against Women. It is a multilateral treaty drafted by the Organization of American States (OAS) in Belém do Pará, Brazil in 1994 and ratified by Nicaragua in December 1995.

8. Law 230, passed October 9, 1996, amended the Penal Code to include interfamily violence.

9. Alemán was an official of the Somoza dictatorship and mayor of Managua from 1990 to 1995. He was the president of Nicaragua from 1997 to 2002. In 1999, Ortega and Alemán signed an undemocratically self-serving agreement referred to as "the pact." The agreement united their two political parties in the National Assembly and gave Ortega and Alemán control over nearly 90% of the legislature, granting them near-dictatorial powers

over the nation. The Ortega-Alemán union controlled the National Assembly and passed legislation that lowered the required percentage of votes necessary to win the presidency from 45% to 35% based on Ortega's low support rate.

10. Daniel Ortega was elected in 2007 (the Rosita case was in 2003).

11. The IMF (International Monetary Fund) is an international financial institution that provides loans and financial assistance to countries throughout the world.

12. In Spanish, it is *el Movimiento de Renovación Sandinista* (MRS). The MRS is a Nicaraguan political party founded in 1995 to reclaim the values of Sandino.

13. Azahalea Solis is a lawyer and representative of the *Movimiento Autónomo de Mujeres.*

14. This is Sofía Montenegro, whose testimonio is in Chapter 2.

15. Marcela Lagarde is a feminist scholar whose primary research focuses on violence against women and femicide.

16. Mesoamerica is used to describe the area spanning Mexico through Central America.

17. The platform is the Beijing Platform for Action.

18. She is indicating the proceedings of the U.N. Human Rights Council (UNHRC) that enforce international human rights law.

19. The Inter-American Human Rights Court is based in Costa Rica and carries out the judicial processes for the Inter-American Commission on Human Rights as put forth by the OAS. The OAS maintains relationships between countries in the Americas and supports and promotes the interests of member states internationally.

20. In 2005, there were 1,000 women across the globe nominated for the Nobel Peace Prize. A book by R. G. Vermot-Mangold, *1,000 PeaceWomen Across the Globe*, was published with their stories (2005, Scalo /Kontrast-Verlag in Zurich).

21. Vilma Núñez was interviewed for this project, and her testimonio is included in the Global Feminisms Project.

22. The Vienna Conference was the second global U.N. conference with an exclusive focus on human rights. Women's rights activists mobilized to ensure that women's human rights were fully on the agenda with the demand "women's rights are human rights."

23. This is a committee that monitors the implementation of the U.N. Convention on the Rights of the Child. Azahalea Solis Roman testified before the UNHRC in 2010 regarding the criminalization of abortion.

24. Five months from the interview, Ortega was up for reelection for presidency.

Sandra Ramos

6

Subjectivation in Response to Patriarchal and Neoliberal Rule

> *We have taken feminist philosophy as a way of making change in this patriarchal structure that oppresses us and keeps us sunken in poverty ... For both neoliberalism and the patriarchal system are responsible, both of them together, for continuing to oppress women, to oppress more than 50-plus 1% percent of the world's population.*
>
> —*TESTIMONIO* FROM SANDRA RAMOS

Although the oppositional ideology that often fuels the pursuit of women's human rights frequently manifests in a discussion of domestic violence, structural conditions in Nicaragua have also led to a high level of violence against women outside the home, including in the workplace. Sandra Ramos cofounded the María Elena Cuadra (MEC) Working and Unemployed Women's Movement in 1994 in response to an intersectional awareness that workplace issues for women involved human rights violations that extended beyond those experienced by men, to include violence. Since then, Ramos has traveled extensively to countries such as Canada and Korea, which also have strong labor movements, to participate in transnational exchanges aimed at sharing organizing strategies for women that are attuned to gendered consequences in an era of globalization and economic crisis.

Because much of Ramos's work with MEC has revolved around organizing women workers in Nicaragua's free trade zones (FTZs) to improve conditions in *maquiladoras*,[1] Ramos and the MEC served as the hosts for an ethnography: *From the Revolution to the Maquiladoras: Gender, Labor, and Globalization in Nicaragua* (Mendez, 2005). More recently, Ramos was involved in launching a national campaign that recognized the ideological nature of violence that resulted in the Comprehensive Law Against Violence Toward Women (Law 779), which was enacted in 2012.

Sandra Ramos was born in 1959 in the capital city of Managua. Like others in the *Movimiento Autónomo de Mujeres* (Women's Autonomous Movement), and those included in this book, Ramos began her political career as a youth involved in the Sandinista student movements of the 1980s. She attended college at the *Universidad Nacional Autónoma de Nicaragua* (UNAN) in Managua and then shortly after helped found the Sandinista Workers' Center, the largest trade union confederation in Nicaragua. Ramos worked on labor issues in this union for over a decade before founding the MEC. When Ramos separated from the Sandinistas to focus organizing efforts on women's rights, a warrant for her arrest was issued that led her into hiding for a year until the Austrian Embassy legally intervened on her behalf.

At several points in her interview, Ramos acknowledged the role of *conscientización* in subjectivation—or the development of an alternative subjectivity that questions authority. Specifically, she highlighted that most people do not immediately come into the world with a nuanced understanding of struggle or inequity, in particular surrounding gender, but that it is a life process that is learned through experience. In this manner, she was articulating the importance of what Foucault (2005) referenced as autonomous pathways to the "truth" that develop through practices of freedom. Ramos's testimonio demonstrates the importance of transnational intersectionality in subjectivation because she exhibits how understanding the interconnections between patriarchy and global capitalism pose unique challenges to the actualization of women's human rights.

> *Sandra, I'm very interested in the work of your organization, but I'd like to ask you to start back further, with your own personal history and tell me a little bit about your childhood, some of your earliest memories, what kind of family you were from, those kind of things.*

Well, I was born in the city of Managua. From my childhood, what I can remember is that it was a childhood similar to that of all the children in this country who grow up with only a mother, who is mother and father at the same time. My mother is a working woman; she worked at the Mercado Oriental.[2] She worked, had a shop there so she could support eight girls; we were eight sisters. I'm in the middle. So my life was normal, as normal as it is for the poor children in this country who have to work with their mothers to be able to access the basic necessities of life.

If there is anything that at this point I can remember is that I come from—that in my life the strongest images and figures are those of my grandmother and my mother. I think their example really marked my life. They are women who worked hard. They were always fair women, women with a big heart, and they are women who marked my life because despite their poverty, despite their limitations, they always shared what little they had with the people around them. My mother's example as a working woman, as a strong worker, also marked my life, and that is the sector of women with whom I work. I studied; I finished primary and secondary school. I went to the university.

Of all my sisters, I am the only one; none of my other sisters were able to finish college.

Why were you different?

Because the conditions were different. They entered the labor force from a very young age, because we all had to work alongside my mother. My other, younger sisters lived different conditions; my mother was able to send her daughters to secondary school, you see, not only to primary school but also secondary school and vocational school. They didn't go beyond that because of the traditional role that we women have been brought up with. It's like life finally arrives when—or rather that our life is over when we marry and we take care of a man. And when we have kids, well that turns into a limitation for women to get ahead. It may have also been genetics, right. Possibly because of my genes because my father is not the same man who is the father of my older sisters, nor the man who is the father of my younger sisters. But also my rebellious attitude. I think from the moment I was born I was rebellious, but also, possibly because of the competition I had, because I was the middle child, the ones after me pushed and the ones before me pushed. So possibly that made me somewhat of a survivor because I really fought to graduate; I really fought to go to college; I fought to become a professional, even having my son. Even as I was mother-father to one of my sons, I kept on studying. Then I got married and had my second son and I stayed in school. I had a fixed goal in my life, and it was that I did not want to follow the same path or the same lifestyle as my sisters.

Can you tell me when you first became involved in the work you're doing now in a centralized way, what was the process?

I lived in what was known as La Bolsa neighborhood; this is the neighborhood behind the cathedral. That was in the center of Managua. My mother rented a place there. And I started to become involved because that area was key. The students[3] were constantly taking over the cathedral, the university students, the high school students. It was like protest central.

What years were these?

We're talking about the '70s, '60 something, because I was born in '59. From the time I was very young I had been exposed to the protests, so that is something that marked me. Every day I had to walk past the cathedral and the palace[4] to get to the central market where my mother worked. On this route, I would bump into all the protests, into the student movement struggle, and I would observe them. Maybe I didn't understand it all, as young as I was. My mother says that a BECAT[5] drove by one day—that's what they called the police patrols that were from the specialized group of the Somoza Guard, and I grabbed a rock and threw it at them. Ask me why I did it, I don't know, but I threw that rock at them because everyone used to say that they were bad. [Laughter.] My mother had the fright of her life because she says that the BECAT stopped, and they said, "Who is the son of a bitch who threw that rock?" and it was me! My mother was very concerned; she even smacked me in the head that day, but I was just a little girl. I think I was in primary school back then.

My life took place within that sector because I studied in the Joséfa Toledo de Ayeres School, which was close to my house. Then, in secondary school I went to the Andrés Bello School, which was also very close to my house. Back then, that whole perimeter was like a vicious circle, full of revolutionaries. I remember that I would beg my mother to let me go to school because for my mother, because of the culture and her being a small-business owner, well, she considered that we should all be businesswomen; it was not necessary to study so much, because she had not had that many years of schooling and she was supporting her family—that was the way to do it. I remember that I would beg for her to let me go to school, and sometimes she would say, "No, you're not going today," and I would cry and cry and cry and cry, because I wanted to go to school. Or sometimes, I remember, there would be strikes and demonstrations at the school, and I would go. I would tell my mother that we had classes, but there were no classes. There was a strike. Those were my surroundings, and it seems that they marked my life.

When I went to college, it happened as well; I was going to UNAN in Managua, and all the heavily involved people from the Sandinista Front were at the UNAN-Managua campus. We would protest all the time. I think I didn't go to many classes because I was out protesting. So, that's how I was making connections, connections, connections until, well, I was involved. I became completely involved with the Sandinista Front, extremely involved. Then came the Revolution, and I began to learn about the workers' unions, well, that the government had ordered the creation of the unions because we needed to organize the entire society, so the workers in unions, the youth as youth, the teachers as teachers, and it all got set up.

So, I became one of the union activists at my job. I became involved with the Sandinista Workers' Centre, the CST[6]; I am one of their founding members. And then I started to take on responsibilities. I think taking on responsibilities happens gradually, little by little, bit by bit. It's a process, right? Nobody is born with open eyes; today I'm going to be a guerilla fighter and tomorrow I'm going to be something else. No, it's a process that you take on, and it's a life process, an analysis of life when you see the struggles that other women and men have and you want to help them overcome those struggles.

But I do think that for me, two great women in my life influenced me: my grandmother and my mother. The men in my life have no weight in my history. I cannot find strong men in my family. I find strong women, determined women who were able to raise their daughters as best they could. So, that's how I became involved. I kept working with the unions until 1994, because I had a falling out with the leadership of the union movement. It was a falling out over the agenda.

We insisted that the working class was not just one class because it is not asexual. Men and women form the working class, and we—in the case of women—we have another demand, not just our salary, not just collective bargaining, not just the right to organize, but the right to a life free of violence, free of sexual harassment in the workplace, the issue of maternity, right, the issue of sexual and reproductive health; that's to say, for women there was a whole other world. But the workers' movement in those times wasn't prepared for these matters. It's like the women, we advanced, and they stayed behind, backwards. There was a point where they believed that what we were doing was weakening the working class of our country. We were diverting the working class from its historic mission, which is the struggle between capitalism and the proletariat, but they didn't understand that within that struggle there is another hidden struggle, which is also important, and that's the women's struggle.

So, the women's struggle led to a very, very, very strong rupture within the Sandinista union workers' movement, in this case, particularly with the Sandinista Workers' Centre, to the point that we decided to leave that space. It was such a violent rupture that the union leaders decided that the women needed to be taught a lesson. So they accused us of a crime. The leaders accused us of stealing sophisticated technological equipment, the air conditioning units, the desks—seems like we stole everything but the men! This was an organization that had security personnel, men with guns, who said that we came at night under the guise of darkness with a truck, in the middle of the night, and that we—right in front of the security guards, because they went to the trial and testified that they had seen us with their very own eyes. Well, why did you not stop me?

So, that was the rupture. We left the organization, and they took us to trial. There was an arrest warrant issued against me, issued by a judge who was also a member of the national security force. But, I did not let them arrest me. I was on the run throughout the country for a year because they were determined to make an example out of me.

What year was it that you had to leave?

In '94, I spent the entire year on the run. Thanks to the Austrian Embassy, the ambassador called for us and offered us two things: political asylum, and I just laughed. How is it that I am going to seek asylum because of these assholes? No, it's not possible. I am not leaving my country. How can that be, if I am a woman who has struggled all her life in this country? How can I leave? So we told them that if they wanted to help us, they could pay for the lawyer. And they paid for the legal services for our defense, and in '95 we won the case! We won the case against all those big shots who were protected by everyone because they were high-level leaders. So, we won the case—well, you see the María Elena Cuadra was organized on May 7, 1994, and on May 9 we already had arrest warrants. So, just 2 days after organizing the María Elena Cuadra, there was an arrest warrant issued against me. What happened to us reflects the patriarchal power that, just as today we see in the acts of violence against women when women decide to leave their husbands, the husbands believe they are the ones who decide how the relationship will end, how, when, and where. They are the ones who are supposed to leave us because when we leave them we hurt their pride, their self-love, their macho love, and that's when they decide to hurt the women, right, sometimes to point of killing them.

What was your role in establishing María Elena?

Well, I'm one of the founders of the María Elena Cuadra organization. I, along with two other people, came up with the idea of how we were going to reorganize, but really it was more like a collective convocation among all of us. We made lots of phone calls and decided to found an organization. Eight hundred hard-working women leaders got together, and we organized the women's movement known today as María Elena Cuadra, and we organized it in six different departments within the country. We were born in the way in which women give birth to multiple children. Usually, an organization starts simple and then gets complicated, right? It usually starts in Managua and then grows. Not us, we were born in six different departments simultaneously.

And how did you name the organization?

The day we organized, on May 7, when we had the large assembly meeting, everyone suggested a name. I proposed the name María Elena Cuadra because she was a woman leader of AMNLAE, the Luisa Amanda Espinoza Association of Nicaraguan Women,[7] and a person we knew. She was a leader, and we know of the love she had for women and her unconditional support, her strong work. But also, she was a woman leader who had died just 1 month before organizing the María Elena Cuadra. So, she had been a member of her organization, and we decided to recognize her work by naming our organization in her honor.

Can you tell me about some of the strategies that you were first using to organize women when the organization started?

Well, initially we decided to call ourselves Movement of Working and Unemployed Women, María Elena Cuadra. Why working? Because we are all workers; that is to say that all the informal work, the unpaid work, the paid work, the concept of workers is to rescue ourselves as active subjects, as subjects with rights; and unemployed because we were going through a crisis in which women were losing jobs, and we wanted to incorporate the women who did not have work, either because they couldn't find work or because they were young women.

So, the first strategies were about making visible the contribution women make to the nation's economy as subjects with rights. We began the work by organizing the working women of the free trade zones because there was a very large number of women there whose rights were being violated. Back then there was no union organizing inside those companies, and, frankly, the unions weren't even interested in organizing women. So, we start to organize the women, to support them in their struggle for their rights.

We also worked with women who were domestic workers, with women who were small farmers, helping them diversify their crops, and providing workshops on gender, self-esteem, human rights, labor rights, providing them with technical assistance to improve the yield of their crops. So, we started off strong, everything that had to do with gender analysis.

Today, the María Elena Cuadra is a strong organization, active in six departments in the country; we have a 16-year work history, and all that work is not just the work of one leader, there is not a single leadership. Each one of us has been in the company of a large group of leaders, in the *barrios*,[8] in the communities, in the workplace. Our leadership is not our own; it is a collective leadership. My leadership represents a collective because I am what I am because other women have worked with me. The recognition that I have and that this organization has is because of the leadership of the thousands of women who participate in this organization, right?

Have you had to change the strategies that you use to adjust to different political climates or historical moments?

No, our strategies have not changed. Our mission, our vision, our strategies have remained the same, and it is the defense of women's rights. The methodology, perhaps, is what has changed. We began with a strategy of not denouncing when rights are being violated, but rather to accumulate strength by educating women to take ownership of their own rights. This is because it does not help that I go out there and report and denounce that someone's rights are being violated, if the rest of the women do not want to. So, we started this process of convincing the women to recognize themselves and to empower themselves to claim their rights, so that once a large group of women is convinced and has appropriated those rights as their own, then the collective action is stronger.

Today, we are a respected organization in the free trade zones because we have also contributed to the education of the business owners to respect our laws, and in our education endeavor we have incorporated what the law in our country says, and when business owners do not uphold the law, we take them to court. But this has all been a process. If 16 years ago someone would tell me that I would seize a company, I would say, Oh dear Lord. How am I going to seize a company? What? How? When? Where? Today, if a company violates the workers' rights, we seize them, but this is because within that company there are now workers, men and women, who are cognizant of their rights. If the people are not cognizant, they will think that what we are doing is crazy.

Will you tell me a little bit about some of the conditions that women are facing in these free trade zones?

Well, like everywhere, even like in the United States and everywhere, the business owners always try to violate the laws of the men and women who work for them. They all come to this country looking to accumulate wealth. That is why they have moved from the countries in the North to the countries in the South looking for cheap labor and a place where they can get away with not obeying labor rights. And that is why our organization is so important, because we know whom we are dealing with, we know that there are people whose mentality is based on wealth accumulation, and not based on distributing the benefits—a capitalist model that strives to accumulate, accumulate, accumulate, accumulate, and not redistribute. The economic model used in the free trade zones is a model that tramples on workers' rights, that makes women sick, that does not have the best work conditions, and that still doesn't offer equal pay to women.

Can you explain the conditions? Can you give me some examples of what women are facing?

Well, for example, in the first years, about 10 years ago we still struggled a lot in the free trade zones with the matter of physical violence against women. The free trade zone isn't composed of one single source of capital; there are Taiwanese, Koreans, Americans, now a Mexican, now a Guatemalan, Honduran. So initially, the first ones we approached to eliminate physical violence in the workplace. We felt there was no place for that. Also, the low salaries just hadn't changed at all. So we tackled this, we tackled the fact that the men and women there were not allowed to organize into unions; they weren't allowed time to go for medical appointments, and also the pregnancy tests to which women were subjected in order to work there. On top of all that, of course, you had to be thin, young, and pretty to work in those businesses.

Why?

Since this country had so few employment sources, right, because it just recently ended an aggressive war in which the North American government[9] had not been able to compensate this country for that, although there was a resolution from the International Court of Justice[10] that it should financially compensate the damages to this country. It was very difficult to get the country's economy going.

When the Sandinista Front loses the elections, the new government, which was a right-wing government, they decide to privatize all the businesses that at the time belonged to the State. So, it was just enormous quantities of people who became unemployed. And to this day, that decision—that decision to end with the national industries, it is still the largest nightmare that we women have in this country. Because, you see, when they dismantled the national industries, all that was left here was to bring in foreign investment, and the first foreign investment to come to our country was looking for one thing: cheap labor, right? Terrible pay, bad working conditions, and also, you have to remember that the infrastructure had been so obsolete that when these new industries came in and occupied those buildings, the people were crowded together. Today, thanks to the struggle of all the women workers, because it is their struggle that leads to results, today the new companies that come here come with better environmental conditions, and the owners of those industrial parks are required to prove good conditions. You might work in what seems like a box, but that box should be appropriate, in good condition.

But there are still problems; they haven't ended, they'll never end while we have this model of production focused on accumulating wealth and not redistributing it. We'll still be fighting over the same thing, to have our rights respected. It's a struggle, and well it's proven that since the 19th century, when capitalism emerged strongly, we've been fighting for the same thing. It's a never-ending struggle. It's not going to end, and what we try to work on is for the coming generations of women laborers to enter this struggle in better conditions, with more equality, not like today where there are so many young women who are not cognizant of their rights. We want the new generation to know what their rights are and to demand them, regardless of who is governing the country, and that any company that comes to this country, comes respecting those human rights that our government has ratified.

I insist that everything that happens in this country is the responsibility of the State, is the responsibility of the big investors, and is the responsibility of the big brands; there are three entities that are responsible for what happens here. Therefore, if we have a government that is more protective of investors than of its own citizens, it will allow for their rights to be violated. But if we have a State that is more of a benefactor of its workers, and is able to combine rights and investment, well that helps to reduce the problems.

You know, the big question that folks from outside, from the North, ask is: Are these factories, these free trade zones, are they exploitation, or are they empowerment for women?

To me, they are exploitation; there's no way around it. Everything else is just a lie; everyone wants to say that since there are no jobs in Nicaragua, well, the free trade zone helps resolve that and therefore it's empowering. Sorry, I don't know who is making that analysis, but whoever it is needs to go back and learn about sociology, about anthropology, about psychology, about economy, and do a more integral analysis. I don't think it is empowerment when women are left crippled with lung problems; I don't think it is empowerment when the working conditions of that repetitive work leave long-term muscular-skeletal effects in the women. No, I don't think it is empowerment to have a production model that won't even allow the workers to continue their studies, when young women form the largest group of women laborers. So, that cannot be empowerment. What the *maquilas* are for this country is a band-aid, a band-aid for the huge unemployment in our country. I cannot see that they have any other role, and I won't give it to them. It would be empowerment—they would be empowering women if they abided by the Codes of Conduct, if they fully obeyed the law, if they created decent working conditions for Nicaraguan women. That's to say, if they were redistributive. How can I say that they are empowering if they do not reciprocate? If an economy is not redistributive, it's only about taking: work for me, work for me, and here's your 3 pesos; work for me, work for me, and here's your 3 pesos. That is not empowerment. That is a band-aid.

I'd like to shift gears a little bit and ask you about the role that feminism may have played in your work, if at all. How do you understand or define feminism?

Well, when I worked in the unions, before beginning my work with women, I thought the working class was all one, that it was a sole working class. I was a woman, but in my mind, the working class was the working class. When I became involved with the feminist movement in this country, and we began the debates, the analyses—because this is a process, nobody is born a feminist and nobody is born knowing about gender; this is learned as we go, right? So, in this learning process, when they name me to lead the Women's Office of the Sandinista Workers' Center, I said to myself, what's this? What am I going to do here? Well, the first thing I did was to go talk to the feminists in this country, so they would teach me. AMNLAE taught me one part; another part I learned on my own from the ties with the women. Well, I started to see the everyday problems that we women have, to the point that I became deeply aware of it and took it to heart, and the feminist movement in this county has contributed greatly to Nicaraguan women.

But, that also depends on how one takes on feminism and what one wants feminism to be; for me, what we are doing is providing workshops for women workers, for the female leaders in the barrios, for the female leaders in the workplace, so that they learn about feminism and that feminism is not a single feminism, that there are multiple feminisms; and that once you tell them, these here are the multiple feminisms, the various theories, pick the one you like the most. I recognize in feminist theory, I recognize that it has the potential to transform women's lives. And it's a way of seeing the economy differently, seeing life differently. So, we believe, and I personally believe, along with all the women I work with, we believe we have to transfer what we know about feminism to the new generation of women. Why? Because when we brandish the feminist philosophy, oh, we were discredited, they'd say here come the lesbians, the divisors, the ones who don't like men, the ones who are going to ruin and taint what it means to be a woman. It was all so horrible, and so many women wouldn't come near us. We suffered discrimination, but we told ourselves, well, we're not going to die because of this discrimination; but we have to teach the women, we have to teach them to understand that men are not inherently right, and that's what we are doing now.

We have a leadership academy, and we are preparing young female leaders from other organizations. We have joined with other organizations to form new leaders who know the ABCs of their human rights, but also have knowledge of what feminism is, because in the mixed sectors, they say, to keep us divided and so women don't demand more respect, they tell us that if we take on feminism, then we are deviating the organization towards something it should not be deviated to. That's why they are so defensive. I live feminism, I live it as a part of my life. Everything that I do, I know it has to do with feminism; it's not just a theory up in the air. Rather, it is a way of living life, of thinking and of working for other women to know and appropriate themselves and make changes in their life. As I see it, that is feminism. What I do is part of feminism. So, yes, I think that the feminist movement has progressed in this country in the way we see ourselves as equals. I think the contributions of the feminist movement to this country are indisputable, and I'm not talking of just the Nicaraguan feminists, but of the global feminist movement that has contributed so much to us, and well, we have also taken that feminist philosophy as a way of making change in this patriarchal structure that oppresses us and keeps us sunken in this poverty. This is not just the result of neoliberalism, for both neoliberalism and the patriarchal system are responsible, both of them, together, for continuing to oppress women, to oppress more than the 50-plus-1% of the world's population.

We talked about this a little bit when we first arrived, but can you tell me about, in your opinion, the relationship between scholarship or academic work and activist work that you're doing?

We work closely with academia. Currently, we have a program with the Universidad Centro Americana [UCA],[11] with the UCA's Gender Studies program, so that when our leaders graduate from our academy, we send them to an advanced program at the university. We work along with the universities, and so the ones who teach our leaders are women from academia. So, for us, a synergy is necessary between academia and empirical knowledge, and these two must join forces to improve the work that we do. So for me it is valid, the academic study, because we conduct studies here and we contact the people in academia to do them. I think that's why all the academic studies that take place in the country have our support because we have very close ties to make that link between what is formal academia and our women. I think that academia has learned a lot, too, and so have we. I think it's been both ways, and that's important; theory and practice should go hand in hand. I think at one point in our history, academia was here and practice was over there, right? So, we would criticize the poor academics and they would criticize us, oh, those women are all activism, activism and they don't think. But then, when we began to work together, the two pillars, we saw that if the two pillars come together, we can do better things for women. And following on that thought, the daily routine of women needs to be written down, because while we are heavily involved in activism, we are actively struggling day in and day out for women's rights, it's important for someone to write it down and compile this history. It's the women who will engage in the struggle for women; no one else will do it. The men are not interested; I still haven't seen any male author, oh Paulo Coelho, or I don't know who, saying how beautiful feminist women are. So, okay, they make some tiny reference, but to really rescue the story of women's lives has always been the work of women in academia or in film who are always there behind us, trying to make visible this effort which I believe is very—very—very important for the future generations, because just like those other feminists in other times did what they did and fought for our right to vote, for our right to citizenship, for a name, a last name. That's why we are so thankful of what you are doing; now that you explained the project and its objectives,[12] it seems like it's a pertinent project, and we thank you for doing it.

You've described the reality that there's often a difference between the law and then what women actually experience. Can you give me examples of when women's organizations have been necessary to make advances in women's health?

Well, as you probably know already, we used to have the right to therapeutic abortions. Unfortunately, a certain political class[13] joined forces with the ecclesiastical authorities to take away a right that had been ours for 100 years. However, we are not just sitting with our arms crossed in the women's organizations. There are women's organizations that are intimately linked to the defense of women's health, of our sexual and reproductive rights, and they continue to struggle every day to rescue the right to therapeutic abortions, also to assist our women with any problems they might have as a result of that prohibition. For example, the National Assembly is discussing what is known as the law on sexual and reproductive health. Sexual and reproductive health, it says nothing about rights, it says sexual and reproductive health. But we are there, we feminist women, we're there trying to get that tiny little concept [rights] in, trying to find room for that little concept because we know that we are up against a huge economic power, because the church is not only an ideological power, but it is also an economic power. So much so that, in order to take away that right we had, had at its service all of the owners of the media, so that the publicity that was shown was extremely cruel to women. Cruel, cruel, cruel, cruel, and we didn't have enough funds to create a countercampaign; we couldn't. It was such a monster, the church with all its economic, patriarchal, ideological power, along with the political parties, and on the other side the women's groups, it was like David against Goliath.[14] So today, we are still working on all and any process of reporting, condemning, and suing for the restitution of the right to therapeutic abortions. Our organizations continue to work to promote a life free of violence. This is another front on which the feminist movement has fought, to make visible that pandemic, that tragedy that we women continue to live because we still do not have a State that is a protector of women and that strives to save the lives of women and allows us to live a life free of violence.

Today, we are also working on a law against violence towards women, including all the *feminicides*,[15] and that law was introduced by 21 women's organizations, including the María Elena Cuadra Women's Movement, and it is now being decided on. We know that the law in and of itself will not resolve everything, but before we didn't even have a judicial framework that would recognize feminicide or femicide. Today, we can now talk of femicide and feminicide as punishable crimes. I think that it is a great contribution of my country's feminist movement and of the women's movement, that we will be able to count on a law that will save women's lives, although the struggle later will be to implement the law, due to all the influences we will have to address, to avoid inequality and also tolerance. Tolerance towards these acts of violence, but this law also addresses sanctions to government employees who do not aggressively act against the wave of violence against women.

You also mentioned that you—the María Elena Cuadra Movement—have addressed some health issues in the free trade zones. Can you tell us about what health issues you've worked on there?

Well, in the first place we have pressured the Department of Labor to issue a ministerial resolution prohibiting pregnancy tests in order to apply to jobs. We have also worked with the unions and the private sector on what is known as the Law on Labor Health in the maquilas. There is a special law to demand better health conditions for workers, men and women, in the maquilas. We have looked into the provisional medical clinics to ensure they are treating women well. Regarding issues of sexual and reproductive health, we have a team of health promoters who are continuously educating women on their sexual and reproductive rights, on sexually transmitted diseases and the use of birth control, because they are very young women and they need to protect themselves, their health, and their lives. To think about things like if they are struggling with one child, well it will be even harder with three; besides, the salaries in the free trade zones do not really allow you to live a decent life. So, we also need our young women to learn to plan. We also have a program to educate male and female workers on the consequences of HIV/AIDS, how to protect yourself. But, we also have a resolution that forbids the companies from requiring an HIV test in order to apply for a job. I think we have advanced little by little, although we still have large challenges, as are the long-term effects on the health of the workers that are caused by the repetitive movement, which is still something we have to work on. But, we have also worked on matters regarding pregnant women and their need for time off. It used to be that when the women started to show, they were immediately fired. It's not that they don't still get fired, but it happens in a less-abusive way. Also, there is a little more protection for the state of a pregnant woman, a little more protection, not the best, but a little more.

At the start of her testimonio, Sandra drew the connection that observing the exploitation of her mother's labor directly shaped the extent to which she would later become involved in upholding the rights of women working in Nicaragua's FTZs. The FTZs in Nicaragua reflected a new international division of labor and an industrialization of the country driven by the economic strategies for Latin America promoted by the Reagan and Bush administrations in the United States. Though already established elsewhere in Latin America, FTZs were essentially irrelevant to the economy of Nicaragua during the Revolution because factories during the 1980s were unionized and State run.

However, as part of a neoliberal initiative to privatize state enterprises, the Chamorro government of 1990 closed a number of state textile, clothing, shoe, and other factories, which set unemployment soaring among women workers who had been the backbone of the workforce in these industries. When the FTZs opened their doors again in 1991, almost all of the women from the closed factories sought and found jobs in the FTZs, although now working for foreign employers that could and did pay poverty-level wages.

Since then, the Central American Free Trade Agreement (CAFTA), an expansion on the North American Free Trade Agreement (NAFTA) in five Central American countries (Guatemala, El Salvador, Honduras, Costa Rica, and Nicaragua) and the Dominican Republic, was passed under the presidency of George W. Bush in 2004 and began to be implemented in Nicaragua in 2006. Since its implementation, Nicaraguan exports to the United States have gone up by 71%. Moreover, some estimates suggest that women make up 70% of the export workforce, with 50% being head of households (Avin, 2006). In 2010, the largest percentage of Nicaraguan maquilas (30%) were owned by U.S. companies that were not meeting the living wage requirement established by the Nicaraguan government. It is in this transnational context that Sandra's awareness and praxis for change developed, but it was not overnight. Sandra expressed the iterative nature of concientización in her own words when she said, "This is a process, nobody is born a feminist and nobody is born knowing about gender; this is learned as we go."

At the outset of this process, Sandra observed in her mother a strong worker, yet one who still could not provide fully for her family. This undoubtedly shaped the life course of Sandra's activism. She began her testimonio articulating an oppositional gender ideology by expressing a deep desire to be different from other women in her family. She had a fixed goal in her life to not follow the same path or the same lifestyle as her sisters. In recognizing this resistance, Sandra identified as a rebel, in part because the ideology or norms that drove her were not the traditional gender norms that guided the decisions of her grandmother, mother, and sisters. Although she was aware that structural conditions impose undue economic hardship on women that necessitates entering the workforce early, Sandra rejected following in the footsteps of her mother and seven sisters. As Sandra was developing her oppositional ideology, an impassioned interest in attending school reflected that she did not want to be subject to dominant power relations that predetermine one's destiny as a girl.

In Foucault's (2005) writing, he argued that "subjects" are often constituted as a production of power whereby the power, or dominant ideology, imprints itself on individuals' immediate lives in a manner that imposes a certain submission to the "truth" behind that power. Foucault proposed, alternatively, that subjectivation reflects a different mode by which the subject constitutes herself. In particular, in processes of subjectivation the truth arises from the subject's own practices of freedom and not from a relationship with an unquestioned authority. Although Sandra's early interests in school or hurling rocks at the National Guard did not yet fit into a strategic plan, in either case her actions reflected the formation of a practice of freedom that would serve as the foundation for an oppositional ideology that valued subjectivity and, by extension, the rights that subjects are afforded. She credited her fight for freedom to deideologizing the limits imposed by gender roles as well as to the examples of resistance and protest that were abundantly surrounding her during her formative years as a child.

Sandra's point of entry to address struggles related to labor rights was the Sandinista Workers' Center, where she served for over a decade before an ideological clash created a chasm between her and those in power. Up to this point, much of the truth that Sandra was operating under was determined by the male-dominated agenda of the Sandinistas. When Sandra insisted that, "The working class is not just one class because it is not asexual," she reflected a subjectivity born of an unwillingness to compromise to the production of gendered power. Although the Sandinista Workers' Center was a place in which Sandra came to understand that the experience of the working class was not universal, exposing the "hidden struggle" of women was viewed as a threat to the dominant narrative, which was rooted in a single-issue focus centered on capitalism. Although the historic mission of the Sandinistas was to resist the abuses of capitalism, Sandra's oppositional ideology challenged this narrative to take an intersectional approach that also acknowledged the abuses of patriarchy for women whose labor was exploited within global capitalism. At this juncture with the Sandinista Workers' Center, Sandra made a move to act with other women to create an organization that would recognize that the experience for women in the factories "was a whole other world" that went beyond salary grievances and collective bargaining to include the right to live free of violence and sexual harassment.

Seeking "space of their own" within the labor movement to address women's rights parallels the experiences shared by other women in the Movimiento. That these processes run parallel across sectors reflect that ruptures were occurring across all of Nicaraguan society whereby women were questioning a male-dominated authority that would not recognize their rights. Like others in the Movimiento, when Sandra resisted the male-dominated Sandinista organization to focus on women-specific issues, she was criminally persecuted. Two days after the MEC collective was organized, arrest warrants were issued for Sandra and her *compañeras*.[16] Sandra problematized the abuses of patriarchal power that led to the false charges. Although she began this line of work with a lens predominantly focused on economic oppression, not yet recognizing herself the "hidden struggle" of women, she viewed the Sandinista retaliation as an abuse of patriarchal power similar to domestic violence or workplace abuse that men exhibit when they fear losing control over women. As has been demonstrated by several other individuals in this book, when women exerted subjectivity by disengaging from their subordinate positions in the gender hierarchy determined by the *Frente Sandinista de Liberación Nacional* (FSLN; Sandinista National Liberation Front), men retaliated in an attempt to halt and silence their efforts. Although the persecution from the FSLN created a limit situation that inhibited the MEC's work for a year, it also opened the opportunity for Sandra and her compañeras to refute being "governable" subjects and instead be autonomous subjects who established rules based on truth that emerged from practices of freedom (Foucault, 2005).

The truth recognized by the MEC organization understood women's rights violations in the factories to be occurring at the intersections of patriarchal and capital interests that superceded the rights of women. This truth is reflected in the naming of the organization: the María Elena Cuadra Working and Unemployed Women's Movement. They called themselves "workers," not simply to reflect that their organizing was occurring in the labor sector, but rather as an ideological reference that underscored the value in viewing women as active subjects, rather than governable subjects, and therefore subjects with rights. Because Sandra's experience of activism with the Sandinistas had further shaped her understanding of inequity and oppression, the praxis she employed with the MEC organization to actualize women's truth involved methodology that is rooted in collective and mobilized interests and, relatedly, rejected the "rescue narrative" that views women as victims. Sandra explained that the methods used by the MEC were driven by the theoretical frameworks of feminism when she stated that, "I know it has to do with feminism; it's not just a theory up in the air. Rather, it is a way of living life, of thinking and of working for other women to know and appropriate themselves and make changes in their life."

Feminist praxis was first demonstrated during the founding of the MEC organization when Sandra described a "collective convocation" of 800 women leaders who came together to establish branches of their labor organization in six different departments in the country simultaneously. The founding of this organization took a planful, coordinated action among a large number of women united in their opposition to the male-dominated Sandinista Worker's Center that did not recognize the need for their representation. However, the success of the organization 16 years later continues to rely on the same feminist structure that rejects authoritarian models of leadership in favor of recognizing a collective leadership that is inclusive of community leaders from the barrios. In this manner, there is a synergistic collaboration whereby each role or position within the organizations— whether it is a founder or members of the communities—is imperative. This feminist structure ensures that they collectively resist and rethink the top-down authority in a way that recognizes the roles of everyone are important.

Sandra's recognition of collective processes and strategies for the defense of women's rights underscore an ideology by which she views others, not just herself, as active and autonomous subjects whose paths ought to be characterized as free, rather than governed.

To actualize a lived experience whereby women in the factories are active autonomous subjects, the methods that Sandra employs through the MEC involve focusing on the structural problems, rather than a "victim-focused" model whereby the organization would serve to denounce cases where women's rights had been violated. Because filing a report for one individual working in the FTZ will not contribute to changes in the system, Sandra explained that their approach is to educate women "to empower themselves to claim their rights, so that once a large group of women is convinced and has appropriated those rights as their own, then the collective action is stronger." Sandra's work through the MEC demonstrates that deideologizing women as dependents that exist as beneficiaries of law led to strategies that informed the new generation to know what their rights were and how to demand them. In this manner, Sandra used her subjectivity to engage in subjectivating, rather than protecting, women who were in economically and physically vulnerable positions in the factories.

The multiple methods that the MEC employs reflect the intersectional nature of the oppression that women in Nicaragua experience. For example, even though much of her focus is centered on the collusion of the State and investors, Sandra also recognized that when it comes to women's human rights, there are several intersecting sources of power when she said that "the church is not only an ideological power, but it is also an economic power. . . . It was such a monster, the Church, with all of its economic, patriarchal, ideological power." As such, one of the methods she employed from the margins drew on the importance of "joining forces" in a manner that recognized that "theory and practice should go hand in hand."

The joint forces Sandra referenced are academia and activism. In particular, Sandra identified them as pillars in the struggle to overcome oppression because they each inform the other; empirical knowledge that emerges from communities informs theories, and those theories, in turn, inform practice that is emerging from the margins. Similarly, "theory in action" to Sandra also meant that women's lived experience needed to be documented to inform theory, and academics, in partnership, can serve as documentarians.

In large part, Sandra's testimonio demonstrates how feminism informs praxis because feminism allows "a way of seeing the economy differently, seeing life differently." In particular, Sandra's testimonio uncovers how collusion between the State and investors represents a powerful intersection of the abuses of patriarchal and neoliberal power because the male domination that upholds the dominant ideology does so within a global economic system that protects foreign companies that devalue the subjectivity of women by disregarding human rights. The method that emerges from Sandra's oppo-sitional ideology to address structural inequity, rather than "help" women in a model that utilizes a "rescue narrative," demonstrates an alternative form of subjectivity aimed at producing citizen subjects not advocating for victims. Throughout her life course, Sandra operated as a citizen subject who was rewriting the rules based on practices of freedom informed by women's truths that have been born through opposing authority, rather than conforming to it.

Notes

1. *Maquiladoras* refer to foreign-owned assembly factories located in free trade zones.

2. The Mercado Oriental is the largest market in Managua.

3. She is referring to the Sandinista Student Movement.

4. The *palace* refers to the National Palace.

5. *Brigadas Especiales contra Actos de Terrorismo* (BECAT; Special Counter-insurgency Brigades) were part of the National Guard police force during the Somoza regime.

6. The *Central Sandinista de Trabajadores* (CST) is Nicaragua's dominant national trade union center.

7. *Asociación de Mujeres Nicaragüenses Luisa Amanda Espinoza*

8. *Barrio* can technically be translated to English as "neighborhood"; however, the word *barrio* carries a connotation more specific to a working-class neighborhood.

9. She was referring to the United States.

10. The International Court of Justice (ICJ) is the primary judicial organ of the United Nations. Based in the Hague, Netherlands, the ICJ settles legal disputes submitted by U.N. member states.

11. The Central American University (UCA) was founded in 1960 as a private, not-for-profit, autonomous institute for higher education focused on public service.

12. On our arrival at her office, Sandra was initially skeptical of our motivations as foreigners from the North and was hesitant to participate.

13. This indicates the Sandinistas under the 2006 Ortega administration.

14. This is a biblical reference to David, a young boy, up against the giant Goliath.

15. The term feminicide, unlike femicide which is broadly defined as the killing of women for being women, is used because feminicide recognizes murders of women are founded on a gender power structure that intersects with other social and economic inequalities.

16. *Compañero* is used to reflect political solidarity with someone who is a partner, colleague, or classmate. *Compañera* is the feminine form of *compañero*.

Bertha Inés Cabrales

7

Legislating from a Feminist Standpoint

*We questioned the power that the patriarchs had, that politicians
had; we claimed that politicians were the main abusers of women,
that the congressmen did not legislate in the best interest of women.*

—TESTIMONIO OF BERTHA INÉS CABRALES

Much of the work being conducted within the *Movimiento Autónomo de
Mujeres* (Women's Autonomous Movement) approaching and following 1990
was focused on legislating, or responding to legislation, meant to uphold wom-
en's rights. Given the increasingly tenuous situation women found themselves
in with the Sandinista dismissal of women's rights, and the neoliberal dismantling of the limited services that sought to actualize some of those rights,
several nongovernmental organizations sprung up in an effort to address the
rights that the State neglected.

When members of the Movimiento began to initiate their separation
from the *Frente Sandinista de Liberación Nacional* (FSLN; Sandinista National
Liberation Front) to focus on women's human rights, three organizations
emerged in Managua to specifically address women's sexual and reproductive
rights. The Itza Women's Collective, which began in 1989, was one of them,
and Bertha Inés Cabrales was one of its founders. Itza was named after an
indigenous woman during the time of the Spanish conquistadors who resisted
enslavement through helping other women perform abortions in cases of
rape by Europeans. Itza's goal is to help women develop a basic understanding
of their bodies, with an emphasis on reproductive health, sexuality, gender
roles, and the socioeconomic structure of the family and its negative impact
on women.

Cabrales has been an integral part of the leadership of the Itza collective for almost three decades. In more recent years, Cabrales joined efforts
with a number of other women's organizations in the Movimiento (led by
the María Elena Cuadra organization, see Chapter 6) to push legislation that
more comprehensively recognized women's human rights by introducing
the Comprehensive Law Against Violence Toward Women (Law 779) to the
National Assembly.

Cabrales was born in 1948 and was raised in the capital city of Managua. She was the only daughter and the eldest of five siblings. Cabrales grew up in a politically active family with a father who was sympathetic toward the communists and socialists. As a consequence of her father choosing political exile because of his anti-Somoza tendencies, Cabrales spent parts of her childhood in Honduras and El Salvador. While attending university, she joined the Sandinista student movement. As an active member of the Revolution, she went on a self-imposed exile to Sweden and worked on solidarity efforts across Europe. The critical thinking about politics that began in Cabrales's youth eventually drove her to collective mobilization aimed at critically questioning legislators who were "playing politics" by upholding or overturning laws that could serve to protect women's human rights. The following testimonio by Bertha Inés Cabrales demonstrates how an ideology that developed to question political power facilitated methods that involved writing legislation that incorporated power dynamics between women and men out of a desire to have laws that would effectively penalize violence against women:

Bertha Inés, I want to start by thanking you for being willing to participate. I know you're probably used to talking about the collective work of the women's movement, but I'd like to ask you to start with your own beginning and tell us a little bit about your personal history. Can you tell me some of your earliest memories, what your childhood was like? Your family?

I was born into a family with a father with communist sympathies. My mother was a housewife, but an avid reader, particularly of political and health issues. I am the only daughter in my family. We are five siblings: four boys and me. I was my mother's first pregnancy and have a twin brother.

What can I say about my family? Well, my father was an orphan. His mother died during labor. Why do I tell you about my father's history? Well, because it has a lot to do with the story of my life. My father studied in a school run by monks. He was not able to continue his studies at the university, like his older brother—who is a historian of Nicaragua—he's a very well known poet, avant-garde, he studied in France and was the eldest. My mother, well, she had nine siblings.

Ever since I was a little girl, they would call me, since I was the only girl, "You are the queen of the house," but it turns out that the "queen of the house" would be sent to wash the dishes, fold her clothes, make her bed. "Queens don't work," I would tell my father. "Why do you make me work if I'm the queen of the house?" He would tell me that modern queens have to know how to do it all, they have to study, they have to do different things. Our immediate family—my father's family was very close, but he had us exiled, he was anti-Somoza. He took us with him to Honduras; we were in El Salvador; wherever he went, he went with his children and my mother, it was incredible. So, I grew up in a political world. For example, my father had communist-socialist sympathies, but I had an uncle who was a conservative; he was one of the congressmen who were then called *diputados zancudos*[1] because they made pacts with Somoza. I had another uncle, the one who studied in France, who sympathized with fascism, with Hitler, and my aunt was a teacher. So, there were always discussions about literature, about politics. I was very young, and they wouldn't tell me to go, so I was there and listened to everything. I believe that this type of family, with these conversations every afternoon after work, where we would all sit down for lunch, my father's siblings, my cousins, everyone, they were incredible conversations, because there were huge contradictions, don't you think?

I studied at a religious school, and so I was educated. My first contact with religion was at school. It was a bit strange because at home we would have conversations; my father did not believe in Mary's virginity. My aunt defended Mary's virginity, so I was raised in this world of great contradictions of ideas, and they filled me with lots of questions. I remember that when we returned to Nicaragua we moved to a neighborhood called San Sebastian, that was a strong working-class neighborhood, where people were also anti-Somoza. This is where the first large protests against Somoza took place, during election time. I would sit on the sidewalk in front of my house to watch all the election movement, and I very much wanted to go and vote against Somoza, but of course I couldn't vote because I was underage.

That was where I saw for the first time how one of Somoza's guards killed a man, a tall man from our neighborhood, who was part of the opposition.[2] This event impacted me profoundly because the man was running and his friend was also running and two guards were chasing them. So then, the tall friend, in an attempt to prevent his shorter friend from being captured, stuck out his leg and tripped one of the guards. The guard fell to the ground and then stood up, furious, and shot him. It was a thin bullet, it made a hole and his back just split open. I saw how his back exploded. That impacted me a lot, and I developed a lot of rage against Somoza. And we were under siege for several days, our neighborhood was; we couldn't leave the neighborhood because the Guard[3] had us surrounded; the entire neighborhood was surrounded with their armored cars, and planes and small aircraft would fly above, and the people were in the streets. The kids and the youth were in the streets and the parents would come out and take us inside, and we would find a way to go back out. So, it impacted me deeply. I think that is what created in me this profound antidictatorship sentiment, and you can see how even today I still have that profound antidictatorship sentiment that I reject what is going on these days. Sure, it's not as crude as it was before, but it's starting to show; when we take to the streets, they beat us with sticks and treat us as if we had no rights. We said with the Revolution, that we had the right to mobilize, and now they are falling back on that.

Well, that's part of the political motivations—the situation that the country was in. There were women who would become involved, and they would ask me, "Why do you want to join the *Juventud Comunista*?"[4] and I said, "Well, because in my house, my father is communist, and I think that it's a good thing." They said, "But you can't be here if you don't think for yourself, you can't be because your father is one, you have to get there, you have to mature." And so that created a boom inside my brain, you see.

Time passed by, and I was in secondary school[5]; I was studying at the Divina Pastora, and there were many protests going on. I wanted to meet Doris María Tijerino,[6] who had been captured. To me, she was a great example of a woman, because she had been captured when she was in a house with Julio Buitrago[7]—I was already beginning to sympathize with the ideas of the Sandinista Front. You never saw the Sandinista Front anywhere, but you heard of them all over the place; it was like a mysterious and striking thing for us youth. So then, when she passed by the school, I was on the second or third floor, and I ran to see her and I told a classmate, "That's Doris Tijerino, she's a heroine." The nuns, scared, came to get us, "Come back inside girls, come inside." So, for me, that was another person who impacted me.

When I left school and went to the university—sometimes I laugh when I tell this story—because when I went to enroll at the university, what I really wanted to know is how I could enroll with the Sandinista Front. At the time, the Sandinista Front was still a clandestine movement, but I was so naïve about the danger that I went into an office and I asked a professor who had a long beard, because the beard, back then, the beard was a revolutionary symbol, like Che[8] and all that. So, I approach him and ask, "Where are the offices of the Sandinista Front?" And the professor looks at me and says, "Don't ask those things in public. There are no offices of the Sandinista Front here, but you can go to the offices of the Student Movement." So then I go to their office and knock and say, "I want to be part of the Sandinista Front; how do I become involved with the Sandinista Front?" And everyone there was just so scared. I remember that among them were Edgard Munguía,[9] Bayardo Arce,[10] Hugo Mejía, and others, and they all said, "No, no, nope. No, this has nothing to do with the Sandinista Front; we are student leaders of the Student Movement." Later, when we got to know each other, they laughed at me, you know; they said "You were crazy; you walked into our office asking if you could sign up for the Sandinista Front, when it was still a clandestine movement." So, I eventually found out how it all worked.

After that, I was imprisoned for a little while, at night, for a few hours. This happened when we would organize protests with the Revolutionary Student Front, asking for the political prisoners to be freed, not to be tortured, all that. I remember that La Aviación[11] was here, and now this is Ajax Delgado.[12] Life is ironic, don't you think?

What did you study at the university?

Well, I became more involved in the political life of the Revolutionary Student Front; we would go to the factories, we went to the *barrios*[13] to hand out flyers from the Sandinista Front. We would have meetings in the barrios, so then the people began to collaborate with us; they'd let us know the Guard was coming, and we would hide in the churches or someone's house.

Before the triumph of the Revolution, I had to go on a self-imposed exile. I had a son, a son born of a romance with someone in the revolutionary groups. I had met a young man from Guatemala who had studied in Czechoslovakia; he was a physicist-mathematician, and we fell in love, you know, student love. He was already a professor and I was a student—but he was not my professor. We fell in love, and soon after I became pregnant at the age of 24. Why do I mention my age? My mother had me when she was 28, which was very strange because back then women became pregnant very young, but my mother married and got pregnant at 28. So, I came from a household with a mother who was a little more—not as young. Although you might say that 24 years old is young, sure, but in the Nicaraguan context, they would say, "What happened? You're not going to have kids? You're not going to get married?" There is a lot of social pressure. But, I decided on a self-imposed exile, and I spoke with the comrades from the Sandinista Front because I was very scared, I was terrified; I wanted to go up into the mountains, and they wouldn't take us into the mountains.

When I was in Sweden, we began to strengthen solidarity with the struggles of the people of Nicaragua. We were able to get Olof Palme[14] to be the honorary president of the committee of solidarity, as well as other well-known Swedish personalities who were social democrats. We did lots of work at the European level; we organized solidarity conferences. After the triumph of the Revolution, I decided to come back. They asked me to stay and help out with the embassy, but I didn't want to stay. I came back and became involved and really wanted to work with land reform. I took an intensive course to learn more about land reform throughout the world: China, France, Chile, Guatemala, and Krakow.

In the early '80s?

Yes, early '80s because I came back in November of '79. I came back when they had the first massive public tribute to Carlos Fonseca Amador,[15] and

I joined that tribute. I got off the plane and I joined. So then, we began working on the land reform training, and I was made responsible for the training at the institute in Ciudad Rivas. Afterwards, around 1984, I was able to get them to relocate me to Managua. The first program I worked on in Rivas was a program where we spoke about women, about women's health, and we talked about abortion—because I had just returned from Sweden, and over there I was able to see how women handled their sexuality; they were free, "*libertinas*"[16] we would call them here, but I say they were free, they had sexual experiences before getting married. It was the complete opposite of Nicaragua. In the environment I grew up in, if you had sexual experiences before marriage, it was a social scandal, whereas over there it was the norm. So, I was inspired by how Swedish women lived their lives, how they didn't have kids at a very young age; they weren't worried about having kids.

The selection process for the second promotion of the Sandinista Front was going on when I asked to be relocated. So, I was sent to an office that was more about party organization, and I didn't like it because I had come from working more on advertising and promotion, and the people who worked there were more open, they liked discussing different things. The people in my new office were more symbolic. I didn't like it, but I had to take it.

That is where I had my first experience in putting together questions for the committees to evaluate the new FSLN militants. I included a question on how they got along with their partners, if they hit them, if they respected them, if they forbade them from participating in politics, because I had seen that there were many militants who were great militants, but they didn't allow their women to participate in FSLN politics. Well, I went ahead and included many questions like this, but my superior said, "No, they'll never approve it." I made my case, and we had a meeting about it in the office, about what relationships between men and women were like, honestly. For me, it was important for the new militants to be evaluated on this, maybe not to measure whether or not they were well qualified to militate in the FSLN, but as a mechanism for self-reflection, so that the men would start thinking about how their relationships with women needed to change. I remember that we had a discussion about this, and the psychologist came and told me, "These questions are good; they're excellent. You should be the one to take them to the regional committee." So, I go present my proposal, the questions, and I make my case and all, and then Carlos Carrión, who at the time was the political secretary, he says, "But with those questions, we won't have any new militants for the FSLN!" What a shame, I told him, but we have to reflect on these things, we need to change the behaviors of our *compañeros*,[17] as well as their daughters and sons. And the proposal was not approved.

I think that was my contribution, based on what I had seen and what I had read. I saw, for example, that in the rural areas in the Fourth Region,[18] men would hit their women or they would burn them. If they walked too far away from the house, they were reprimanded by having their feet burned, or little girls would have their private parts scalded if they wet themselves. That had an impact on me—how could there be so much cruelty in a relationship? All those things I had seen, I wanted to ask questions about. Well, after that—there's a compañera I want to mention, Rose Mary Vega. She was the political secretary in Managua and had been my supervisor in Rivas. The FSLN named her to be coordinator for AMNLAE[19] in Managua. She called me and asked if I wanted to work with her.

Were you already a member of AMNLAE?

She brought me in, I think it was in '86 or '87. I loved working with her because she was very open minded; we talked a lot, we had long conversations, sometimes we agreed and other times we didn't, but she was a woman I could have a conversation with.

They asked me to create a training plan for the AMNLAE leaders and to see how the leaders could then replicate it in the barrios. So, we draw up the plan and she approves it, but there's some resistance from the various leaders because they were used to working with issues related to party politics. For example, AMNLAE made the rucksacks for all the mobilized individuals, both the reserves as well as those in the military service. That used to be the work that AMNLAE would do.

So, we need to transform it so that it does more work related to the politics of women's rights, independent from the party. There were big contradictions; there was resistance, and there were changes at the leadership level in many regions of Managua. But, there was nothing going on that really worked on issues regarding women, and it was difficult because there was a lot of labor-related resistance. We discussed this at AMNLAE, and we said, why is there resistance if it's something that helps women advance? I think there were some expectations that we would lose the status quo.

We had to work without funds—AMNLAE did not give us funds for the work we did; we had to go and look for our own funds. I came here as part of the party's structure, but I wanted to make it clear that I didn't have to work according to the party lines, but that we had our own lines—and we wanted to integrate them into the party—which were to benefit women. They accepted this diplomatically, but in practice they didn't. Some time later, we had discussions at the AMNLAE assembly. It was on March 8, there were three groups that wanted to really go deeper in our work regarding violence towards women, to go deeper in our work regarding the reality of pregnancies that were forced into being through rape. We shared those ideas with three leaders. There was Nora Meneses from Xochitl,[20] Luz Marina from 8 de Marzo,[21] and there was me, with Itza, representing the collective. However, before we weren't a collective, we were grouped as a territory under the FSLN. So, we struggled in the assembly, but really we had arrived there with the idea of becoming independent from AMNLAE and from the FSLN. We had some meetings amongst ourselves and discussed how it was impossible to change the ideas of AMNLAE's management. They wanted to remain within the FSLN, while we wanted to focus on women's issues.

You were talking about Itza becoming independent from AMNLAE?

We weren't called Itza. We relied on the participation of women from the entire zone surrounding the lake: from San José Oriental, from Edén, from San Cristóbal, because we worked in the barrios. We didn't have a house,[22] so some women would let us use their yards to do our work or for discussion sessions or reflection sessions. We used their yards. We didn't have an office or typewriters, just backpacks, paper, and the desire to create change.

And were all these women members of AMNLAE?

AMNLAE was the only women's organization that came out of the Revolution. So, any woman who wanted to work for the Revolution had to be part of AMNLAE. Many of us opted to work with the FSLN—we were inside the party. But, we learned that there were also organizations that shared our thoughts of autonomy; we talked about autonomy from the FSLN and from AMNLAE, and so then we began to assume that concept of autonomy—to have political autonomy, ideological autonomy, to do what we wanted to do, to transform the lives of women, to deal with subordination, with the multiple forms of oppression, such as violence, abuse, rapes, all of that. We were utopic; we had big dreams, really, and we were dreamers. But, we also liked to finish the work, and we worked hard to do so, we didn't just stay at dreams.

After that, we realized that the unions were also being heavily criticized; there were many processes of detachment that were of a political-ideological nature—there were detachments at the ATC,[23] and leaders from CONAPRO,[24] which was for those with professional degrees, where Milú Vargas[25] and other compañeras worked, there was a newspaper from the Revolution—a magazine called *Gente*.[26] I want to mention this because we really lived that periodical, which was led by Sofía Montenegro.[27] And, well, Sofía she would write whatever she wanted to write about, because she had very progressive ideas, and we always read it. I don't think she ever realized that we read it. We would buy it, and we discussed what she wrote about in the barrios. It was like a support pamphlet for us, in terms of reflecting on our work. We also looked for what Clara Zetkin from Germany[28] wrote or for Inés Armand's letters to Lenin.[29] We would read them, try to learn a bit about them, and then we would share it with the people. So, the people inside the FSLN would say, "These women are crazy—teaching the people theory! What do the people care about theory? What the people are interested in is having food and having good health." So, there was this Machiavellian manipulation going on that said that theory is something for intellectuals and what not. And we would say, no, no, theory is born out of reality; it picks up on reality and converts it into theory. And what's more, you do know, Marxism was theorized and you [the FSLN] followed it. And what about Lenin? He was a reader and was also an author. And who, then, made decisions? It was the proletariat. Why the proletariat? Because his ideas reached them. His ideas had something to do with their lives—labor exploitation and all that. Later on with feminism, it was European feminists, who theorized, and sure, they were highly educated, but their writings also feed our reflections.

So, we began to break down those stereotypes that theory is for intellectuals. After that we had our cry for autonomy. This was the Festival of the 52%, where we said that women are 52% [of the population], and we want to be free, we want autonomy, we do not want violence, and we do not want prejudiced sexuality. After that, we had a meeting which we called—after a strong discussion—"United in Diversity." That's when the networks formed, the Network of Women Against Violence, Network of Sexuality, the one for health, the one for economy, about six or seven networks in all, and of all of them the only ones that remain are the Network of Women Against Violence and the Health Network.

The autonomy, we translated that to the people by establishing ourselves as nonpartisan and as secular. The organization doesn't have any religious beliefs; we explained what secularism is and that each person can have their own, individual religious beliefs. We are nonpartisan because we do not answer to any party. We are feminists because as women we want to have a different power, we want to change the relationships between men and women.

After that, it turns out that in order to request funds we had to have legal status [as an organization], so then we began debating, did we want to have legal status? We needed funds to continue the work, because our staff, those of us that were working, we didn't have money for our life expenses. For example, we had workshops at the factories, and they would give us clothes. The women leaders at TricoTextil[30] would say, "Well, we'll trade: You train us, and we'll get you clothes." But, we couldn't keep on living that way. Another example—our first house was a house that had been confiscated. So, we went to the FSLN's regional committee and asked, "Do you plan on using it?" They said no. So, we took it, and the metallurgy workers donated the iron railings, a few iron chairs, and the sharp edges of the chairs would tear our clothes, so they came in, and they would sand them down. Meanwhile, we provided people with training. There was a real feeling of solidarity, but we couldn't keep on living like that.

We submitted paperwork, and in '92 we were given legal status. In '94, we had everything in place, and we began to work on small projects. We had a small project worth $500—oh, did we stretch out those $500—I don't know how many months it covered!

Later, we became more consolidated. We spoke up to join the Network of Women Against Violence and well, the "feminist movement," and we grew and took more interest in issues related to women. We questioned the power that the patriarchs had, that politicians had; we claimed that politicians were the main abusers of women, that the congressmen did not legislate in the best interest of women, but rather against women's interests. We began to publicly question those in power; we organized large mobilizations to demand the National Assembly create laws that would penalize violence against women. And today, we are still trying to get a law that would penalize violence towards women.[31] We are working on it and waiting to see if and how it is approved.

Bertha, can I switch gears a little bit and ask you to tell me briefly about Collectivo Itza specifically. How did it start, and what are the areas of focus?

The Itza Women's Collective began, like I said, in '89, '90, or '91. We were groups of women, groups of women from the barrios and decided to work as a collective. Many of the founders are women that still continue to live in the barrios. Afterwards, we incorporated other compañeras who worked in the different grassroots movements and were very active women. After that, the collective began to feel that we were starting to voice many of our demands to the State, and the State did not respond. For example, we started to see how we could obtain an office to support the women from a legal perspective and later how to demand access to health care. However, the area that first worked out well was education, the area of education that we later renamed "area of feminist training and community organization," and we decided to do this in order to clearly outline the areas that the collective worked in. Because, you see, in the beginning we became involved in everything, and we couldn't do that; we had to divide our work and decide who will take care of what. So, that's how we reorganized.

The AMNLAE coordinator asked us to turn in the first house to them because they were going to start a clinic for female laborers. So, they asked us to hand over the premises, and we responded that the house did not belong to AMNLAE. But, since they already had the funds to begin their project, they said, "Well, we have a house that we can—well, you could see it and if you like it. ..." She was very curt. So, we took it, and they agreed to hand over the deeds to the house. Up to this day, we still have not received the deeds,[32] but we're here, and so now we are trying to get this house officially in our name, as the collective.

Is the collective active on the femicide bill?

Of course; we joined 18 other organizations in the María Elena Cuadra Movement[33] to work on a proposal for a new law because we had been asking for a new law since 1994. So now, we are waiting. We're also working with the Network of Women, which also was active in both proposals; they took that proposal to the Supreme Court.

Can you tell me how the femicide law is different from the family violence law from the '90s?

Well, the Law Against Domestic Violence, the main definition of it is that it is violence within the family, and so it doesn't reflect the power dynamics between men and women in the way we want, in a law against violence towards women and against femicide, because femicide is a product of those power dynamics and that control that men have, that's the biggest difference. We're demanding that they go back and include all the contributions the various organizations have given them and that the law be reoriented because it really is a pressing issue.

Every day, the newspapers report on women being killed by men. Yesterday, there was a story on the radio and in the papers about a woman who was killed in Ciudad Sandino by her partner because another man had walked by the house and had asked for some water, so the woman gave this man some water. Her partner saw this and said, "This is how I wanted to catch you," and killed her! Killed her because she gave a glass of water to another man to drink. The day before, in Chontales, a woman was beaten to death with a hammer. So you see, day after day we hear of all these cases, and in these last months the killing of women has been even crueler. We need our legislators to stop playing politics when it comes to this law, because that's what always happens; it's what happened with abortion to save the life of the mother; that was a process in which the FSLN negotiated with the other parties, negotiated with the church, and they repealed the abortion law and penalized it. So, now we don't want that to happen; we don't want this law to be taken advantage of, we want it to be forceful so we can respond with it and end all the femicides happening in the country.

Every day, the killings of women are crueler; the rape of girls is—for example, in the Department of Madriz, where we have this shelter, it's a calamity the way these girls are raped because after they end up pregnant, the Ministry of Health forces them to breastfeed. How can the Ministry of Health force a girl who was raped and became pregnant to breastfeed when all she feels is a profound rejection? At the shelter, we have told her, "You do not have to give birth; no one can force you to have this baby, and you can put it up for adoption." But, this girl's mother is the one who has the authority to make decisions, and she decided she wanted to raise that child, and when this girl leaves the shelter, she is going to come face to face with this reality. With this particular girl, we were able to get her to continue her studies, but that's a very rare case. In general, girls who become pregnant after being raped don't go back to school.

And what does the government do? What does the Ministry of Education do with these girls? They exclude them and expel them, because they were raped and became pregnant. And all the while the rapist goes free; yes, the rapists, they're out there, free. We are in a complete state of halt regarding the right to live, to live our own lives. So, that is what we are focusing our energy on, our struggle, and our demands, against all that because those are strong powers. And in a country that calls itself secular, it is a break from the Constitution to approve laws of a religious character. A country that says it is respectful of human rights—does not actually respect human rights. A government that says it believes in gender equality, what kind of equality is it talking about? Gender equality becomes visible through concrete actions, through policies, through programs, and through specific budgets. We don't have trust in the government, due to our national history, but we have to keep up the battle, we have to keep fighting.

Can you talk about the role of La Boletina[34] *in the struggle?*

It's from *Puntos de Encuentro.*[35] We use it as a tool for reflection with the women in the barrios during the workshops. The way it's written helps and encourages women to read. At Itza, we have produced other magazines, for example, our first, which is on the issue of abortion—this was on purpose, it was at the same time as they were penalizing all abortions. We also questioned the role of the church. We have produced another one about sexual abuse. This magazine, or newsletter, has been used by teachers in the schools, by leaders, and by *promotoras.*[36] This is a tool that even got us into some schools so that the teaching staff can learn about the dynamics of abuse, so they can detect and refer, so that they can help and assume some level of responsibility as members of an educational institution.

We have another one that was very well received and made its way to Guatemala. This is a newsletter on the genesis of women's subordination. We were very subtle and called it "The Dirty Trick History Played on Women."

It's written like a story, a bit like Paquín,[37] but with a lot of questioning, and it reflects on what life was like for primitive women, collectively, and how later on, as time went by women's bodies and lives become privatized. Then, we see how the struggles of many women have made history, and we reflect on that, for example, women's suffrage. What was it like? Also, the right to be a mother or to not be a mother—we are not required to become mothers just because we are biologically women and we have the capacity to become mothers, to reproduce, but it's a decision that belongs to each woman. So, we incorporated this analysis in the story. That newsletter is a big source of pride for us, because it took many years of hard work, and we were able to produce something concrete that is actually used.

I'd like to ask you about the role of feminism in all these years of struggle for you. What does feminism mean to you?

For me, it has meant how to question the power men have, question the system, yes, the system, because these are things you live through, a lifelong process. It's not something you start out with but it evolves, you begin to think, to compare it to life, to compare it to the policies of the country. So, it's about questioning the whole established social order where men are the "the model," so to speak, of how it's done. They are the ones who have the power in the household and in the relationship, and so they dare to be abusive, because the system guarantees that nothing will happen to them. Feminism breaks with that traditional control of men over women. For me, it means a philosophy of liberation, a philosophy of liberation at a personal level because that liberation, we don't see it there, in other people; we see it at a personal level and also in women as a collective gender. That's why it's easier for us to voice all these actions with the other organizations, because we know that alone, we could not do it—because the system is so strong, so heavy. For me, for example, within feminism I have been able to know many different feminist currents. In Latin America, feminism was born out of the Leftist movements and now we are questioning the Left. Within the Autonomous Women's Movement, we say that *we* are the Left. We are questioning power; we are questioning power dynamics; we are questioning the oppression dynamics, different oppressions, the indigenous woman, the Black woman, the Misquito woman,[38] Garífuna,[39] white, rich, poor, student, young, or a woman who never had the opportunity to further her studies. We all cross that tragedy of subordination of multiple oppressions. For me, feminism is the way for women's liberty, and we women have the right to be free.

And are you a feminist?

I am a feminist; in our organization, we see ourselves as feminists, and that we are secular and nonpartisan. We discuss this with all new staff, so that they clearly understand our philosophy. It is part of a philosophy that we delve into each day, a philosophy of life for women. Just like the Greek philosophers talked about philosophy, the feminists scrutinized philosophy and claimed that it belonged to men. In their mind, philosophy was all about the big Greek and French philosophers, but the lives of women were not within that philosophy, so it's the feminists who rescue women's philosophy; they are the ones that bring attention to the power dynamics, bring attention to the oppressions, bring attention to the health and sexual life of people.

You've talked about how some national policies affect women's lives in Nicaragua. I'm also interested in your opinion about international policies, in particular neoliberal policies; do you think they affect women in Nicaragua?

Obviously, they affect them because when we talk about gender policies, it's always done from the *machista*[40] point of view, and they see us women not in the way that we want to feel and see ourselves. The vision they have is one that sustains that subordination. They sell it as a great opportunity for women, but we don't want opportunities; we want to transform the power dynamics between men and women. For example, when we talk about gender and development, what is that? We don't want that, if we can't break away from that pattern of subordination, that pattern of violence, that pattern of seeing feminine sexuality from an androcentric point of view, right. That's how I see it, really, and that's why it's hard when we try to request funds and then we read the gender policies of the donor, we see it as suspicious. So, we say to ourselves, maybe that's why we don't get the funds—that thing they say that if women were rich, then they wouldn't have the problem of domestic violence. Women with money suffer from domestic violence; women who have resources suffer from subordination and other oppressions. So, it's not just about having money, but about owning it, about having it to spend it on ourselves. What happens when both women and men work? Where does his money go, and where does her money go? How is money managed within a relationship? Do the women set some money aside for their own entertainment and healthcare? At least in Nicaragua, the answer is no. But, men do set aside money that is for their entertainment. The money women make goes to cover family expenses. So, where are the so-called gender policies? This country has a long history in which we women take on all the responsibilities for raising the children. We are not the only ones who should be raising them. Some men are waking up and getting involved; some men are becoming conscious of this, but systematically this situation persists.

From the outset of her testimonio, Bertha described growing up in a "political world" whereby her family, who represented a diverse political

spectrum during the Revolution, held intensely political conversations during her youth. Unlike Sofía Montenegro (Chapter 2), however, Bertha was not
excluded from participating in these conversations. In fact, conversations that
reflected a contradiction of ideas about the political turmoil that was envelop-
ing her neighborhood and country as a result of a war being waged, in part
over global economic pressures, served as the foundation for the development
of Bertha's critical thinking. Moreover, during her youth, the violent death
and civilian control that characterized the Somoza regime developed into
what Bertha called an "antidictatorship" sentiment. These early experiences
and perspectives led to an ideology that strongly opposed strict governmental
control and repression, instead privileging the idea that the people had a right
to collectively organize and protest to make demands for their rights. Bertha's
initial actions toward these aims were to join student movements.

At the outset of her interest in antidictatorial activity, Bertha's oppositional ideology was further developed by the influence of others in addition
to her father. For example, when she joined a communist youth group out of
a budding interest to oppose the dictator and align herself with her father's
anti-Somoza political leanings, she was pressed by peers to think more critically about her beliefs and how she had formed them. Similarly, although public protests were abundant at the time, Bertha recalled a protest in support
of Doris Tijerino, one of the women to participate earliest in the Sandinista
Revolution and someone Bertha identified as a "heroine." These early experiences shaped Bertha's thinking and motivation to join the Sandinista Front in
order to participate in efforts to end the dictatorship. In fact, Bertha enrolled
in a university, in large part, just to enlist in the Front and learn more about
how she could contribute to change. Over time, as an active member of the
FSLN, the constant threat from the dictatorship led Bertha to take a political exile in Sweden after giving birth to her first child. She did not return to
Nicaragua until 1979, only after the Revolution triumphed and the dictatorship was no longer in power.

As a member of the FSLN, Bertha was actively engaged in a social revolution whereby people were mobilized around an interest in confronting the
economic devastation and oppression that resulted from years of dictatorial
and foreign control. Although grave social inequities stemmed from decades
of economic exploitation, the unified focus on capitalism among the FSLN was
magnified, in part, because abuses of patriarchal power drove a singular focus
that served to sustain male dominance in agendas aimed at social change. It is
in this context that privileges the fight against unchecked capitalism that the
broader, intersectional, nature of the oppression of women began to reveal
itself to Bertha.

Shortly following the triumph of the Revolution, Bertha described
the FSLN colleagues with whom she worked as "symbolic," suggesting that
although they were Sandinista in name, they did not share her oppositional

ideology in regard to rejecting control and repression of people. More specifically, Bertha extended this ideology to include the control and repression of
women, whereas her compañeros did not. For example, Bertha deideologized
how FSLN militants treated their wives with control and violence, thereby
disallowing women's political participation. She drew parallels between this
use of control and restriction and the manner of restricted participation that
people witnessed during the dictatorship.

In an attempt to create institutional change that recognized the systemic
nature of men's control over women, Bertha proposed to her compañeros that
they add items to an assessment of new FSLN militants to query whether they
mistreated their female partners. As evidence of the symbolic nature of FSLN
ideology, Bertha's male colleagues denied her proposal. Despite being presumably united around achieving transformative change, Bertha's compañeros
acknowledged that with the criteria implied by her questions, there would be
slim enrollment of new militants. Thus, not only was male participation privileged over female participation in FSLN activity, but a blind eye was actively
turned on women's rights.

Although Bertha's proposal for evaluation was not approved, her actions
reflected resistance as defined by María Lugones, whereby resistance to
oppressive structures is not necessarily the end goal of political struggle or an
outcome, but rather a beginning—an emergent behavior that moves toward
justice and liberation (Lugones, 2010, p. 746). This is important precisely
because liberation psychologists suggest that although dominant power structures are often unremitting and sustain the limits of a situation, they are also
situations where possibilities begin (Martín-Baró, 1994). Bertha's testimonio
is a near-perfect illustration of this process because her oppositional action
demonstrated both the limits of power *and* the emergence of possibility. Like
her parents, Bertha was not satisfied with the lip service or symbolic discourse
of equity reflected in the dominant narrative of her compañeros and wanted
to deepen the conversation. The iterative stages of this "deepening" would
eventually lead Bertha to move from symbolic solidarity to solidarity aimed at
transformation through questioning political leaders who did not legislate in
the interests of women's rights.

Therefore, a proposal for change was rejected by her male compañeros;
the experience served as the catalyst for being offered a position in AMNLAE,
the FSLN-affiliated women's organization, which would ultimately position
her to separate from the FSLN so that she could more directly question men's
political power. Initially, as a member of AMNLAE, unlike her original FSLN
appointment, Bertha was able to return to the conversations of her youth that
held depth, disagreement, and critical thinking. Despite a more open environment, however, Bertha quickly came to see that the perspectives held within
AMNLAE were just as "symbolic" as those held by FSLN members in her prior
position.

Although AMNLAE was the largest collective mobilization of women within Nicaragua at the time, the efforts of members focused on FSLN party politics, rather than on ideological change that could transform the conditions in which women lived their lives. For example, instead of being organized around an oppositional ideology, AMNLAE was organized around women's participation in the Revolution through gender role congruence (e.g., sewing). As a result, when Bertha initiated efforts toward change that were related to the politics of women's rights, members of AMNLAE routinely rejected those efforts.

The limits of male-dominated FSLN power were unremitting even among an organization of women. This may be somewhat counterintuitive if not for considering Audre Lorde's thesis that, for women of privilege, change may be "threatening to those women who still define the master's house as their only source of support" (1984, p. 2). Bertha made sense of the women's resistance similarly when she said, "I think there were some expectations that we would lose the status quo," reflecting that many women were willing to tow the party line for the advantages that participation, however marginalized, afforded them.

The extent to which Bertha's efforts were effectively being denied once again served to strengthen her collective interests, and her praxis for change began with taking theory to the people. Bertha problematized the FSLN attempts to keep feminist theory from women as a form of control to keep women from being educated and mobilized. She astutely pointed out that the very Revolution in which they all fought was deeply informed by Marxist theory and drew a parallel between how Marxist theory reached the proletariat in the same way was that feminist theory was reaching the barrios.

Because Bertha believed that "theory is born out of reality," she and her compañeras hosted workshops and trainings based on how women's rights (e.g., violence, sexuality) were related to political power and subordination. This praxis was used once again at Itza when magazines created for workshops were designed to raise women's awareness about a number of human rights that were being marginalized by the government (i.e., abortion, sexual abuse). Some of the magazines being produced at Itza reflected feminist theory and oppositional ideology regarding how power functions to keep women in subordinated positions, in titles such as, "The Dirty Trick History Played on Women."

Bertha's actions demonstrate that theory and oppositional ideology are important components of resistance. The praxis that emerged from this theory is also evident when Bertha described the creation of the Movimiento. Dictatorial use of politics and policies that created a system of patriarchal control among the FSLN were rejected, and methods informed by political autonomy, secularism, and feminism were used instead.

As Bertha began the process of separation from AMNLAE and started mobilizing with her compañeras to address women's rights, she learned that across several other sectors of society (e.g., in labor unions, as represented by Sandra Ramos in Chapter 6; agricultural organizing, as represented by Martha Valle in Chapter 8; and journalism, as represented by Sofía Montenegro in Chapter 2), women were being marginalized or politically persecuted by the FSLN due to women's political and ideological demands related to women's rights. These massive chasms in ideology led many women to separate from the FSLN to enact an oppositional ideology that rejected control and repression of women. Bertha stated that, "We began to assume that concept of autonomy—to have political autonomy, ideological autonomy, to do what we wanted to do, to transform the lives of women, to deal with subordination, with the multiple forms of oppression." In seeking not to have political powers corrupt their goals, the women established autonomy by declaring themselves nonpartisan and secular. This deideologization of the traditional structures of power underscored Bertha's, and her compañeras', interest in rejecting the parameters set by the "powerful" to control and repress the marginalized. To deideologize power, the women would need to transform the "system [which] upholds privilege not rights."

To do this, as members of a coordinated group, the Movimiento "spoke up" by questioning the "power that the patriarchs had. . . . We claimed that politicians were the main abusers of women, that the congressmen did not legislate in the best interest of women, but rather against women's interests." In one of their first concrete actions as a collectively mobilized group, they organized large demonstrations to demand the National Assembly create laws that would penalize violence against women. This action reflected a large public questioning of power that drew attention to the role that politicians and legislation could play in either denying or promoting women's human rights.

Although a law focused on "family" violence was passed in 1996, Bertha and her compañeras rejected the fact that the focus on family in the domestic violence law did not reflect the power dynamics between men and women in a way that recognized how a system of violence against women is sustained or reproduced. Bertha's continued deideologization of patriarchal power led her to participate in the mobilization surrounding a new "feminicide"[41] law as a means to demand legislative protection for women's right to live free of violence.

In 2011, Bertha united in mobilization with several other organizations surrounding the design, promotion, and passage of stronger legislation regarding violence against women. Her commitment to this law reflected the same oppositional ideology she had demonstrated when generating the proposal at AMNLAE because the law underscored that threats to women's safety are a product of power dynamics whereby men have control over women. Recognizing the continued limits of a congress that did not legislate in the best interests of women, Bertha stated that, "We need our legislators to stop playing politics when it comes to this law." The "strong powers" that women were up against were rooted not only in the power men had over their partners or spouses but also at the intersection of the patriarchal and religious authorities that colluded to approve laws of a religious character.

Nevertheless, despite unremitting obstacles, Bertha's individual and collective experience of *concientización*, or the iterative nature of her analysis and action, has fueled an oppositional ideology regarding women's rights that has been used to build laws suited to women's situations in Nicaragua. In a continued rejection of the "symbolic," Bertha approached the conclusion of her *testimonio* with the belief that "gender equality becomes visible through concrete actions, through policies, through programs, and through specific budgets."

Examining Bertha's psychology of resistance allows us to see how an ideology that developed in her youth that opposed dictatorial control evolved over time to question the power that patriarchs and politicians have over women. Bertha's opposition to control and repression, and her belief in the right to mobilize in the pursuit of human rights, led her to increasingly problematize the control the Sandinistas exerted over a women-driven agenda. Like many of her compañeras in this section of the book, Bertha reflected on the process of concientización and understood awareness as something that evolves, through action and various attempts to create structural change even in the face of limit situations that shift. She drew a parallel between patriarchal power and dictatorship when she described that men who have the power to be abusive can do so because the system guarantees that nothing will happen to them. Feminism, as a praxis for Bertha, "has meant how to question the power men have, question the system, yes, the system."

Notes

1. *Diputados zancudos* are "traitors."
2. She was referring to the FSLN.
3. "The Guard" refers to Somoza's security regime, the National Guard.
4. *Juventud Comunista* is the "Communist Youth."
5. In Nicaragua, secondary school is equivalent to 11th or 12th grade in U.S. high school.
6. Doris María Tijerino was a female commander of the Sandinista Front who was captured and imprisoned in 1978.
7. Julio Buitrago was a member of the FSLN killed by the National Guard in 1969.
8. Ernesto "Che" Guevara was a Marxist Revolutionary who was a major figure in the Cuban Revolution and has since become an international symbol for revolution.
9. Edgard Munguía was a member of the Sandinista Front who was tortured and killed by Somoza's Guard in 1976.
10. Arce continued FSLN involvement and was Daniel Ortega's top economic advisor at the time of the interview.

11. La Aviación was a prison where political prisoners were kept and often tortured.

12. Ajax Delgado is a public gym run by the government and named after a martyr of the Revolution.

13. *Barrio* can technically be translated to English as "neighborhood"; however, the word *barrio* carries a connotation more specific to a working-class neighborhood.

14. Olof Palme was a Swedish politician who led the Swedish Social Democratic Party from 1969 until being assassinated in 1986.

15. Carlos Fonseca Amador was the founder of the FSLN; he was killed in 1976 before the Sandinistas took power.

16. *Libertinas* translates as "libertine," "licentious."

17. *Compañero* is used to reflect political solidarity with someone who is a partner, colleague, or classmate. *Compañera* is the feminine form of *compañero*.

18. The Fourth Region is a narrow region located between Lakes Managua and Nicaragua and the Pacific.

19. *Asociación de Mujeres Nicaragüenses Luisa Amanda Espinoza*.

20. The Xochilt Acalt Foundation for the Comprehensive Development of the Indigenous Women of Sutiava is a women's center that began as a clinic in 1991 and has since evolved into an organization with a variety of different focuses, all of which revolve around the empowerment of women.

21. Ocho de Marzo is a women's collective that advocates for women and offers services relating to domestic violence and reproductive health, as well as offering job training classes and workshops open to the public.

22. Many established organizations had meeting spaces they referred to as houses.

23. The ATC is the Association of Rural Workers (*Asociación del Trabajadores del Campo*).

24. CONAPRO (*Representantes de la Federación de Asociaciones Profesionales de Nicaragua*) is the Nicaraguan National Confederation of Professionals.

25. Milú Vargas founded AMNLAE.

26. *Gente* was a supplement of *Barricada*, the official Sandinista newspaper that focused on issues related to gender and sexuality.

27. Sofia Montenegro's testimonio is in Chapter 2.

28. Clara Zetkin (1857–1933) was a respected socialist in Germany.

29. Inés Armand was a French communist and feminist made famous by her alleged affair with Lenin.

30. TricoTextil is a garment company.

31. The Comprehensive Law (779) was under review at the time of this interview and passed in the Assembly in 2012, although it was amended in 2013.

32. The deeds had not been received nearly 25 years later.

33. A testimonio from one of the founders of this organization, Sandra Ramos, is in Chapter 6.

34. *La Boletina* is a feminist magazine produced by Puntos de Encuentro, a feminist organization started in 1991 that works on violence against women.

35. Puntos de Encuentro is a feminist organization based in Managua that develops communication activities, training, and research for social change

36. *Promotoras* can be translated to "promoter," "advancer," "forwarder". In this case, it is being used to refer to someone who promotes women's human rights.

37. Paquín was a Mexican comic strip in the 1930s.

38. The Misquito are a Native American group of people often of mixed race and often speaking Misquito creole English and Spanish.

39. Garífuna are a group of people living in Central America of Caribbean or West African descent.

40. *Machista* indicates a male, typically chauvinist, point of view.

41. The term feminicide, unlike femicide which is broadly defined as the killing of women for being women, is used because feminicide recognizes murders of women are founded on a gender power structure that intersects with other social and economic inequalities.

SECTION TWO

Summary: Intersectional Ideology

LEGISLATION AND WOMEN'S HUMAN RIGHTS

In much scholarship that is written about women's human rights, the focus often centers on the role of international rights discourse in legislation. Although international treaties do play a part in the efforts of the women included in this section of the book, their *testimonios* also demonstrated how psychological processes of resistance were imperative to employing a rights-based discourse that would be conducive to structural change, rather than simply putting band-aids on existing problems. Moreover, all three women in this section (Violeta Delgado, Sandra Ramos, and Bertha Inés Cabrales) made clear that, despite the use of international discourse and transnational collaborations, the oppositional ideology driving their interests in women's rights, and the laws proposed to protect them in Nicaragua, were not based on foreign ideas or practices that were imported. Rather, legislation surrounding women's human rights in Nicaragua emerged from efforts rooted in an ideology that opposed the structures of authority and domination that were not adequately serving women locally. Moreover, the oppositional ideologies that women in this section of the book held all shared in common an understanding that the intersectional abuses of patriarchal and neoliberal power collude and needed to be transformed legislatively for women's human rights to be actualized.

Although it is true that examples of legislative efforts in Nicaragua took place in a specific location at a particular time, it is also true that the tension between human rights and the privileging of capitalist interest that has emerged in the context of neoliberalism has created struggles the world over; they are not isolated to the majority world. For example, in 2015, several U.S.-based companies (e.g., McDonald's, Monsanto) used a 2010 U.S. Supreme Court ruling that corporations are people with human rights to fight against new laws that were being enacted to protect *human* rights. In one case, McDonald's (and other franchises) sued the city of Seattle over a new $15-an-hour minimum wage law, arguing that mandated wage increases violated corporate personhood rights to determine wage setting. This example demonstrates how the omnipresence of neoliberalism can function to threaten human rights all over the world. This makes what the women in Nicaragua are doing even more important. The activists in this section of the book demonstrated how to enact and uphold legislation driven from an awareness of and opposition to the intersectional nature of a predominantly male judiciary system, which colludes with corporate interests to dismiss human rights violations. Because parallel processes of collusion occur across the entire globe, moving oppositional methodologies from the "margins" of the *Movimiento Autónomo de Mujeres* (Women's Autonomous Movement) in Nicaragua to the "center" could contribute to change aimed at justice for women in far-reaching places.

Similarly, although throughout the world many women's rights violations are discussed as health problems or as a consequence of "cultural" norms, international data demonstrate that almost without exception women *everywhere* in the world are disadvantaged by power differentials (Grabe, 2013; United Nations, 2012). Taken together, the *testimonios* in this section suggest that to be effectively positioned to put forward laws for women, enhance women's agency as subjects with rights, or run programs that bring the understanding of rights to communities, it is necessary to employ an intersectional ideology that opposes a social order whereby men retain power and use it within a capitalist system that, by design, violates women's rights.

For example, Violeta's story helps illustrate that an oppositional ideology that views women's experiences as valid sources of knowledge can facilitate an understanding of violations against women as systemic and in need of transformation via legislation that upholds women's right to live with dignity. Violeta's efforts underscore how a transnationally intersectional perspective influences awareness and action because her oppositional ideology to the treatment of women in Nicaragua led to her to strategically use international discourse and alliance to build awareness and put pressure on the Nicaraguan National Assembly to enact laws to protect women from violence. Sandra's testimonio highlights how *concientización*, or bottom-up action and analysis, is an iterative process of learning that enhances one's contribution as a citizen subject by facilitating others' positions as subjects who know and can claim their rights within a transnational system that marginalizes their experience. Bertha's testimonio underscores that oppositional ideology needs to come from the margins to create change by rejecting a "symbolic" form of politics in favor of legislation that questions abuses of power and serves to protect the interests of women. All three women opposed abuses of power and tried to restore them through legal action related to women's rights—creating laws, using human rights discourse to monitor factories, or educating the masses in feminist theory that explains how gender subordination puts women at risk for rights violations.

These targeted methodologies demonstrate that simply opposing the dominant ideology, absent of action, would not create opportunities for change. In fact, most of the women in this section experienced marginalization from the FSLN (*Frente Sandinista de Liberación Nacional* [Sandinista National Liberation Front]) when they attempted to move their ideology from the margins to the center through action. A psychological analysis demonstrates the role that oppositional ideology played in their resistance and tells us, in part, how they did it. All of the women in this section understood that conceding this ideology in the face of limit situations would only lead to band-aid solutions that continued to sustain the intersections of power that subjugated women and denied their rights. The collective action that was engaged, guided by an oppositional ideology that recognized the systemic nature by which men had power over women, generated the required mobilization to have an impact on the design and proposal of legislation. It was clear that what was necessary for rights to be actualized were not laws *for* women but laws made and upheld *by* women who understood the intersectional abuses of power that women experienced.

Given that many countries have laws that only serve to address consequences and take care of victims, the processes and methods used by the women in Nicaragua can serve as a model for feminist activists who live in countries that have legislation that is lacking an understanding of power and therefore does little to address the structural conditions that lead to women's rights violations. Although the findings suggest that strategic work in the area of legislation is a necessary part of addressing women's human rights, women in the Movimiento are also aware that legislation is just one part of the process, and that having one's rights enshrined in law does not necessarily mean they will be recognized. A number of barriers, including cultural norms and lack of cooperation from the State, still exist that impede the actualization of rights. One sector in Nicaragua that has worked doggedly to address cultural norms, the agricultural sector, is the focus of the next section. The agricultural emphasis in the Movimiento began during the Revolution when a number of steps were taken to remove institutional obstacles that traditionally prevented women from gaining access to land, resulting in the emergence of rural feminism.

SECTION THREE

Agriculture
FEMINIST RURAL ORGANIZING

In addition to the obstacles inhibiting citizen democracy and women's human rights that occurred in the 1980s and 1990s in Nicaragua, the consequences of the global economic policies of the same decades also introduced or exacerbated several structural factors that contributed to rising levels of gender inequity and marginalization (Naples & Desai, 2002). This was especially visible within the area of property rights, with pervasive gender inequities in land ownership, in particular, recognized as a structural problem inhibiting women's rights in Nicaragua (Peña, Maiques, & Castillo, 2008). Moreover, the feminization of agricultural labor in the countryside was also becoming particularly acute during the same time period as massive numbers of rural men joined the war, leading to an increase in the percentage of rural women workers from 20% to 40% by 1985 (Kampwirth, 2004).

In response to these gendered patterns, the Sandinista's Agrarian Reform Laws of the 1980s recognized equal rights for both sexes and were acknowledged as among the most forward-looking reforms in Latin America because, in theory, they made it possible for women to become direct beneficiaries of land allocation. However, data from the rural titling office indicated that, in practice, between 1979 and 1989 women accounted for only 8%–10% of beneficiaries under the agrarian reform. The small gains made during the 1980s were eroded under the neoliberal agrarian legislation of the 1990s that began during the Chamorro administration. By the early 1990s, the former state-oriented model of agrarian reform had been discredited in favor of counter-reforms that focused on privatization, or the individualization of land rights, which was thought to be more conducive to export-oriented agriculture (Deere & León, 2001).

Women leaders in the peasant movement recognized that rural women's subjugation in Nicaragua reflected not only global economic policies that put pressure on agricultural production and access to land but also abuses of patriarchal power that determined whether women's productive capacity and land ownership were valued in this context. The third and final section of the book examines how a psychology of resistance influenced members of the *Movimiento Autónomo de Mujeres* (Women's Autonomous Movement) to transform structural conditions in agricultural contexts so that women's participation in rural society, namely, through production and their right to own land, could be more fully actualized.

For over a century, Nicaragua's economy has been focused primarily on its agricultural sector, with the United States being its largest trade partner, receiving approximately 60% of all of Nicaragua's exports. During the Somoza dictatorship, private property rights were emphasized in order to favor export-oriented, large-scale commercial agriculture. Under the dictatorship, rural land ownership was concentrated among relatively few affluent Nicaraguans, including a disproportionate number of Somoza's family members and friends, who operated farms producing goods for export, largely to the United States (U.S. Agency for International Development [USAID], 2011; Walker, 2003). During the Revolution, the Sandinistas reversed Somoza's policies through agrarian reforms by expropriating large landowners' property for redistribution to cooperatives and small landholders for use as State farms oriented toward domestic food production. In the 1980s, women gained access to land mainly through the cooperative movement, which enabled women to engage in agriculture on a more independent basis than previously. However, although nearly 4,000 women joined farming cooperatives in the 1980s, less than 1 in every 10 cooperative members were female (Rocha, 2002).

Although feminist scholars have highlighted that rural women have always been more oppressed than their counterparts, mobilization among rural women in Latin America has generally been low (Deere & León, 1987). Nicaragua is an exception to this rule. In fact, mobilized action by women in the Movimiento has been crucial to women's improved access to land in Nicaragua. The agricultural emphasis in the Movimiento Autónomo de Mujeres began during the Revolution when a number of steps were taken to remove institutional obstacles that traditionally prevented women from being recognized as producers or owning their own land.

The *Asociación del Trabajadores del Campo* (ATC; Association of Rural Workers), the principal *Frente Sandinista de Liberación Nacional* (FSLN; Sandinista National Liberation Front) labor organization for farmers that was founded in 1978, was one of the first FSLN labor unions that formed a Women's Secretariat, in 1983 (Kampwirth, 2004). The efforts of women's chapters within organizations such as the ATC or UNAG (*la Unión Nacional de Agricultores y Ganaderos* [National Farmers and Ranchers Union]) attempted to raise awareness of women's problems and mobilize grassroots support around specific gender issues, encouraging the formal recognition of women's rights and access to land with promising legal results. For example, in 1995 a major legislative leap was taken by the Nicaraguan Women's Institute by introducing provisions to agrarian legislation that encouraged joint titling of land to couples, thereby recognizing married women's rights to land (Act 209/95, Article 32). However, as evidence of cultural norms, the term *Joint* in the Joint Titling Act was interpreted literally as "two persons" within the family unit. Hence, this act did more to promote joint titling for men (fathers and sons) than for women.

Two years later, in 1997, the Inter-Institutional Committee for Women in Rural Development was established with the aim of introducing a gender perspective into agricultural policies, and in 2000 the Rural Titling Office approved a declaration of the principles of gender equality and a need to incorporate a gender perspective into all its policies and programs. Nevertheless, despite considerable legislation that positions Nicaragua as cutting edge in mainstreaming gender in agricultural policy, the relatively low percentage of women landowners reflects the reality that women's rural participation remains restricted by cultural practices that prevent the recognition of their role in agricultural production and property ownership.[1]

Thus, as was similar across the other sectors included in this book, rural women leaders needed to branch away from the male-dominated FSLN leadership that characterized the agricultural unions and that prohibited the full actualization of rural women's rights. The chasms that were occurring in the FSLN agricultural unions, and the increasing need to promote rural women's capabilities, led to the proliferation of rural women's organizations in the mid-to-late 1990s. These included organizations involved in the Movimiento such as the *Centro de Mujeres Xochilt-Acalt* (Xochilt Acalt Women's Center) in Malpaisillo, the *Comité de Mujeres Rurales* (Rural Women's Committee) in León, the *Fundación Entre Mujeres* (La FEM; Foundation Between Women) in Estelí, and FEMUPROCAN (*la Federación Agropecuaria de Cooperativas de Mujeres Productoras del Campo de Nicaragua*; Federation of Agricultural Cooperatives of Rural Women Producers) in Managua. In the current phase of land privatization driven by global economic policies, women in the Movimiento have an important role to play in promoting awareness of rural women's capabilities and securing women's land rights.

The women included in this section of the book recognized that formal equality before the law was not sufficient for women to achieve actual equality of outcomes in an agrarian context. This is consistent with the theory of gender and power (Connell, 1987), which postulates that institutionalized gender-based inequalities grant men disproportionate power in society and result in male control and dominance in a number of areas. It has been demonstrated that gender norms based on these power differences create a risk environment that legitimizes and perpetuates women's subordinate status (Glick & Fiske, 1999).

In the context of agricultural Nicaragua, one of the principle consequences of neoliberal policies has been the growing labor force participation of rural women. However, there is a disjuncture between the value of men's and women's productive capacity, whereby men are socially recognized as agriculturalists and women regarded only as "helpers," irrespective of the amount of time they dedicate to agricultural activities. This gendered perspective has been bolstered by the cultural exclusion of women as landowners. Because land ownership in majority world countries reflects dominant roles and elevated status in society and is a sign of power and dominance, the social structures surrounding land ownership help sustain gendered imbalances in power (Grabe et al., 2015). Feminist scholars suggest that notions of land ownership share core ideologies that are embedded within constructions of masculinity and femininity and the "proper" roles that men and women should assume in public spheres (Deere & Leon, 2001; Grabe, 2010). Rural women leaders in the Movimiento recognized that being valued as an agricultural producer and owning land would substantially challenge traditional gender roles and thereby hold the possibility of transforming the conditions in which rural women could exercise agency and, in turn, confront aspects of their subordination.

The women included in this section of the book therefore recognized that rural strategies related to production and land must focus beyond economic aims to a restructuring of the social relations that constrain women. FEMUPROCAN, one of the predominant rural women's organizations in Nicaragua, held its first assembly in 1997 and was founded with the task of mobilizing rural women producers into women-only cooperatives to ensure support for women to grow and sell crops sustainably. A *testimonio* from Martha Heriberta Valle, the founder and current president of FEMUPROCAN, is included in Chapter 8. La FEM, an organization in northern Nicaragua that focuses on land ownership, not only promotes ideological, economic, and political empowerment of rural women through projects such as diversified and organic production and prioritizing food sovereignty but also focuses on violence against women by creating community networks of rural defenders, an education program promoting literacy, primary and secondary education with a focus on gender equality, and the promotion of sexual and reproductive rights. Diana Martinez, the founder of La FEM, is the focus of the final chapter of the book.

The two women included in this final section rejected the dominant ideologies that served to sustain the marginalization of rural women and worked to create collectives whereby women's experience and productive contribution were valued so that a new reality could drive women's experience and expression of rights. The *testimonios* in this section reflect how two women, working from different social positions, both *deideologized* the marginalized experiences of rural women in a manner that led to the shared goals of enhancing the value for women's agricultural production and land ownership with the strategic aim of elevating women's human rights.

Note

1. As of 2015, only 15% of women in Nicaragua hold a title to land in their names, with the majority of most rural women cultivating land that is not theirs (International Fund for Agricultural Development [IFAD], 2015).

Martha Heriberta Valle

8

Deideologizing the Material *and* Social Conditions of Inequity

*'The poor and women cross the same paths.' ... We must have
programs of greater significance or scope since we women are the
ones who drive the world economy.*

—*TESTIMONIO* FROM MARTHA HERIBERTA VALLE

As a prominent leader within the rural social movement in Nicaragua, Martha Valle cofounded *la Federación Agropecuaria de Mujeres Productoras del Campo de Nicaragua* (FEMUPROCAN; Federation of Agricultural Cooperatives of Rural Women Producers of Nicaragua) in 1997 and currently serves as its president. Valle is a trained agronomist and longtime activist focused on organizing rural women in agricultural cooperatives. During the Revolution, she was dedicated to strengthening peasant organizations, first through her affiliation with the underground FSLN (*Frente Sandinista de Liberación Nacional*; Sandinista National Liberation Front) organization, *la Asociación de Trabajadores del Campo* (ATC; Association of Rural Workers) and later through *la Unión Nacional de Agricultores y Ganaderos* (UNAG; National Farmers and Ranchers Union). Under the Somoza regime, organizing within cooperatives was prohibited, thus forcing initial efforts at mobilizing peasant farmers to underground, clandestine efforts.

After the Revolution, UNAG was created under the new Sandinista government in 1981 to voice the needs of small-scale producers and defend the rights of farmers to have access to land. Valle was elected as the head of UNAG's women's section to direct the *campesina*[1] movement and eventually went on to be a regional vice president. However, because male colleagues were persistently opposed to women's attempts to increase their access to and participation in decision-making within UNAG, several women eventually found it necessary to break away and set up their own organization that would create a space of their own, FEMUPROCAN. Valle was one of the cofounders. Valle is also a formerly elected deputy of Nicaragua's National Assembly.

Valle was born in the 1950s in the city of Darío, in the Department of Matagalpa, approximately 60 miles from the capital of Managua. Like many other women included in this book, Valle began her political career organized with the FSLN. However, unlike many of the others who taught literacy, as an uneducated member of the peasant class Valle did not join the Sandinista student movements of the 1970s. Instead, when Valle joined in 1974, she became active in the radical rural movements that were sweeping Nicaragua by becoming a community organizer united with peasant groups in their struggle.

That Valle would become a key leader of a peasant movement as a woman is a crucial part of her story. From the beginning of her interview, she described how being a member of the peasant class intersected with being a girl attempting to find meaning in a social context that privileged the contributions made by boys and men. Valle emerged from the limited situations in which she found herself as a woman working for change to cofound a federation for *campesina* women that bypasses the conventional structures of class and gender that have directly marginalized and excluded the participation of women. Her testimonio demonstrates how rejecting both the material (i.e., economic) and social (i.e., gender) conditions of inequity that violate the ability of individuals to live with dignity led her to develop the subjectivity necessary for enacting the political activity required to transform the structures whereby rural women would be recognized and valued for their productive capacity.

Martha, I know you're used to talking about your organization, but I'd like to start the interview today talking about you and asking questions about your own history. Could you tell me something about your early years, your childhood, maybe what kind of family you're from? What kinds of things do you remember from when you were very young?

In the first place, I want to thank you. In conversations a few minutes before, what I was telling you is that for me it was a big deal when Carmen Diana[2] also had this interest. There are times when talking about yourself is difficult, but I'm going to give it all I've got. I'm going to talk about successes and failures. I was born in a community that was around 20 communities or regions; there weren't schools. And my parents had 14 children. Of them, I was the first daughter, the oldest daughter. We were producers of basic grains and livestock. We didn't have potable water; we didn't have electric lights; we would use oil lamps for light.

I was born in a community they called Las Pilas in the city of Darío, in the Department of Matagalpa. The whole family worked; there were 31 of us in the house. The whole family was illiterate. For climate issues, it was a very dry zone—we had to go to a cold and rainy area that was called *La Montaña*.[3] In La Montaña, we had to go 8 hours on mule for the coffee production, to arrive to sell in the Department of Matagalpa. In this world that surrounded us, men and women both worked. This is how we were able to be efficient producers of something. But we never had shoes.

How old were you when you started working in the fields with your family?

At age 8, I was the tortilla maker, and I went to the orchard. This work that we did together as a family—to fight to have nourishment and to have a better harvest—gave us the great virtue of being efficient, and at the same time it broke with the traditional structure. What are the traditional structures in the country? That the girls don't work. But, my father said that all of us had to work so all of us could have goods. This virtue that God gave me and that my father taught is one that gave me the strength to fight from the time I was very young until today. I want to turn 60 and then go back to the *finca*,[4] to farming.

I didn't know how to read, and so I would visit a young woman who had arrived from Managua, and she had me read sections of the newspaper. I learned to read but not to add or subtract. With the triumph of the Revolution, the first thing I did was study in adult education classes. There I completed sixth grade, I began secondary school,[5] and I completed an agronomy technical certificate—already having three children.

How old were you when you did that?

I started at age 27. That's why I believe that humans aren't defeated when we have this desire to grow and to serve. I always looked for something to grow, introducing some technology, for better productivity. In our farm, we had more than 14 items that we produced. We made soap, we had sugar cane, and we made candy, syrup to flavor—what you call *rapadura*.[6] We had 12 *manzanas*[7] of coffee. We planted about 15 manzanas of basic grains, we had citrus, we had *musaceae*[8] plants that were the plantains, the bananas, et cetera.

This was all on your family's farm?

It was a diversified farm that was just our family's. We would grind 20 pounds of corn per meal. We all had to get up at 2 in the morning, we all prepared food: While I made tortillas, the guys ground the dough, my father got the corn to be made into cuttings for the next day. And at 5 in the morning, we all went to the fields to work. If there is something that I have always valued it's that my father didn't differentiate—despite not knowing the term *feminism*—the different gender roles. We did it out of real necessity, and he was proud because we—all us girls—produced results equal to those of the boys. When I was 13, my father told me, I had asked him for a horse that was very pretty, a beastly horse, and he told me, "I'll give it to you if you break him." So, I tell him, "He'll throw me off." "No," he tells me, "If you—look, I'll pull him—if you see that he's going to throw you, take this tamer, this bridle, and put it on, restrain him, because you aren't going to let yourself be hit by anybody." And this stuck with me because it was during my adolescence, and I think this gave me a lot of strength.

So then when I began to read, I was the one who kept track of the coffee, I priced the cows, et cetera. And all of this was coming together to make me a woman who made a lot of decisions. I got married when I was 16, but I also started getting involved in movements that were about farming. And we began to work for the communities.

When I began to work, I met a coworker—I was a woman with many abilities, productive; I was a woman who left her mark on the house; I also drove vehicles, this gave you strength. Then, this colleague who worked with me, one day said that I couldn't continue there because I was more illiterate than—he wanted to look for people who had at least finished school.

How did you get involved in the Front?

Everyone around me didn't know how to read and write either, and the 20 communities around me didn't know to read and write. I dreamt that human beings could have a school. When the fight with the FSLN began, I joined in '74, but I joined the community groups in their struggles. This meant community organizing, looking for productive options. There was a ton of violence. It was sometimes forbidden for youth to go out at 6 in the afternoon. Logistically, we began to act as couriers for the groups in the banana camps. There was also a line that would take *compañeros*[9] from here, from Managua, to the south, to Rivas, Tola, Carazo.

What kind of strategies were you using at the time to organize people in rural areas?

Well, in the first place, someone has to motivate you—peers come to you, and they tell you that things aren't going well, things you're feeling, too. In that moment, it wasn't just anyone who risked doing that. There was a death sentence then. But, the reality is that we saw that the country worked with an attitude as if we were animals. They went by and if they knew that there was a guerilla there, then they would sweep the area; the area would be bombed. This was hurting from the inside. With those notions, you began getting involved in activities. You have to start by collaborating, and you begin entering into the process. I liked it because it was a struggle. The motto that we had, it was only workers and peasants that made it to the end.

The dream that I had was that one day the country would have light, would have water because we would pull a cart to get water 7 kilometers away, my whole life since I was a child. So, we would think: One day—if the people win, we will someday have water, light, just like they have in the city. But also, those challenges come from—once when I was an adolescent, I got on a bus with my grandmother. I was already about 14, almost a young lady, right, but I was carrying a sack with the hens' eggs, the milk curds, to sell in the city. I got on the bus. I don't know how you call them, trucks, or whatever. I got on, and when I got on there was a woman with nice glasses, and she looked at me and she covered her nose and I began to cry. Because dirty peasants had gotten on and she did that and I just cried. I grabbed my grandmother, and I told her, "I promise you, I promise you that I am going to fight so that one day I can be in power and transform"— I didn't say transform because peasants don't say transform, but I said this: "One day I will change this so they don't look at us like animals." And since then, this is my principle, because I cried and cried and cried until I got off the bus because the woman covered herself and I felt coldness, pain.

Battles don't come so easily, but they come with these feelings, right. So, that was one. And when people tell you, "This one doesn't know how to read," the reality is that at a natural level, we're also thinkers. I was a woman who applied the best techniques, and I didn't know how to read well. So then, what is it to only create values of hard work, of a vision? We didn't say vision, we only said this, "We want to live well, have enough food, never to worry about shoes." I put on shoes when I was 14 years old. But my dream was one day to do something and lead a municipality, a department. When the Revolution happened, I began to study; I finished sixth grade, I finished secondary school. And, I began to study for a technical degree in agronomy. I already had children. I completed it at age 36, a 2- or 3-year degree. This gave me strength and I was able to do the first movement that happened here in Nicaragua in the decade of '79, the peasant movement.

Can you tell us a little bit about what you were doing right after the Revolution?

The whole time I was dedicated to strengthening peasant organizations. I started at the ATC, the organization where we worked, it was underground work, and I started with the triumph, that's where we began to organize.

Tell us a little bit about the ATC first.

Sure; the ATC was an underground organization that worked with the revolutionary movement of the Sandinista Front. It started because when the workers organized, their rights were violated, they couldn't have an organization here; there were only clandestine organizations. When the triumph happens, the ATC defended the unions and the workers. But, we belong to the producers, so then we began a peasant movement. The first meeting was December 14 of 1979. In '81, we created the peasant organization that is called the National Farmers and Ranchers Union. But, the people from the ATC as well as the people from UNAG were comrades in the struggle. Then, I became the first provincial president of this campesina movement. They elected me. I don't know why.

As a woman?

Yes, but this woman had won, like I said—what my father left me, he didn't leave me an inheritance. He left me strength, this vision. I have been strengthening that with better techniques, but he told me that he was teaching me so that a man or my husband wouldn't hit me. You have to be strong. And he told me a very important slogan. He told me, "The poor and women cross the same paths." But, when we see them, he tells me, among those who have money and those who don't, at the end everyone ends up in the same bag, but the women suffer more, he tells me. The majority of men hit women. You have to defend yourself because you're my daughter and I adore you; you are going to defend yourself. That's why I swore to him, I'm going to marry someone whom I can dominate. I think I accomplished that. [Laughter.] I think I accomplished that. Yes, that's it. My husband didn't drink or smoke. Actually, I was the smoker. [Laughter.]

Sometimes, I have looked at it like this ... my nerves, they almost didn't exist. I was never afraid, and this was a dilemma. And I think also that I raised very good children; I think that many people who know them admire them. They said how did I dedicate time to my children if I was working day and night. I told them that it's not the hours but the quality that's important. I think it has been a tough fight. I've worked since I was 8. I was a girl who went behind an oxen planting beans and corn. This has given me strength. When do you think it is that one finds her weaknesses? When one wants to make a small jump, then you find the idiocracy of the small towns, and that's when things begin to move.

When I was regionally elected in the organization, there were guys who said, this woman is almost illiterate, she didn't finish secondary school, we need technicians. So, we created an all-around technical assistance, technicians to tend to the production, technicians for the procedures. Then, I said, well, I've done it all but the women, I've left them behind. I worked until '84 only with 27,000 men organized in the organization that I coordinated. There were also colleagues there who were on the regional directorate board, but I was the coordinator. Later, I became vice president.

Were you treated differently as a woman working for this organization?

Yes, of course. The elements of work contradict those of the culture. What are they? While we were together as a movement, the only struggle that existed was the power of the presidency. There was a colleague with a lot of passion and knowledge about production; he was elected. They say he won, but the truth is that I had two more votes than him, but the agreement was, you go. I want the vice presidency because I want to work on a topic that I haven't worked on, and that was to work with campesina women because in the 27,000 people we had, we had 819 women. And, these women only participated—but not actively—it was like "Oh, we need to have women," so they would bring women. And sometimes they [the women] didn't even know why they were there. My struggle was to change these work roles because they would say to me: "So? We have women here; there are women and men here in the organization." Yes, but the women don't make decisions, they don't plan, and they sure aren't the presidents of the cooperative. They are the wives of the members. And when they bring them, that's when we have women. That is where we have to make our fight.

Thinking back to what you were doing in the '80s, how did you get from where you were in the mid-'80s to what you're doing now here at this organization?

Well, that is the circle I'm working on. I'm organizing, right, trying to microsynthesize all of the aspects. You cry, you sing, and the truth is hard when you had to fight. I really do consider that things are cultural because we women are the ones who have the boys; our sons are men, we raise them and I think from age 1 to 5 is when the boys figure out the story of their lives. So then when it comes from outside, you at least fight part of it within. I can't have a child and make him sweep outside because others go by and shout, "Hey *cochón!*"[10] So then, you have to convince this boy that it's not like that; you have to explain that to him.

So, I was the regional president of the National Farmers Union, and I broadened the national council. I very respectfully directed the midsized producers. While I was there, I plant the idea that it's necessary to organize women in collectives. They tell me, "You're crazy; that's divisive." I tell them, but this isn't a big deal—it's so that they identify [with the organization] and learn to be coordinators, presidents, secretaries, and it's very important. So then they say, well, you'll have to take it to UNAG's national conference. We proposed, it was four—eight women who brought this up. These women proposed that is was necessary that the organization's planning and statutes state that women should also participate in the cooperative movement. So, we held on to that, and we tried to open a women's section. They tell me I'm crazy. They tell me, "Now you screwed up," a colleague tells me, Alciro Rodríguez is his name. He says, you screwed up, now you're going to be with women. Then, they come and say to me, one of them says, "C'mon, let her do that."

So, I had my first meeting in a co-op that is called Oscar Fabricio, and I talk with the president of the co-op, and I tell him, I want to have a meeting with the women because we want to organize them. We call them together, and a colleague from the executive committee of the cooperative tells me, "You already screwed it up, Martha." Then, he told me, "First you organize us, now you came to organize the women and you come saying that we have the same rights." We're talking about 1982. Then, he comes and he says, "How is it that women have the same rights? A woman doesn't have the right to pass out drunk in the street." "They'll grab her, tipsy, drunk with liquor." So, I tell him, "You don't even have the right to pass out drunk in the street either because"—look, I used a vulgar word but it's because they respected me and I told him, "If you pass out, and some ass goes by and rapes you, is that a right? That's not a right. And it's also not a right for a woman to pass out in the street. Rights are different. Rights," I told them, "are that the woman works equally or that you work equally with her or that she works equally to you, and you work together for the legacy of the finca that you have." I had to use techniques they would understand; I tell him, "For example, if you die tomorrow, and this woman doesn't know how to work in the finca, what does she have to do? Look for another man? Do you want another man to ride your horse? [Laughter.] That's it, "Would you like someone to ride your horse?" "Of course not," they tell me. But, I was using a double entendre, right, about the woman. Well, that's what we want, that now you and your wife both manage. She can decide when she'll enter into a relationship, but she's not going to decide to do it because she's ignorant of how to manage the finca. So, these were the methods that I started using because in the countryside you couldn't openly have a confrontation.

We selected a group of women, 63 women, because they still weren't accepting the concept of my work on a national level. So, I go on and I make a group and I ask them if we are willing to launch a rebellion, and we were going to do it while working. So, I arm the 63 convinced women and go to make the proposal at the regional council of UNAG. They start to tell me that I'm a woman, "You're crazy. Campesina women aren't going to leave their houses, not going to spend 1 month away from home." So, I tell them, why don't you let me do the work to see if I can convince them, just like I became a contributor to this organization that allowed us to have a campesino movement. But, campesina movements are not men's movements; they are men's and women's movements. A member of the executive board stood up and said, "Let her do it." But, this meant let her do it without resources—without resources.

I began to visit a women's collective in Matagalpa, directing it at the time I think was Magaly Quintana and Gloria Ordoño. They were women that—they had another idea. But, the reality is that they were also fighting.

I said that we had to be tactful to continue and also to have economic power. They contradicted me; they said that I was fighting for economic reasons. But, I was fighting because my sector, if it remained dependent, it couldn't make decisions. If you don't work, you're in your house, you have four children, five children, eight children, how are you going to make a decision? Are you going to grab the eight children and leave? Because in everything else, you don't have rights; there are no jointly owned deeds, no jointly owned lands. So then, the woman has to grab the eight children and leave. Who would give her shelter? Nobody with eight youngsters and everything, nobody is going to give her shelter. And worse, if she's illiterate, where is she going to go? Will she head to a city? These are the terms that are important for understanding a situation in which one could decide to have more participation.

I'm talking about 1983, and I put together a brigade that was called—the first group was María Castil Blanco, after a campesina who was killed by the Guardia while pregnant. Two groups, or three—people like you—came to visit us from Holland, from Switzerland, from Spain, from everywhere. So, we asked for their collaboration, not money. We asked if they could provide us with some necessary everyday medical products, and they offered us a few boxes, but I asked them to visit us as well. I went and recruited three midsized producers—these women with their resources. And, I take the women from the cooperatives. Then, we made the brigade and we left. But, the war was happening, and there were already pockets of war.

So then we were carefully going, the brigade arrived, we cut coffee, they paid us, and this payment that the woman had, I told them to save it because we would take care of the food, medicine, and those things. After 15 days, we took them to the city in a bus, also with the collaboration of people, so that they could buy what they had one day dreamed of having. One said that what she had dreamed of having was an electric iron because she ironed with one that was put over the fire, made out of cast iron. Another said that she had dreamed of having a set of eye shadow to wear makeup. Another said it was a cot, so she bought herself a cot. And, we took all of this to where we were staying. We were in the mountains. We got wet every day; we didn't sleep, but there we were.

Later—aided by our colleagues who were promoters—we called all of the husbands for a get-together; we were making lunch in the mountain. We made it easy for everyone to get there. Then, she lined up the cot, she says, I bought this cot, take it with you. The other says, look how I bought these dishes for the kitchen, this iron, take them for me, and here is some money for you to buy me eggs from that other hen, because you told me ours are brooding. You understand?

Then, we made a movement with action and reflection. The brigade was playing an organizational role, teaching and every day we gave each squad a president, we gave it the name of a cooperative. Every day, we had a different executive board. The objective was to rotate and build unity. Then, we went to another finca, with a cooperative, and we went deeper into the mountains.

Martha, can I ask you to jump forward—

I only want to finish this little bit. Then, I tell the compañeras who were in the city, "Get the media; we're going to finish." We had already been there since November; we were already in December, and we hadn't left. "Get the media." And, they got the media, and the local media came out with big headlines: "The María Castil Blanco Women's Brigade refuses to leave [the mountains] until the National Farmers' Union approves the line for women's work." We got into contact with Silvia Torres, a woman who is a researcher and at that time she was a journalist with *Barricada*.[11] Another one worked for the press. And, we got them together, and they got great headlines. The National Committee for the Sandinista Front immediately says they are going to go see those women. At that time, you know that when a chief, a president concedes—even the regional, national, the national organizations—we felt so big that not even a tree was as tall. And that's where they promise to have a line and section for women.[12]

We made it with a little work, but with a lot of effort. We were mobilized from November until January 8. Not a single woman left; we fought but with the support of the women from the ATC, the women from AMNLAE[13], the women from the women's collective, the women's movements and women from other countries, from Europe and from other places. I lost contact with all of them because email didn't exist then, only telephone. On one of these occasions Diana Deere also came. We have very little contact now with these great women who, if some have died or if they're alive, they're going to have something to tell because they are women who in some way have fought and have helped.

I never was able to pressure to achieve a goal; the goal should progress flexibly and should continue developing. That's why there are times that I have contradictions with some organizations because I don't think that because I set a goal in a plan, then we have transformed the women. This is a process that you enter into. Sometimes, women still advocate the fight for their space as women, and sometimes those women are still abused. That's a brutal step backwards, and we are still fighting. I would say that those who fought in the '60s or in the '70s; it's just that every moment with a different style, a methodology, a vision.

What is the vision now? What strategies are you using now?

Well, first we have to value the context. At the beginning, the fight was to make a federation within the organization. A group of women like Matilde, me, Morena Díaz, Berta Vargas, um—I don't want to forget anyone, but I forget, it was a small group like—Rosa Emilia Reyes, Guillermina, we were about 20 women, and we now had a section, we began to fight. We asked the National Farmers' Union why they had allowed the men to make a men's federation, but why didn't they want our women's movement—that had almost 12,000 women—to make an incorporated women's federation. They told us that this was divisive. So, we said, we don't think we'll do them harm. We made them a proposal, that the UNAG was a confederation and that we would became a federation. They told us no. I was heading the entire movement, because I was the only director. Then started the ups and downs.

Look, there are people who came just to manipulate. I was accused of sexually harassing one of the secretaries of the national organization. That's the first thing they did. At that time, I swear, I never heard of it. I made a determination—this is why I talk about wisdom and tact— I tell her, "Look, it's none of this. I know that they gave you a nice car, they gave you $5,000 but I am going to tell you something, as I haven't done this and I'm going to give a sworn declaration, I'm going to say it's true." She backed off. That this would humiliate me—that this was going to make me give up my participation in the movement, from making a women's movement or a federation? I mean, so that I wouldn't have this adrenaline, this energy, they gave me an obstacle and barrier saying that I was sexually harassing my colleague. This means that I would step aside and leave it at that, but no, I decided to face this head on. So, in this way I defeated this professional woman. And we continued working.

And that's how you started this organization?

So we continued working, and they tell us, "Go ahead, create your federation."[14] But, they cut off all of our resources, they cut off the projects from our section, they cut off our vehicles, they cut off everything, and they left us—they left the women who supported us unemployed, Matilde, Morena, Berta, all of them, they all end up unemployed. And, they took our access to vehicles. They took everything. So, we ended up with nothing. So then, I aim for something different; I aim to launch myself into politics. While the others continue the struggle and I launch myself and I win at the national level, I win second place of all the deputies in this country. And within the Assembly, I win with a percentage of—almost half a million votes, so I am a choice deputy. My salary is injected into this federation so that women can go on with that, and we negotiate.

The people from the UNAG want—the time for elections comes up, and Daniel Núñez[15] tells me, Núñez is the name of the president, "Look, let's negotiate. If you give the vote to us, we will support the federation." I mean we'll make a sworn declaration with a lawyer. We declare the federation, but do you think the organizations give money just because we say that we are a federation? With what I made in the Assembly, we rented a house, I bought a car, I bought an air conditioning unit, a computer, and I put it in. I'm saying it clearly because sometimes people don't know it because we don't say it. And finally, a little help for the compañeras to mobilize. I invested it all in that.

I'm a deputy who left [the Assembly] with the same shoes, but I was able to become a deputy. Later, I set out to be the director of the party and I was able to get into the leadership of the Assembly. I was able to become part of the management, and the day that the Sandinista Front won here, that I said, "Now you've got it, you have more people than you need, I don't want to work here because I'm still with the campesinos." You can imagine 9 years or 16 years working in the opposition. The day that you have power and they get it and you say, no, I don't want anything because I needed to understand policy. Nobody can defend themselves if they don't understand the policies. Nobody can defend themselves if they don't know how the economy works.

What I do want to make clear is that when we are women with goals, women are more persistent. We are able to give birth and work the next day. We are able to have a child, care for him, and sometimes even make his food. We are capable. And I think, they say that men don't respect us. How is that? When you are taking power, you are respected, and this is important.

Can you tell me a little bit about your definition of feminism in your work?

Look, I think that the processes, the processes—it's that there is some confusion here. Here [in Nicaragua], when people hear about feminism, they think you're a lesbian, that you're—well they say everything, bisexual, that you're this, that you're that. I interpret feminism as my fight, as an ideology in defense of women, with the different expression that everyone has decided to make theirs.

Do you call yourself a feminist?

I do call myself a feminist because I'm fighting, and I think that it's part of my fight and it's part of the principle and that each person, as they say, can play with the ball they want.

I have one last question. In your opinion, are there international economic policies that impact women in Nicaragua?

I think that talking about gender politics, what has happened is that the focus that it had in one decade, the focus it had in another decade, what has changed is the language at the political, economic, and family level. But, there is still a lot of underestimation of the role and what we are capable of doing as women. I'm going to explain why. You can be a great professional, but you are always confused with something. There are men who don't understand a thing, but they have an efficient secretary, but they are morons. So then, there is still a lot to fight for. There is a lot in this real, real space, this real space for women's expression, both at the organizational level and at the personal level, her decisions. And, we still lack the application of so many laws that we have that aren't being applied in real life. And global policies are still bound to the media. Here, when they talk about women, they talk about the environment—of going to plant a tree. The programs are for vegetable gardening, you understand. They're not of much significance. We must have programs of greater significance or scope since we women are the ones who drive the world economy. And you ask me why? Because you say that the economy is driven by a corporation, a bank corporation. But, that's not how it is, the ones who make the products—all of us little people.

There are many women who are secretaries. But they aren't the directors of universities, in the United States, for example, or in other countries. There's only a few of them, you need tweezers to find them, and ask Carmen Diana about it.

Can you tell me a little bit about the relationship between scholarship like Carmen Diana's and the activist work you're doing?

Look, Carmen Diana[16] has always had a focus on women's struggle for land acquisition, for women to become empowered, and that is something that I really admire. She's a great woman. She came to share with us here in the country, to share her ideas with us. And, we have shared with her because a professional also has to get feedback from the product in order to be a good professional and it's the informative part. And, we give feedback for those concepts that they are focusing on in the world. We think that it's a great role, and to tell Carmen Diana, I hope a thousand women come out with her thinking. There are also a lot of very smart women here, and I think the Revolution gave us a lot of space. Here, even though we had the Revolution, we didn't accomplish everything. We have to keep fighting.

Martha, I wanted to thank you very much for your time and for sharing so much of your story with us today.

I want to tell you that I'm not perfect, and I have made mistakes, too. Just by walking, you make mistakes; he who doesn't work doesn't fail. Or he who doesn't work never has faults. He who works always finds problems and sometimes makes a lot of mistakes, but the good part is to never give up. And, I think that my whole youth went by in this fight with a lot of hits and a lot of misses.

I appreciate your sharing your struggle with us. We can learn from you.

The reality is that in a 40-year process you've had tough, difficult battles that you can only win with great effort. I hope that the coming generations follow us like we have followed other women who had already struggled. I read Domitila Luz, I read about women in the free trade zones from the United States; I love documentaries. Every one of them is one of us even though they are no longer living.

Martha began her story by painting a powerful picture of a childhood greatly influenced by issues of resource scarcity and illiteracy. She had a salient recollection of her social condition, vividly portraying a girlhood of poverty by narrating details such as the lack of potable water, electricity, and shoes, at the same time painting a richness of family values, resilience, and dignity that emerged from extraordinarily limited conditions. We begin to witness a pride in her familial values when she discussed the role her father played in her life. She described a learned virtue in being hardworking in the context of an environment where one had to "fight to have nourishment." Rather than questioning the asymmetry of the system, strategies (e.g., hard work) were employed with the aim of maintaining a positive sense of self and with the desire to acquire social and material reward. Martha described hard work as a virtue, rather than a burden shouldered predominantly by communities disenfranchised by economic struggle, reflecting the seeds of a deep-rooted dignity that would serve as the manner with which she conducted herself throughout her life.

At the same time that Martha was negotiating her status as a youth from an impoverished peasant household, the lens through which she viewed her experience was clearly gendered. For example, to explain the role she had in her family, Martha shared that under traditional gender norms in Nicaragua, girls did not work. In reality, girls and women in Nicaragua *did* and do work extraordinarily hard; rather, it is that "women's" work was not considered of as much *value* as the work produced by boys and men. What emerged early in Martha's story is that, with the help of her father, she deideologized gendered notions regarding whose work mattered. In other words, as a young girl Martha rejected the dominant ideology that suggested whether someone should be permitted to make a substantive contribution should be dependent on gender and instead believed that the contribution of girls' and women's work should be of equal value. The formative experiences of having one's work, as a girl, be of value in traditionally male-dominated domains would prove crucial to Martha's later success as an adult woman seeking to create opportunities that allowed for and valued the political participation of women in rural communities.

It is clear early in Martha's story that even as a child her identities as a peasant and a girl intersected in a manner that uniquely influenced her experience. Her deideologization of both the material (i.e., poverty) and social (i.e., gender) conditions that limited rural women's life experiences would serve as the platform by which she conducted her life's work. In particular, despite critical awareness of these intersecting obstacles, Martha continued to see potential in this limited situation by demonstrating her belief that "humans aren't defeated when we have this desire to grow and to serve." Martha's resistance to being defeated, even in the face of unremitting obstacles, demonstrates how important it is to examine the manner in which oppositional methodologies emerge from the margins well *before* focusing on empowering "outcomes" (e.g., the establishment of a campesina organization).

About midway through her story, Martha described an early childhood encounter with classism while on a bus with her grandmother. This early account of being publicly mistreated by an upper-class woman because Martha was viewed as a dirty peasant girl is tragic in its tone and produced a highly emotional reaction in Martha that reflected shame surrounding her peasant class status. Martha's response to this encounter assumed such a significant place in her narrative that it may be viewed as a turning point—an episode that suggested a transformation in the life story or that marked a considerable shift in critical awareness (Hammack, 2010). Prior to this experience, Martha had described an internalized pride in the virtues that accompanied the hard work required by impoverished conditions. However, the cruelty of the experience on the bus awakened a sense that it was not she, by virtue of her poverty, who was somehow flawed and in need of change, but rather it was the social and material conditions of inequity that demanded change. This reconstructed understanding of her experience resulted in some of Martha's earliest skepticism and awakened a strong sense of social injustice in her narrative, where she sought to reconcile the social inheritance of poverty with a plan to become a leader with the power to transform social conditions.

Martha's deideologizing of the structural conditions that determine the experiences of poverty and gender likely contributed to her decision to pursue secondary education as a mother having already had three children. Because of the oppressive cultural and political climate that existed for women during the Somoza regime, accessing even basic education was a revolutionary act. Martha's decision to pursue education was strategic; she articulated, clearly, the role of literacy in her struggle to defy the odds of poverty and gender that created the contours that were limiting her employment. Although she discussed literacy as a necessary starting point in her goal of being a working woman who could make a substantive and valuable contribution, it was also viewed as a vehicle through which to achieve political and social liberation for other women. The determined resiliency that was rooted in Martha's childhood is evident here: She not only saw possibilities for advancement in severely limited situations but also resisted the social obstacles constructed for women and rejected traditional norms by grasping new possibilities.

In particular, Martha did not halt her education with literacy training, but rather completed an advanced degree in agronomy, which she directed toward her efforts to enact social change as an active leader in the peasant movement. Thus, rather than being complacent with bettering her own life with the advancement of educational success, Martha engaged in frequent, regular, and committed action aimed at transforming the material and social conditions for those living in impoverished rural Nicaragua, reflecting choices and behaviors characteristic of liberatory change (Martín-Baró, 1994).

Through an iterative process involving committed action, we observed Martha deideologize the structures that justify the oppression of poor peasant women throughout her story by witnessing her reconstruct women's lived experience as rooted in inequity and the scarcity of resources. In the process, Martha developed an alternative vision—one whereby she dreamed that schools, food, and water were resources afforded to all people based simply on the condition that they are human. She vowed, as a young girl, to transform the structural inequities that imposed dire living conditions on the majority of those in rural communities, conditions whereby basic needs were not met and people were viewed as animals. Yet, it is clear that to actualize her alternative vision, Martha repeatedly, at each new stage of change, had to defy traditional gender roles. This began, for example when she spoke with pride about engaging in traditionally male activities such as agricultural labor as a child, learning to read, and driving vehicles for work. Her defiance to tradition was also evident when she discussed focusing on change from "within" by educating her son with a different ideology—one that rejected traditional gender roles that would serve to sustain the marginalization of women.

Martha brought this approach of "fighting from within" to her position as a leader within the peasant movement with the ultimate goal of changing the structural conditions in which peasant women lived and had their subjectivity denied. On assuming her role as a regional coordinator with UNAG, the male directorate threatened the post Martha held by first calling into question her literacy skills and then later collectively attempting to block her efforts to include the work and contribution of campesinas in the peasant movement. When these unremitting obstacles began, Martha maintained, in the company of her male colleagues, the oppositional ideology that she learned from her father when she declared that women and men's work on the farm should be equally valued and that doing so was a matter of human rights. Moreover, she underscored to her male colleagues that having rural women substantively participate as decision-makers in the peasant movement should not be viewed as controversial; rather, it should also be viewed as a matter of human rights. As has been demonstrated by most women in this book, Martha's story reflects how male compañeros displayed neglect and outright dismissal of matters of particular concern to women.

Despite the seemingly continued obstacles Martha experienced working within the system of patriarchy, she emerged seeing herself as a "winner." Yet, this is not because she was elected to the very kind of position she had dreamed of—one where she could organize around issues relevant to rectifying the social and material conditions of peasant women—but it was because she believed she had inherited the power of resistance from her father, a power that has afforded her an alternative vision and the strength to pursue it. In recollecting lessons from her father, Martha recalled a message that, in its simplicity, underscored his understanding of structural power and marginalization when he informed her that, "The poor and women cross the same paths." Martha seemed to attribute this directed message to planting an early awareness that readied her to take risks from a position of fearlessness. It is from this position that she confronted the male-dominated leadership in the peasant movement by problematizing not only the shortage of women who were involved in UNAG, but also the extent to which they were being represented in a tokenized manner that denied their subjectivity. Martha astutely observed that women were invited to meetings only to fill seats when she acknowledges that women were present, "but the women don't make decisions, they don't plan, and they sure aren't the presidents of the cooperative. They are the wives of members. And when they bring them, that's when we have women."

In being vocal about her resistance to dominant structures within UNAG, Martha's demands for greater inclusivity and recognition of women's rights were met with ridicule and obstacles intended to keep women (including Martha) in their marginalized positions. Thus, although Martha's experiences as a poor rural producer shaped her commitment to the peasant movement, her experience as a woman in the peasant movement shaped a pervasive dedication to women's rights.

When she initiated efforts aimed at increasing women's subjectivity by demanding that the statutes of UNAG formally state that women should also participate in the cooperative movement, she was met with open and direct resistance from male colleagues. Rather than conform to the obstacles present within the male-dominated structure, Martha used her position as vice president to organize campesina women into collective action aimed explicitly at problematizing the exclusion and devaluing of women's economic contributions. She organized a women's collective with the intent of fomenting a rebellion that would have campesina women's work recognized and valued, in part, by demonstrating women's productive capacities. This experience was so powerful to Martha that when I attempted to interrupt her story, she ensured that she was able to finish making her point—which was that it was only through collective action—a rebellion—that women advocated and won a fight to be recognized as subjects in the peasant movement.

Throughout her testimonio, Martha underscored the need to understand context. The context most relevant for women in the peasant movement involved an intersectional understanding of gendered power and poverty that were affected on a worldwide scale by global economic policies. In this context, Martha problematized the fact that women's roles and capacities were underestimated, and that women remain in undervalued positions, rather than holding positions as decision-makers with power. In deideologizing this experience, Martha suggested that, "We must have programs of greater significance or scope since we women are the ones who drive the world's economy." Martha's story illustrates how she developed her own subjectivity in iterative stages; her consciousness surrounding inequity began early, but her resistance unfolded as she armed herself with more tools for the fight she began as a child. Martha's testimonio demonstrates that when one engages in action and is met with resistance, change can occur when operating from a marginalized position that holds true to deideologizing the dominant ideologies that justify oppression.

Notes

1. *Campesino*, in Spanish, is a peasant, or a person living in a rural area. *Campesina* is the feminine noun.

2. Carmen Diana Deere is a development economist specializing in Latin America. As of this writing, she was appointed as a professor in the Food and Resources Economics Department at the University of Florida. She has conducted extensive research in Nicaragua and written several books on women and agriculture.

3. *La Montaña* means "the mountain."

4. *Finca* is most commonly used in reference to coffee plantations but can also be used (in this instance) to refer to farmland or an estate.

5. Secondary school is similar to high school in the United States. Primary school is grades 1–6 and secondary school is grades 1–5 (corresponding to grades 7–11 in the U.S. system).

6. *Rapadura*, also known as *panela* or *piloncillo*, is the leftover solid that remains after boiling sugar cane juice. It is used as a sweetener instead of sugar in many traditional sweets in Latin America.

7. One manzana is equivalent to approximately 1.72 acres.

8. *Musaceae* are flowering plants; banana trees are an example.

9. *Compañero* is used to reflect political solidarity with someone who is a partner, colleague, or classmate. *Compañera* is the feminine form of *compañero*.

10. This is Nicaraguan slang and loosely translates to queer or fag; it is often used in a derogatory manner.

11. *Barricada* is the name of the official FSLN newspaper.

12. The success of the brigades resulted in the First National Meeting of Peasant Women and played an important role in persuading the male leaders of UNAG to agree to the formation of the Women's Secretariat in 1987.

13. [Asociación de Mujeres Nicaragüenses Luisa Amanda Espinoza (Luisa Amanda Espinoza Association of Nicaraguan Women)]

14. This refers to FEMUPROCAN. The male leaders of UNAG stepped up their pressure by limiting the women's resources in the hopes that they would not be able to formally secede from UNAG. The women were not swayed by the intimidation, and on November 20, 1997, they formally founded FEMUPROCAN.

15. Daniel Núñez was president of UNAG.

16. At the time of Valle's most recent visit with Carmen Diana Deere, Deere was the director of the Center for Latin American, Caribbean, and Latino Studies at the University of Massachusetts, Amherst.

Diana Martinez

9

Deideologizing Land Ownership
STRUCTURES THAT INTERRUPT MALE DOMINANCE

We began linking the purchase of land with feminist thinking,
becoming aware of our identity, of how women have been
constructed, to deconstruct the model that was the obstacle to leaving
the kitchen, and work in the field.

—*TESTIMONIO* FROM DIANA MARTINEZ

In the effort to elevate rural women's human rights in Nicaragua, several organizations emerged in the mid-1990s to increase the likelihood of women owning the land from which they produced. *La Fundación Entre Mujeres* (La FEM; Foundation Between Women) in Estelí is one of the most prominent, and Diana Martinez was its founder. Martinez is trained in sociology and international development and has, for her lifetime, combined activism and scholarship with the aim of improving women's labor conditions in rural communities. Like Martha Valle (Chapter 8), Martinez's involvement in peasant organizations during the Revolution was first through the FSLN (*Frente Sandinista de Liberación Nacional*; Sandinista National Liberation Front) organization, *la Asociación de Trabajadores del Campo* (ATC; Association of Rural Workers). And, like many of the other women members of FSLN-affiliated organizations, Martinez eventually broke away from the oppressive male leadership that characterized the ATC to begin her own organization with a focus on gender equality.

The initial aim of La FEM was to create an autonomous space for rural women that challenged the traditional, male-dominated model of rural development and to promote women's rights. Because La FEM was founded on the theoretical understanding that control over resources would facilitate women's autonomy and subjectivity, women's land ownership has always been a key aspect of La FEM's mission. La FEM currently operates as a female-led cooperative of women organized from rural communities to grow and sell fair trade coffee, predominantly to an international market, while simultaneously supporting and promoting women's rights in a number of areas, including education, violence, and reproductive health.

Martinez was born in 1958 in Managua, the capital city. As a youth, she attended elite private Catholic schools, although she expressed an early desire to understand the inequities experienced by the laborers on her grandparents' farm. As a young adult, her parents sent her to Guatemala to live during the Revolution, which is where she began her university studies. After returning to Nicaragua, she studied sociology at the *Universidad Centro Americana* (UCA; Central American University) and at the same time pursued the experience of "being a worker," in part because the efforts of workers and peasants were viewed as the route to change during the Revolution. In 2008, some 24 years after being in college for the first time, Martinez returned to the UCA to obtain a master's degree in gender and development. Although Martinez is a member of a privileged class who was afforded the ability to pursue university education, her commitment to the peasant movement and the manner in which she deconstructs processes of power for rural women place her role and contribution solidly in *el campo*.[1] The following testimonio by Diana Martinez demonstrates the importance of land ownership for rural women in deideologizing what it means to be a woman in a manner that can bring visibility and value to women's agricultural work:

Diana, I'll start by asking you questions about your personal history and life and the work that you've done and any insights you might have about your work and the context of the women's movement. I know you are probably more accustomed to talking about the history of your organization, but I would like you to start by telling me some of your personal history, your early years, a little bit about your childhood, your family. What are some of your earliest memories?

I was born in 1958. I'm about to turn 53, and I am the second daughter of an upper-middle-class family. When I was born, my mother and father who is from Matagalpa—she from Estelí—lived in Managua. In the first years of my life, I studied at the Purity of Mary school. It was a school run by nuns in Managua. And then, my family decided to come to Estelí because my father was a banker.

What was the name of your school?

The Purity of Mary high school. It was a religious school run by nuns, only girls, only women. And upon arriving in Estelí, I enrolled in another convent school called Our Lady of the Rosary. They are conservative religious schools, convents. In that time, they were only for girls, for women. People from the dominant class in Nicaragua studied there. In secondary school, for example, my classmates were the daughters of the Cubans that had settled there after the fall of Batista. There were many people at the nun's school, many farmers and people linked to Somoza.

It was a school that served the dominant class, one that very few people had access to. And ever since I was young, I think I had a sensitivity for the inequalities that existed, for example, the way that the female workers that were employed in my home were treated, as well as some of the sexual abuses committed against them by my father. One time, I found a woman who was employed as a domestic worker about to be sexually abused by my father. He didn't go through with it because I had walked in. And at the time, that was the most normal thing in the world.

How old were you when you were remembering this?

I was 8 at the time. Yes, and I would go to my grandparents' farm in Matagalpa. They had a large coffee farm. And at the age of 8 or 9, I would notice the huge gap there was between the workers and families that lived in the main house. I developed a friendship with the cooks. I would go to the places where they would sleep. You see, they had racks and rails that would go very high up, and they lived in very bad houses. And they would eat beans and tortillas. Also, at that age I would observe how my grandmother would take care of the financial matters, because at the farm there was a large supply outpost for workers, like a grocery store, and the workers, when she would pay them, much of that payment stayed at the grocery store where they bought cigarettes, soap, sugar, and other household items that they needed. And I was always asking questions about this, and it connected me with people. I would ask them about how they would spend their money. Were they happy? Were they not happy? Did they like working there? And many times, I would give my things, well whatever I had on me at the time, like clothes, my watch, my rings to the little girls that lived there. I always kept friends in that place; I would always tell them that I would return the next year.

Many of my cousins would also go there during vacations. Out of my many cousins, however, I was the only one that would even approach the world that the workers lived in. Well, that was when I was still very young. And when we came to live in Estelí, my father had become the manager of the bank and my mother returned to live in my grandfather's, my maternal grandfather's land. He had 1,200 manzanas² of land here in the north. And I enrolled in another school, but at around 13 or 14 years of age I organized my first domestic workers' literacy group.

Oh wow! Do you remember what year it was?

I came to Estelí in 1971, one year before the earthquake. And I studied the first year of secondary school at Our Lady of the Rosary. I was about 13 years old, so it was in '72 that I organized a study group with my mother's female employees and two aunts and a neighbor. It was a group of five women, and we had a little book—a type of book that is known as *coquito*, and it was used to teach reading. Their bosses, the owners of the house, would let them have these classes with me because I was, uh, me.

What did your parents think of you doing this?

Well, they had always thought that I was a little strange, you see, because when I was 15, I had stopped going to mass with them. I actually became involved in a revolutionary Christian movement that was based out of the church called Calvarios, in Estelí. Here, there was a priest who was a great figure in the Revolution named Father Julio César López. He was Colombian, and he is still alive. He connected many youth in this Christian movement to the Revolutionary process.

What happened is that after the Revolution, he became reactionary. But, for a time he played a very large and important role. For example, in Santa Cruz I would frequently go with him and lecture about the need to renounce the dictatorship, and this was a method to familiarize myself with and build new perspectives from an evangelical opinion about the poor and not from the church's gospel. And, I would go on Sundays, sometimes with my parent's permission, other times without, to these communities.

When I was in middle school, things got intense around the years '73, '74, '75 because that is when the organization of the FSLN really came into prominence. But, in the year '76, I was already very involved with the people in the FSLN. So then, my parents decided that I should leave Nicaragua, and they took me to go live with my sister in Guatemala. There, in 1977, I finished secondary school in another all-girls' school in Guatemala, which was called the School of the Sacred Heart for Young Women. And, I was really hurt by that decision, the imposition that my parents had put on me, because all of my friends were going into hiding, and there was a very strong consciousness among many of the youth that opposed the dictatorship and were ready to die for the cause of liberating Nicaragua from Somoza. I left because I had no other option at the time, and I finished secondary school there. And then my parents decided that the following year I should study at Rafael Landívar University, which is like the Jesuit university in Guatemala. They came to enroll me there and everything, but I was only there for about 3 months because I had decided for myself to go to the University of San Carlos, which is the national university, and there I studied political science and sociology.

At the university, I shifted the Christianity that I learned with Father Julio, the revolutionary Christianity, to Marxism. In reality, I became an atheist and Marxist [laughs]. I left in '78, when Estelí had a large insurrection. I had the strong urge to go participate, but it was not possible to come during the insurrection, so in January of '79, when I could leave

Guatemala, I left the university to come back. I flew to Costa Rica so that I could work in an underground hospital in the city of Liberia, where there were forces from the Southern Front. Here, they attended to the injured guerillas from the Southern Front. I stayed in the city of Liberia for many months until the 20th of June, when I returned to Nicaragua and came to Managua. I couldn't come to the plaza on the 19th, so I came the following day. And then, my parents came from Guatemala, because at the time they had decided to leave due to the war. And when I came to find them, they told me that they no longer wanted to see me because I had lost my virginity, because I could not get married now according to their plan and I had turned my back on all of the values that they had taught me and because I had made a life for myself. And so I was no longer welcome in their home. So, I then I returned with only the clothes I was wearing, and my boots, to Managua, because I had to make it on my own. And, well, because of the struggles in my life and because I was no longer involved with the FSLN, I returned to Managua, and I found contacts who let me live there temporarily.

At the end of November, a new school in sociology had opened at UCA, and so I decided to withdraw from Guatemala and continue my second year of sociology in Managua. And at that moment, I had the idea that only the workers and peasants would make it to the end. To quote Sandino, "Only after you focus your strength will you attain victory." From that point on, I truly wanted to become a worker. And then, I involved myself in a factory that belonged to Somoza. Under Somoza's time it was called the "the factory to come," and then the revolutionary government attempted to fix it up, and they called it the Tecnixa textile factory, a textile company where I learned to be a worker, a textile worker. I was a driver for a very large machine that would make cones, cones that would later be converted to make giant pillars. And in those years, I wanted to erase from me the remnants of the petit bourgeois that remained in me and become a worker in the kingdom of heaven . . . contradictory, I know [laughs].

In what years were these that you were being trained in the textiles?

In '82. Yes, '82, end of '81, '82. In the end of 1984, I had managed to combine my work at the textile with my university work. But, it was very difficult because I had to meld two very different worlds, and scheduling conflicts would arise. One week, I would go to work at in the morning and get out at 2 in the afternoon; the following week, I would start at 8: 30 in the evening and get out at 6 in the morning. And then there was 1 week where I could not attend classes. But I had informed the dean that I was having difficulties, and well, being a Marxist as well, the dean said that he would evaluate me by giving me a special task in assignments around the theme of goodwill and the subject of the labor movement. For example,

I did many assignments to make up for my absences, such as how did things work, how were they produced, and wealth in the factory for example. These were political economy classes, and I could combine them in that way. I also had a special concession on the part of the university because missing a whole week was a lot.

When I was in my fifth year of sociology, some friends sought me out to participate in an investigation, and I became a research assistant in a very important study, the first feminist investigation from Nicaragua. But in reality, I was not an assistant; I participated as if I was a member of the research team. And the study is called, "Women in the Exports in Nicaragua" by Clara Murguialday, Ana Criquillion, with women researchers from the Center for Research in Agricultural Reform. We were eight researchers, and over the period of 2 years we studied the conditions of the workers in three export areas of production. And this work is published by INIM[3] of the Sandinista government's women's institute. And there began a period in my life where I was a researcher, very early—because this study was finished in 1985. It was the first feminist study in Nicaragua from the ATC.

And when did you start working for La FEM?

Well, after I participated in that study, I then went to the Sandinista government's Women's Institute to work on a research project on the female workers in the textiles where I had worked. And there I found a perspective on gender that developed from a Nicaraguan woman, who is still alive to this day, who had always lived in the US, named Paola Pérez, from her and her work at Berkeley, I think. We studied the conditions the female workers were in, we studied the industry, and it is called, "Gendered Industries and Women in Nicaragua," and we did that work in '87. For me, it was a great satisfaction to study something in regards to the work that I myself had done as a textile worker. And I, using the results from the study on the female agricultural workers, attempted to create a political proposal to organize the women agricultural workers in the ATC. And I stayed working there during the final years of the Revolution in conjunction with the Women's Secretariat of the ATC.

Can you very briefly explain the ATC for us?

The ATC is a farmworker's organization that represented one of the biggest historical claims to—for the rural world and for the poorest people of Nicaragua, because the capitalist system and the dictatorship unleashed immense abuses to workers in the rural and city areas. And on these farms where, for example, where my grandmother, where I would visit, many people that had farms also had workers in states of absolute exploitation and vulnerability and denial of rights, in conditions of exploitation, where there were no labor regulations, where there were no contracts, social security, and where the people were less than a person. Only the Sandinista Revolution and the ATC could change these situations for the fieldworkers organizing agricultural unions for groups of producers; coffee workers had formed unions for the first time, banana workers, sugar workers, tobacco workers, cotton workers, all goods that Nicaragua exports.

Were there other women involved in the ATC at that time?

Oh, yes, there were some; there were many women that had a shared experience, the horror of having been kicked out of the ATC. For example, Olga María Espinoza, a diligent worker that in actuality was a great leader in her time, she would work with Edgar Garcia to lay claim to land before the Revolution was won. There was also María Teresa Blandón; she worked in the ATC during the last years of the Sandinista decade. There are also other women that are still there, and some new, but many of the women that had positions that were in favor of women had a falling out with the male leaders. Because, well, at first they were open to our demands, but then when issues about equality and power came up, the leaders would abandon us. You see, this happens in all of the left-wing corners of the world, and the ATC was no exception. It was a mixed organization; we had all given our all for the Revolution and for the ATC, but those who were our beloved comrades during the war would not compromise for our demands in regards to gender and women. The best thing for them to do was expel us from the organization. There were various fallings out during the '90s and in the years before the '90s and then they continued, of course. And me, well I was kicked out from the ATC here in Estelí in 1993, when I was the director of the women's health program named *Flor de Pino*.[4] It was a clinic that attended to all of the workers from the tobacco fields. And then, there was a bit of a scandal; they insulted me, they caused me a lot of harm to get me to leave. They accused me of a lot of things that were simply not true; they did it to get me out of the ATC. And that is how they did it.

What reason did they give you for kicking you out?

Well, you see, there was this director named Imelda Gonzales, and she was a representative of the Women's Secretariat and I was the director responsible for the program. The men would take advantage of us and make us fight, the two most prominent leaders of women. She would say that I did not respect her and thought that I wanted to replace her and was not acting in the best interest of the workers, that I was operating the clinic in a secretive way. All of her accusations had to do with money, and that was an intentional tactic to make the women lose respect for me. And they said many false things like that, that I was stealing money, that

I did not respect the Women's Secretariat, and that I was a woman from the bourgeois. They accused me of things that had nothing to do with anything, especially considering that I had a very difficult time in my life attempting to deal with trying to separate myself from my upbringing.

What do you think the real reason was they kicked you out?

I think that they kicked me out because, in my opinion, there was a connection between feminism and the ATC where there were women like Olga María, María Teresa, and because we were the women who had the moral authority to confront and demand from the leaders that they make compromises that would favor women. And the national board and regional board would not want to admit to anything that I would say. I was very influential with the women who worked in tobacco, I was very respected by them, and I had influence. So, they did not support this because I think that they acted in a way that was very inconsistent with their principles. And, I think that with everything that they did, people realized what they had done because all of the workers were complaining that I was gone, and they came to see me at my house. And through the program, I had acquired a few contacts with organizations in Austria, and those organizations would send letters to the national ATC and protest over my firing. That came with a great political cost to the national board, to the ATC, and the people of Managua because this is where the headquarters are located. It was very painful; it was one of the biggest crises in my life. And because of that, a group of women in Austria had supported me for a time. They had allowed me to stay with them for a period of 2 months in Austria so that I could think about a new program that I could create, and from that came the idea to create a foundation among women. The lesson that I learned was that in mixed organizations it was not possible to work towards a real agenda that was in favor of gender equality. I had to construct legitimate organizations, transparent organizations, and create them with the women that it would affect in the process. Without autonomy, we would not be able to do anything either—autonomy from the state, from partisanship, from the mixed organizations, and from the directors. Only women could do something on the behalf of women. Therefore, I had to create La FEM.

In what year was that?

La FEM was founded in 1995.

Can you tell me briefly about what some of the strategies or the aims of La FEM were when you started?

Yes, because we thought that La FEM was simply a historical continuation of the ATC, a process of the Revolution. The situation of the '90s to '95 worsened the conditions; the people's living conditions got much worse in Nicaragua due to privatization and because of the structural changes in place brought by Violeta Chamorro's government.

Can you explain those structural changes briefly? What was it like during the Sandinistas, and how did Chamorro change those policies?

Yes—of course—we had this great revolutionary State where we had free education, free healthcare, scholarships, social programs, programs for production. A great State that assisted cooperatives, there was child care available in rural areas; there were collective agreements between the workers and the institutions or between the companies they represented. There were rights that never had existed. But, when I saw the changes Violeta was making, the State began to collapse, it was weakened completely, and it left the population in peril.

For example, healthcare was privatized, education was privatized, we began to feel as if we no longer had a roof over our heads. And, they began to return land that belonged to Somosistas, and new people would come and claim their land, and other capitalists would emerge to look and take advantage of the privatization of Nicaragua. Then, obviously the people from the fields are always left behind; they were ignored even more, and under these circumstances the need to create an alternative form of resistance led to the birth of La FEM. I had to do something, but my experiences at the ATC were very hard, and we decided that this organization would not have professional women, or women from the upper classes as leaders, but rather the women from the communities would be the maximum authority in the board of directors.

And thus La FEM was born out of the women from el campo. Only I am not from el campo, but I already told them about my past, and that in my heart I feel that I am from el campo myself. And in La FEM we have a board of directors that is still the same people from when it was born, but we are in the process of transition that will continue until 2013. And it has been a great thing that we have created with those 12 women from the founding committee. We have made this happen with a high responsibility of women in institutional power, not simply as the beneficiaries.

That is the difference, that these women have had a strong role in policies of La Fem. And, one of our priorities was to buy land for women, thinking that without the land we could not make structural changes regarding the status of subordination, because we also thought, to transform subordination, it is essential to have gender awareness. Both are complementary, with no consciousness of gender, the land is useless given to the women, because men make the decisions on the land, because she cannot imagine any other form of being a woman. But, there is no purpose to gender awareness if the women do not have land and the resources necessary to be productive.

For this reason, in our strategy, we began linking the purchase of land with feminist thinking, becoming aware of our identity, of how women have been constructed, to deconstruct the model that was the obstacle to leaving the kitchen, and work in the field, to leave the housework, and to dedicate ourselves to visible work and recognition outside the home. And, that is the long process that we lived in order to create awareness and work to purchase the land. And we have also developed other strategies at the same time to educate adults, healthcare programs on proper self-care, educate them about parts of the body, control of their sex lives; they control their reproduction, and now, after 15 years, the possibility that some women can recognize that they have alternate sexual preferences. In the rural world, it is rare that a woman is a lesbian, for example, and this is a huge thing. We have partners who are recognized as that, and that makes us very happy, too.

Have your strategies working with women changed over these 15 years?

We have maintained stable strategies that stem from a conversation about the theoretical concepts that are in the best interests of women—for example: the battle over land, education about protection based on gender, the themes of sexual and reproductive health, the fight against violence, the creation of self-governing organizations, for example, economic power, the creations of cooperatives and having our coffee be a part of the fair trade market. These have been our strategies, and we have all walked it together these last 15, almost 15, years. Sometimes, we advance more than others, but to achieve what we have achieved, it is due to the fact that we have maintained in our perseverance and stuck to our strategies. These aren't short-term changes; they are long and process-driven, profound changes that cannot occur overnight. But, we have to make many things better. For example, the theme of sexual diversity is a very salient and important issue in the community. Fifteen years ago you never would have thought about those things.

There are also things that we are doing well, for example the fight against violence, and we are advancing in our coordination efforts with the Office of Public Affairs from the State. The women connect here—now we are one of the strongest organizations in Estelí—when there is a case of *feminicide*,[5] when there is a trial against the perpetrators, a case of sexual assault, and all those types of incidents. But, we stick to our causes; we use the same strategies when fighting for equal rights for rural women. And, violence is in the heart of all of these incidents.

When you address these other issues, are you working with other organizations in Nicaragua?

Yes. La FEM works in a women's group called the Feminist Movement; there about 18 organizations from different parts of the country, all very different.[6] We have a sense that we women are not too intellectual; we are women, organizations that bring together ordinary women in the neighborhoods and communities to do daily work in the fight against violence against women and to empower women. And, different movements are aligning themselves with our feminist movement. Other groups, like the lesbian organization Artemis, many trans women that are awakening to the cause, are aligning themselves with our movement.

La FEM feels very comfortable in this space because we can really enrich ourselves by learning from how women from the Afro-Caribbean Network, from the Caribbean coast live. With the Ocho de Marzo of Masaya, and all these new groups like Pink Flag, they give a face to the new feminism, the different, rural feminism, we could not imagine before, one that is different from the feminism of the very, very middle class, high, urban, upper class, right? That is what had been considered feminism, but this feminism that we defend, that we created, we believe is possible, is a feminism embodied in the actual processes of the lives of women.

Can you define feminism for me? The way that you mean it?

All right; for me, feminism is a proposed policy. It is an alternative means for change that is in favor of equality for women. It is a proposal, a concept in relation to the inequality of genders; we cannot believe there to be a feminist that is against abortion, one that is against sexual and reproductive rights and liberty for women.

Can you tell me a little bit about the importance of rural feminism?

Well, the truth is, hmmm, I think it's fairly new because, at the beginning of feminism, or what we call difference-based feminism, where women, Black for example, share common ground with white feminists in the northern countries. Also, in this feminism of difference, and in this diversification of sectors, there are women who have been finding feminism in rural organizations that are doing work with this focus. Then, there are women who feel identified with feminism especially because they are learning decisions about their life, especially as they are recognizing the autonomy of all, because they are demanding from their partners, equity, equality, respect in sexual relationships. And some have sexual choices, as they have yet to discover, but which are in conflict with his sexual identity, and in feminism they found an answer.

A few days from now, we are going to hold a forum with all the women there, at least in the communities where La FEM is. Three transgender women who are part of La FEM, and are from el campo as well, and at least two lesbian couples, which could not have come out if it weren't for La FEM, because they feel that in La FEM is a place where they are respected, but it is just a start. I think rural feminism is not only producing coffee, not only owning farms, not only having education, because there are many women in La FEM that will have their high school diplomas in 2013. Of the women who have started to teach themselves to read in La FEM, they will finish their bachelor's degree as well. It is a privilege to organize a rural women's movement. When we brought together 1,500 women in Estelí to protest feminicide, for example, we made May 9 a day of action and mobilized 1,500 women in Estelí. We are a movement, and the call to arms that we have is huge, the respect that we have for communities, for the struggle we have, is great.

You've offered a really complete definition of feminism. Are you a feminist?

Yes.

I'd also like to ask your opinion about the relationship between scholarship, or research and activism, and the organizing you're doing with La FEM.

Well, only since 2008 did we begin to see a connection for the first time in Nicaragua. For example, there is a master's on gender and development being promoted in the UCA, and that promoted the feminist movement that we belong to. Actually, I was chosen as one of the Women's Movement to go to the master's program, and it was a wonderful thing for me because I had not studied for many years since I left the university in 1984. I hadn't returned to the university and had many years of practice and participation and had no academic link. In the beginning, I was so afraid to enter the master's because I thought I would not be able to study with so many young people. But, it was a very enriching experience, and I could organize my ideas in the academy of the master's program, systematize my thoughts, to find myself there, in the analysis, and analyze and give meaning to a lot of the things that I had done and still have to do. Research is still underdeveloped. But, there currently are other graduates, other master's. And to me, in the future I would like to participate in some feminist research since it is research that initiated my thought process and was also my starting point.

You mention also during the Revolution that the State was responsible for healthcare. But, can you tell me in recent years, what is the role of women's organizations in meeting women's health needs? Is the women's movement necessary to address health, or are the government's laws sufficient?

Not at all. The government maintains a very androcentric conception of women's health. The mother and child pair is what dominates conceptions.

That is to say, it prioritizes prenatal care for women, newborn care, pregnancy. There are many women that the government wants, at all costs, to be recognized for the Millennium Development Goals[7] and to do something about the high rates of maternal mortality that the country has and make it drop. They put a lot of effort into that, but they limit women from being seen from the State's perspective as an integral subject, where not only reproductive health counts.

Paradoxically, the government worries about reducing maternal deaths, but they have made a suspension in the Penal Code, Article 165, criminalizing medical abortion. And, since 2006 the feminist movement and women have been carrying out a struggle for reinstitution of therapeutic abortion. In Nicaragua, one of the things that most threatens the lives and health of women is the abrogation of the article due to concessions made by the Sandinista government to the Catholic Church during the 2006 election year. So, all these years have passed and no one in the government cares that thousands of women die as a result of the criminalization of therapeutic abortion. Therefore, health conditions are not favorable, and there is no chance that things will improve any time soon. So, much of our agenda is based on our fundamental belief in the reinstitution of therapeutic abortion, but we as feminists not only want to be able to perform therapeutic abortion, but elective abortion as well. It is essential that therapeutic abortion is in our agenda in this period. The country has, well, the issue of violence to tell the truth. There is a large amount of abused women, and violence of all kinds is also a public health problem. And, we have an increase in AIDS and HIV cases, and women, groups and groups of women, housewives, who are infected and no clear policies for prevention, no policies that see us women as subjects, leading to our lives and our health, because the State has a conception of women as beggars and not as subjects of rights.

Switching gears, I also want to ask you if, in your opinion, you think any of the current international economic policies or neoliberal policies are impacting rural women in Nicaragua today?

Of course, it's true. Unfortunately, the World Bank money continues to determine the fate of Nicaragua. And, there is no clear break from the government with these multinational institutions. In Nicaraguan agriculture, we still see the use of GMOs[8]—they don't promote organic farming. There is a dependence, technology given in the field as development, and prioritization of the economy, linking, for example, the rulers of the country.

Are there ways that those policies impact women in particular?

Women find it more expensive to produce beans and corn in el campo. Rural people are migrating because the soils have lost the quality because there is environmental deterioration since there is little water from natural resources, and all of this has to do with a set of global policies. That is to say, the way climate change and the emission of gases from rich countries affects Nicaragua is that it produces damage. It is not that we cut trees here exactly.

I don't know if someone is taking responsibility for the promotion and support to rural economies and the security and food sovereignty. This government has made food sovereignty laws, but the implementation mechanisms are not visible, and we are still without real proposals for rural development, sustainability in the country.

You mentioned that you have some relationships with women's organizations in Nicaragua, but do you also have relationships with organizations in other countries that work with you in solidarity?

Yes; here in Nicaragua we have, as I mentioned, the feminist movement. We have local links in order to give us strength against the things that happen locally and that are affecting the lives of women. Internationally, we have relationships with women from Honduras that are part of the resistance, who are rural women. Our relationship with them is a priority, these rural women that are fighting against the dictatorship.

That is something very important in Honduras in this moment because there is an agrarian counterreform process that is taking away lands and giving them to the men and women farmers that reformed in their favor. We invited these women to do an interchange a little while ago, and we are participating in strong alliances with them. We have— well, in the entire region—groups that we are interested in strengthening partnerships within el campo, especially people that also have feminist visions.

We are very interested in maintaining a contact with the rural organizations from the region and in the United States. Our strongest and most valuable relationship is with WCCN[9] and with Just Coffee.[10] It is the most beautiful thing that has happened to La FEM to get to know them because we have found a possibility to feel supported, not so much financially, but in the fight, in the struggle that we need to move forward and to find a market that is favorable for women.

We say that women found a window to heaven, not only because of the price, but also the human qualities that are at Just Coffee, because of WCCN. We know that is truly a group of solidarity from all points of view. And, we have partnerships with our colleagues from Germany, that is a solidarity group that has existed since 1980, and with them we also have a very close political relationship. And, very close solidarity groups in Austria, with the women coming from the old brigade that came in the '80s to cut coffee and cotton, to help with the Revolution. We maintain those ties, such as Peace With Dignity, a Spanish organization that has positions very much in favor of equality and very respectful of our processes and is supporting us financially in the economic empowerment of women and in all ideological processes. La FEM is now like an international area [laughs] because it has made itself increasingly multicultural.

Diana was raised with an elite upbringing, in part, because she was the granddaughter of landowners who engaged in large-scale agricultural production staffed by domestic workers. These large-scale farms, while benefitting the owners, served to produce the majority of Nicaragua's foreign export, mostly to the United States. Large-scale coffee production, in particular, for which Diana would be involved throughout her life, began in 1850, and by 1870 coffee was the principle export crop of Nicaragua. In 1992, just 3 years before La FEM was started, more land was planted with coffee than any other crop. Therefore, Diana's experience, both as a privileged youth and later as a rural activist, cannot be interpreted outside the transnational context in which the experience of land and labor predetermine one's social status and lived experience in Nicaragua.

The salience of Diana's youth is peppered with awareness of her privilege. She was aware that the schooling she received was not accessible to most and existed largely to serve the dominant class. That she is knowledgeable of the number of acres her grandparents owned (approximately 2,000) suggests further understanding that her family was securely positioned in the dominant class. Diana's social location as a privileged youth shaped her understanding of inequity through the observations she had on the farm her grandparents owned.

Diana problematized the conditions of sexual or labor exploitation that she observed, leading her to deideologize, from a very early age, the structures that justified the social oppression of the domestic workers on her grandparents' farm. For example, she demonstrated an early curiosity of workers' economic experience and livelihood by questioning an economic system that sustained positions of servitude that functioned to barely allow sustenance for the workers, yet abundance for her family. Through observing the sexual exploitation of female staff, Diana also began to deideologize misuse of power from a young age by recognizing what was considered "normal" and rejecting it. Although dominant ideologies surrounding gender allowed the sexual mistreatment of domestic workers to be "the most normal thing in the world," Diana reframed these experiences to be sexual abuse that was committed by someone in power (her father), thereby reconstructing understandings of lived experience through rejecting the dominant ideologies that justify social oppression. Therefore, at an early age Diana was beginning to critique an economic and patriarchal system, her grandparents' farm, which sustained positions of marginalization and power in the context of global pressure to do so.

As a child, Diana's desire for equity first manifested itself in a somewhat-uncritical manner when she gave gifts to her family's staff as token gestures to demonstrate her belief that everyone deserved to have these things. This perspective started to shift when Diana began committing action to activity that could change lives in her immediate surroundings. For example, her efforts became more structural and strategic when she organized a domestic workers' literacy group. Although not a member of the peasant class or part of the National Literacy Brigades, Diana staged her own insurrection at a young age by hosting literacy training for staff employed by her family. She was permitted to subvert the natural order that employers counted on simply because of her social location—she was the granddaughter of a man with substantial land holdings and the daughter of parents who viewed her initially as eccentric, but not a threat.

A formal rejection issued by her parents that came in early adulthood perhaps served as a catalyst for Diana's motivation to more fully distance herself from her social class and past and more strongly align with the peasant struggles. Although naturally she could not shed the privileges with which she was afforded and shamed by, Diana made a conscious decision to increase the solidarity she had with the workers in the labor movement by becoming a textile worker. Although she was also a university student of sociology, Diana was driven by a Sandinista slogan that was frequently used by FSLN leaders in the 1980s: "Only the workers and peasants will persevere until the end, only their organized force will guarantee victory" (Ryan, 1995). The FSLN, which united around overthrowing a dictatorial capitalist model and imperialist ruling class, placed higher value on a force of workers and peasants and thereby marginalized members of the bourgeois who were regularly questioned as allies in the struggle (e.g., Sofía Montenegro, Chapter 2). In this context, it is not surprising why Diana, who deideologized the structures upholding economic inequity, would yearn to "erase . . . the remnants" of the bourgeois and become a worker.

Although Diana did gain experience as a textile worker, her testimonio reflects that it was through combining seemingly disparate experiences—a student of sociology, a researcher, and a textile worker—that she began to hone a praxis that would involve using theoretical and empirical understandings to implement structural changes for rural women. As both an engaged researcher and an employee of the ATC, Diana was uniquely positioned to engage this praxis. In particular, it was possible that she could directly apply the theory and understandings from research findings to the practice and policies being employed with rural women in real contexts. Although the ATC existed precisely to elevate labor conditions for fieldworkers whose labor was exploited in the interests of an international market driven by export demand, it was also driven by a male-dominated agenda. Therefore, women's interests fell second to the global economy and third to the FSLN male leaders' agendas (which were also intimately tied to economic interests). Thus, although Diana was well positioned to enact change, when she took a stance within the ATC that favored women's interests, she was marginalized by male leaders of the FSLN, who used tactics that would lead to her expulsion from the organization. As has been narrated by several women in this book, regardless of one's background or the sector in which they worked, the aggressive marginalization from male leaders within the FSLN was something nearly all women leaders experienced during this time.

Diana's incentive to start a women-centered rural organization was therefore shaped by her own marginalization from a male-dominated organization that was not only disinterested in rural women's experiences but also acted aggressively to ensure they could not be represented. Diana described the limit situation that was created by being ousted by her *compañeros*[11] as "one of the biggest crises" of her life. Nevertheless, from this experience emerged methods that were women centered, change focused, and rooted in the belief that "only women could do something on the behalf of women." Although it was apparent that women-centered spaces were needed, the founding of La FEM in 1995 also coincided with privatization efforts being imposed by a neoliberal administration that was enacting policies that further exacerbated men's structural power over women. In particular, it is well documented that when land is privatized and parceled to individuals, titles are often administered to male heads of household (Deere & León, 2001). This was particularly true in Nicaragua, despite legislation aimed to interrupt these norms. Therefore, it was the intersection of patriarchal control and neoliberal capital interests that created the imperative for organizations like La FEM.

Diana's experience as a rural activist positioned her to have the understanding, analysis, and skills necessary to found an organization that could address the systematic inequity faced by working rural women in the context of globalization. For example, the methods Diana employed to create La FEM reflect the ways in which she deideologized patriarchy in this particular context. She strategically founded the organization in a manner in which "women from the communities would be the maximum authority in the board of directors," recognizing that an alternative form of resistance was necessary because the global capitalists, who take advantage of privatization in Nicaragua at the expense of women workers, would continue policies with the support of male leaders in her country.

In Diana's analysis, she clearly articulated a praxis in which the methods used at La FEM are rooted in a theoretical framing that understands gender and rural women's lived experience in the context of patriarchal and neoliberal policies that serve to disenfranchise women. Thus, rather than applying band-aid "empowerment" solutions that could address short-term needs, Diana suggested that, "We have maintained stable strategies that stem from a conversation about the theoretical concepts that are in the best interests of women." These strategies involve deconstructing dominant ideology in a manner that values the experience of women and recognizes that structural changes (e.g., land ownership) are necessary for women to be able to act as subjects in their own lives who can make decisions with agency. This became particularly clear when Diana stated that "we began linking the purchase of land with feminist thinking, becoming aware of our identity, of how women have been constructed, to deconstruct the model that was the obstacle to leaving the kitchen, and work in the field, to leave the housework, and to dedicate ourselves to visible work and recognition outside the home." In deideologizing gender in this manner by deconstructing traditional gender roles and their relation to land, Diana described the strategic nature in which La FEM promoted women's land ownership. She matter-of-factly spelled out that "without the land we could not make structural changes regarding the status of subordination," underscoring the critical role of resource control in structural change.

Moreover, like other social movement actors and scholars, when Diana noted that expanding women's control of land ownership is one way of altering women's status and addressing imbalanced power relations between women and men, she also underscored that a critical understanding of gendered relations is a fundamental aspect of altering women's experiences. This element of her praxis was reflected when she said that, in addition to land, "We also thought, to transform subordination, it is essential to have gender awareness." Diana suggested that in gaining the power that may come from land ownership, women also needed to reconstruct and reorient deeply engrained systems of gendered relations. Thus, in this example, the development of critical awareness, in addition to control over resources, was an essential component in achieving the capability to competently challenge established systems. Therefore, although strategic gender interests may be met through women's land rights, the praxis implemented at La FEM recognizes that ownership may not be sufficient if women are not also made aware of their rights through some level of organizing. Similarly, like many examples of change that were shared by other women in the *Movimiento Autónomo de Mujeres* (Women's Autonomous Movement) and represented in this book, Diana articulated an understanding of how comprehensive change involves process. For example, while the full expression of women's sexuality may have been an unexpected outcome related to agricultural production or land ownership, Diana related this outcome to "rural feminism" because, rather than focusing on differences, rural feminism is focused on how structural shifts in power allow women more autonomy and greater agency in decision-making that have an impact on their lives.

Toward the end of her testimonio, Diana stated, perhaps not surprisingly, that she would like to be involved in research again because "it is research that initiated my thought process and was also my starting point." This awareness reflects the synergy of Diana's efforts over her life course. She began her most committed efforts toward change as a student; she worked diligently to bring theory to practice even when it meant losing her job, and although she founded a successful organization rooted at the intersection of women in the context of international development, she still sought additional study through a master's program. This trajectory reflects not only the synergy of her praxis—with theory and practice regularly informing the other—but also the important role of committing to the rejection of patriarchal and capitalist ideology at each stage to aim for long-term, transformative change.

Interestingly, despite deideologizing the social structures that upheld her own privilege as the granddaughter of large-scale coffee farmers, Diana wound up, in the end, on a large-scale coffee farm. But, the farms at La FEM are farms where women are producers who are accountable to each other through cooperative arrangements, who own the land from which they produce, and who are active subjects in making autonomous decisions regarding the products of their labor. Deideologizing the gendered nature of land ownership led to the production of citizen subjects—women landowners who create sustainable living conditions, rather than the exploitation and marginalization that Diana witnessed on the farms of her youth.

Notes

1. *El campo* means in the "countryside" or "field."

2. This is equal to 2,088 acres.

3. INIM (*Instituto Nicaragüense de la Mujer* the Nicaraguan Women's Institute).

4. *Flor de Pino* translates to "Pine Flower."

5. The term feminicide, unlike femicide which is broadly defined as the killing of women for being women, is used because feminicide recognizes murders of women are founded on a gender power structure that intersects with other social and economic inequalities.

6. There are 18 women's organizations that were historically affiliated with the Movimiento but during the 2006 restructuring identified themselves as part of a newly identified feminist movement.

7. Of the 8 U.N. Millennium Development goals, one of them was to promote gender equality and empower women.

8. [genetically modified organisms]

9. The Wisconsin Coordinating Council on Nicaragua (WCCN) was a nonprofit organization originally founded in 1984 as part of the U.S.-Nicaragua "sister city" movement aimed at political activism and solidarity with the people of Nicaragua during the war. After the war ended in 1990, the mission of WCCN shifted toward microfinance services to improve the lives and communities of the working poor.

10. Just Coffee is a coffee cooperative in Madison, Wisconsin, that works to transparently document where the coffee came from, who grew it, and how the consumer's choice affects the farmers in a real way. Available on the Just Coffee website (http://justcoffee. coop/) are links to their contracts with farmers, the prices they pay to them, and more.

11. *Compañero* is used to reflect political solidarity with someone who is a partner, colleague, or classmate. *Compañera* is the feminine form of *compañero.*

Summary: Agriculture

FEMINIST RURAL ORGANIZING

Although much has been written about how women's role in agricultural labor and systematic differences in land ownership between men and women contribute to structural inequality and to poverty among women, most of the attention to this issue has come from the disciplines of economics, development, and sociology. Despite the invaluable contributions made by these disciplines to understanding the role of land and gender in the context of globalization, the *testimonios* in this section of the book demonstrate how a psychology of resistance is a crucial element to enacting structural changes that will advance rights for rural women. As rural activists within the *Movimiento Autónomo de Mujeres* (Women's Autonomous Movement), Martha Valle and Diana Martinez narrated the importance of understanding that devaluing women's agricultural production and denying equal property rights, particularly in a country where women have become increasingly involved in agricultural production, serves to reduce women's social, economic, and political status. Both women demonstrated that deideologizing the gendered structures that justified and maintained women's subordinate status in rural contexts was a crucial component leading to transformative change.

In particular, the *testimonios* in this section demonstrated that changes in laws alone were not enough to bring about significant social change for women. For example, in Nicaragua there are laws regarding women's rights to productive employment and land ownership that allow women equal opportunity to that of men. Nevertheless, cultural norms and practices perpetuated by dominant patriarchal and neoliberal ideologies interrupt women's rights in a manner that serves to sustain dominance and subordination. The women in this section demonstrated that a necessary step in changing these norms involves deconstructing the dominant ideologies that allow structural inequities to continue. The intersectional understanding of the nature of gendered oppression that was articulated by both Martha and Diana reflects how rural feminism emerged to address the role of resource control in larger global processes that have gendered implications for women's rights.

Although Martha did not use the term *rural feminism*, in particular, both she and Diana articulated a feminism that is guided by intersectional understandings of gendered oppression by emphasizing process and distinguishing rural feminism from a "difference-based" feminism. Martha defined feminism as "an ideology in defense of women, with the different expression that everyone has decided to make theirs." In other words, the focus is not on the *difference* between rural women and other women, but on processes that manifest particular obstacles or concerns that are relevant for the advancement of women working from a particular location. In the case of rural feminism in Nicaragua, there is a focus on understanding how women negotiate their relations with men based on other dominant social locations (e.g., poverty, sexual orientation) and, specifically, how these locations interact with women's access to land and land rights in the context of globalization. Thus, a natural starting point in rural feminism is focused on land and agricultural production, but the emphasis is on the process that emerges when women are valued as agricultural producers and/or granted control over land.

What was revealed when Martha and Diana deideologized rural women's lived experience is the intersectional nature of power, lending strong evidence to the processes articulated by the theory of gender and power (Connell, 1987). In particular, the findings illustrated in the *testimonios* in this section demonstrate the social dynamics of gender by linking institutional power to interpersonal relationships in a manner that explains both structures and processes that put women at risk and hold promise for change. For example, the structural power that was afforded to women producers in Martha's story reflects how the experience of being valued in a global economy has an impact on the relational power with male partners in a manner that holds promise for actualizing the rights of women producers. Similarly, the institutional power afforded to women landowners at La FEM demonstrated how shifting structural norms to allow women to own land had an impact on their status, thereby increasing agency and relational power allowing decisions, such as identifying as a sexual minority, that would not have been previously possible without the power afforded by changing structures.

Because rural women in Nicaragua are facing a context dominated not only by patriarchal norms but also by increasing global pressures imposed on the government for privatizing resources (i.e., land), the *testimonios* reflected how mobilization greatly facilitated women's access to property and related resistance in this limited situation. The effect of mobilization lends support to Freire's (1970) theory that consciousness raising occurs through group forums as a means to bring about empowerment, rather than relying on individual complaints. From this perspective, focusing on individuals would do little to alter the social structures that need to shift for change to be actualized. Liberation psychologists similarly argue that progress is not an individual psychological task, but one requiring social changes and political organization (Martín-Baró , 1994). Evidence from the *testimonios* suggests that a combination of structural changes and psycho-political education facilitated women's awareness of their agricultural roles, resulting in transformations in gender relations. In other words, although women's access to land and landownership may be a fundamental require-ment of social justice for rural women, workshops and education regard-ing how land relates to other fundamental rights within society and the women's relationships are critical for establishing equality between women and men. Because women continue to face the risk of land alienation in the presence of imposed privatization from global pressures, mobilization and organizational interventions that facilitate consciousness raising and train-ing may be necessary for women to actualize their rights.

The social construction of land and dominance, especially in the con-text of the political contestations involving land in Nicaragua, created a limit situation that enabled poor peasant women to stand up to powerful leaders and defy their efforts to deprive them of land and agricultural opportunity. Although the struggles by the rural poor are not always successful, the context of peasant movements within the Revolution in Nicaragua led to the rise of a mobilized rural feminism, a feminism theorized and practiced by women in *el campo* that takes into account the distinct needs of women who work or produce from the land. Martha's and Diana's *testimonios* shed light on how the role of land and resource control was deideologized, demonstrating that noneconomic conceptions of resources (e.g., land) are an important building block for conceptualizing how gender relations are constituted, maintained, and reproduced over time and how they can be altered to establish greater equity between women and men.

Conclusion

HOW A FEMINIST FIGHT FOR JUSTICE FROM THE MAJORITY
WORLD INFORMS LIBERATORY KNOWLEDGE

This book detailed the ways that collectively organized women from the majority world generated activities of a new "citizen subject," one that was autonomous from political parties and the power that ruled at the intersections of patriarchy and global capital. Employing a transnational feminist liberation investigation into the "psychology of resistance" allowed for an examination of the ways in which women develop their subjectivity through critical awareness and challenge power-based structural constraints to resist and rethink structures of social domination. Although each of the *testimonios* included in this book could stand alone to reflect individual psychosocial processes, they were framed by common experiences of sociopolitical oppression that demonstrated how the dominance of global capital intersected with male political agendas to exacerbate threats to women's human rights. The oppositional methods that emerged from the margins of this intersection have much to contribute to feminist liberatory knowledge related to women's human rights in an increasingly globalized world. In particular, the psychological mechanisms and methodologies that led to the emergence of new citizen subjects within the *Movimiento Autónomo de Mujeres* (Women's Autonomous Movement) offer several key lessons that can inform social change agents globally as well as contribute to theorizing about feminist liberation and justice.

One of the key lessons that emerged across stories was that within the Movimiento, the construction of local knowledge was viewed as an invaluable perspective from which to generate action. Transnational feminist scholar Leela Fernandes suggested that despite the interest in transnational feminism moving away from stereotypical views of non-Western women, a narrow focus has developed in much scholarship that has created a binary of marginalized

233

women from the majority world and elite scholars who are engaged in the production of knowledge (Fernandes, 2013). By expanding on traditional investigations in the current project, findings from the *testimonios* challenged this binary by demonstrating that knowledge was being constructed by all of the women involved.

Knowledge construction within the Movimiento occurred in a dialectic of awareness and action that was used to drive social change aimed at transforming structures that would enhance the actualization of women's human rights. The methods by which local knowledge was privileged were reflected in countless ways across sectors. For example, in working on violence against women, Violeta Delgado operated from the standpoint of women to demand changes in legislation by viewing women as informants with important lived experience, rather than viewing them as victims. Similarly, in the development of her own subjectivity, Yamileth Mejía expressed a desire to be like women who knew "so much," underscoring the importance of knowledge in processes of change. Once Yamileth herself was positioned as a "knower," she privileged the subjectivity of other women by recognizing that, as community members, they were sources of invaluable knowledge. In doing so, Yamileth deconstructed traditional ways of teaching and learning by recognizing and valuing the knowledge among the women with whom she was working. Likewise, Martha Valle believed that rural women, regardless of formal literacy or education levels, were equipped with invaluable knowledge that should be of a substantive, rather than tokenized, form of information in community decision-making. These methods emphasized the importance of subjective experience as the basis for knowledge and change.

The privileging of local knowledge in these manners led women within the Movimiento to be inclusive, generate citizen participation, and create structural changes that led to the advancement of women's rights. Actions taken within the Movimiento (e.g., creating democratic spaces, proposing legislation, forming rural rebellions) used women's wisdom and experience as vital sources of knowledge and the starting ground for change, rather than importing an international agenda. This method and the mechanisms employed demonstrated evidence for the possibility that changes can emerge from "limited situations," when the methods used are built based on the experiences of real women. Another cross-cutting theme that emerged from the *testimonios* that reflected key lessons was how the concerns regarding violence against women were used to drive collective mobilization and action within the Movimiento.

Although an aim of the project was not to focus on violence against women, every woman included in this book spoke about the problem of violence and in particular discussed it as a matter relating to women's human rights. As mentioned in the Introduction, there exists a general interdisciplinary concern that the use of an international human rights discourse in majority world contexts is a Western imposition. Yet, at the same time, it also is true that countless issues raised by the women in the Movimiento are in fact *not* discussed as human rights violations in countries from the North (e.g., in the United States, access to reproductive healthcare is not generally discussed as a matter of justice or human rights). Nevertheless, the leaders included in this book discussed becoming involved in the Movimiento precisely to engage in the "defense of rights" (Juanita Jiménez), to be part of "citizens fights for rights" (Sofía Montenegro), to work as a "defender of human rights" (Yamileth Mejía), to attend human rights conferences (Matilde Lindo, Violeta Delgado), to monitor factories where workers were "subjects with rights" (Sandra Ramos), to "legislate in the interests of women's rights" (Bertha Inés Cabrales), to value women's agricultural labor as a "matter of human rights" (Martha Valle), or to engage in "fighting for equal rights for rural women" (Diana Martinez). Indeed, collective action in the Movimiento emerged precisely because male-dominated authority would not recognize the need to focus on the protection of women's human rights. One of the human rights violations, in particular, that was brought up by every woman included in the book was violence against women.

Examining the psychology of resistance in Nicaragua helped to unveil how transnationally intersectional experiences may be important for addressing violence against women in some key ways. Multiple narratives illuminated and elucidated an important approach to antiviolence activism by situating violence against women at the intersection of patriarchy and global capitalism. For example, violence against women in factories was practiced both because of women's subjugated status relative to male supervisors and because of the role of women's labor in a global economic system. Therefore, actions aimed at change needed to recognize that the global and gendered nature of poverty and patriarchy sustain these practices. In another example, leaders of the Movimiento strategized actions that could reduce violence against women by implementing structural change (e.g., land ownership) that would lead to enhanced resource control among rural women in the context of globalization.

Addressing both gendered relations *and* the role of the global economy in privatizing land and profiting from women's agricultural labor played important key roles in actualizing rights for rural women. In other words, across sectors an understanding of the collusion of patriarchal control and neoliberalism resulted in resistance that emerged from the "between" spaces of local, national, and global influences. Although many of the *testimonios* demonstrated how violence was an experience that shaped many of the women's lives, they reshaped it through their political engagement with the State, the dominant political ideologies in Nicaragua, and international organizations, in particular the United Nations. This is an important analysis that is sorely missing in contemporary antiviolence organizing within the United States, for example. Perhaps the limited use of a human rights discourse in the North may prohibit an understanding of what perpetuates violence against women, thereby impeding progressive change and legislation.

Another potentially unexpected finding that emerged from the text was that all of the women interviewed identified themselves as feminists, offering great insight regarding the meanings of feminism(s) and how it is being claimed in Nicaragua. To avoid assumptions made about feminism in the majority world, each woman was asked explicitly about her identification and understanding of feminism. Although asking the question highlights the co-constructed nature of the knowledge that emerged from the answers, having asked it revealed that all of the women either defined feminism as an intersectional approach to understanding power and/or claimed it as a platform for concrete action. For example, Sofía deideologized the universalizing of women and argued that women from various backgrounds have different demands and therefore distinct contributions to make toward change.

Similarly, others (e.g., Yamileth Mejía) reflected an intersectional perspective held by many women in the Movimiento, which was that feminism was not simply about the inequities between women and men, but rather an ideological framework through which to understand any form of discrimination that violates the rights of all human beings. Only one woman (Matilde Lindo), however, explicitly underscored that respect "between women" is important by being clear that there are multiple dimensions in which women can participate in the collusion of power that oppresses other women. The framework adopted by these women is important, in part, because many of the women astutely explained, "Feminism, it's not just a theory up in the air. Rather, it is a way of living life, of thinking and of working for other women to know and appropriate themselves and make changes in their life" (Sandra Ramos).

The shared theoretical understanding that different oppositional ideologies could meet to enact effective means for transforming dominant power and political institutions drove strategic efforts that heavily emphasized collective processes. By diversifying women's participation and recognizing women's different social locations, different demands and different strategic efforts (e.g., a newspaper that showcased women's concerns, rebellions organized among peasant women, legislation rooted in oppositional ideology) led to a multi-prong praxis.

Theory, to the extent that it informed oppositional ideology, was an important element in this praxis. As such, a synergy between activism and scholarship was articulated by several women in the Movimiento. Again, although the methods used in this project placed primary importance on the voices of the marginalized, women were explicitly asked about the role of scholarship in their social change efforts. This question, in particular, could generate a certain affirmative evaluation given that I, as the interviewer, was a scholar.

Nevertheless, several women spoke in concrete ways about both the importance and the role that theory and scholarship played in their social change efforts. For example, because Bertha Cabrales believed that "theory is born out of reality," she and her *compañeras* hosted workshops and produced readings that used feminist theory and oppositional ideology to understand how power functions to keep women in subordinated positions. Diana Martinez's story reflected a lifetime of honing a praxis that involved using theoretical and empirical understandings to implement structural change for rural women.

Similarly, for many of the women leaders in the Movimiento, an understanding of theory and scholarship led to methods that promoted education. For example, in the free trade zones, Sandra Ramos used education to empower women so that a new generation of women would know their rights and how to demand them. This strategy was very different from what others (Violeta Delgado) observed in visits to the United States and Europe, where even under the best of circumstances, individuals whose rights had been violated were often treated as "victims." The importance of educating, rather than "treating" or "helping" women, was connected back to the development of citizen subjectivity for most of the leaders. For example, in reflecting on the threats that neoliberalism posed to women's rights, Matilde Lindo underscored the importance of being educated about politics because in the absence of it women "are even being drawn farther from really being a subject, a political subject."

Another major element of the feminist praxis enacted in the Movimiento was what Juanita called "organizational diversity." The feminist structure that was set up within the Movimiento, at large, and within each organization in which the women interviewed worked, was constructed such that women could collectively resist and rethink top-down authority in a way that recognized everyone's roles as important. The methods used to accomplish this involved prioritizing women's leadership (e.g., Diana Martinez's organization positioned women from the communities on the board of directors), creating democratic spaces where women, regardless of their social location, could make decisions (e.g., Juanita Jimenez was instrumental in creating political spaces that deideologized male-dominated authoritarianism) and have participation that was not tokenized (e.g., Martha Valle recognized that having women included in quotas was not a substantive way of diversifying the peasant movement). These efforts of diversifying collective action were enacted with the shared understanding that an alternative form of resistance was necessary because otherwise the interests behind global capitalism would continue policies with the support of male leaders at the expense of women's rights.

Finally, another crucial element of feminist praxis was enacting laws that attempted to legislate women's interests. Thus, one of the major lessons that emerged from the text was how feminism can be used as a platform for action. For the women in Nicaragua, feminism was not a side project, but a theory that informed a praxis that had the power to transform institutions that were misappropriating democracy, legal claims, and women's labor to abuse power.

Another striking lesson that emerged was the awareness that feminist praxis involved a *process*. This was clearly articulated when Sandra Ramos said, "This is a process, nobody is born a feminist and nobody is born knowing about gender; this is learned as we go." However, in psychology the prevailing approach to gender research has been to conduct gender comparison tests to examine differences (or similarities) between women and men (e.g., Hyde, 2014), rather than to more closely examine the processes involved in the psychological phenomenon surrounding gender (Marecek, 1995). As important as this approach has been for documenting various phenomena, investigations focused on gender differences presuppose an essentialist model of gender that, perhaps without intending to do so, suggests that women, as a group, have universally shared experiences, relative to men as a group. This approach also overlooks differences between women and the contexts in which they live. Adopting a transnational framework that understands gender justice in the context of multiple levels of oppression allowed for the examination of psychosocial processes behind oppression and resistance that are critical for creating the transformations necessary for gender justice.

In investigating these psychological processes, the women in Section One of the book demonstrated that the understandings that emerge in limit situations can be used to problematize social conditions—in other words to view conditions, rather than individuals, as problems that require solution. This, in part, involves rejecting dominant ideologies (e.g., traditional gender ideology, the ideology of meritocracy, neoliberal ideology) in a manner that allows for an alternative subjectivity—one poised to challenge and change the rules. These psychological mechanisms, and the actions that result, are not the end goal of change but rather key elements in a crucial process. For example, problematizing control of participation and knowledge in society led to the creation of democratic spaces for women.

In Section Two, examples of *conscientización* reflected the very iterative nature of change as an ideological process whereby analysis and action developed together to contribute to change over time. The activists in this section of the book demonstrated that enacting and upholding legislation that was in opposition to a predominantly male judiciary system, which colluded with corporate interests to dismiss human rights violations, involved the conscious production and re-production of resistance that built on prior action and achievement within the Movimiento. Processes of conscientización generated the required mobilization to have an impact on the design and proposal of legislation.

In Section Three, the leaders of the peasant movement understood that conceding an oppositional ideology in the face of limit situations would only lead to band-aid solutions that would continue sustaining the intersections of power that subjugated women and denied their rights. The collective action that was engaged in a rural context was guided by deideologizing the systemic nature by which men had power over women and reconstructing understandings of lived experience in a manner that led to structural changes (e.g., land ownership). Structural changes were viewed as necessary for women to act as subjects in their own lives who could make decisions with agency. The psychological processes of resistance allowed the women in this book to move their level of interest and analysis from their individual selves to a structural analysis that informed transformational change. As Moane (1999) stated in an analysis of gender oppression, "A liberation psychology aims to facilitate breaking out of oppression by identifying processes and practices which can transform the psychological patterns associated with oppression and facilitate taking action to bring about change in social conditions" (p. 180).

In telling their stories of triumph in this book, the women demonstrated that a feminist, liberatory psychological process was imperative to employing a rights-based discourse that would be conducive to structural change, rather than simply putting band-aids on existing problems. Nevertheless, across all three sectors, without exception, processes of resistance were met with political persecution that was meant to intimidate and silence, reflecting the imperative for solidarity and cross-sector, urban-rural alliances.

Although the exact experiences, methods, and strengths of the women interviewed in this project will not generalize to all individuals, the realities of experiencing oppression while simultaneously holding oppositional ideologies and methodologies toward rights abuses can be applied to other situations. Women in Nicaragua have come together in organizations, networks, and a social movement to tackle problems of democratic participation, legal rights, violence against women, labor, agricultural production, and land ownership. They have altered the ways in which society, the government, international institutions, men, and they themselves evaluate their own experience. They have struggled to bring the issues of basic human rights to the forefront of public consciousness, to organize against patriarchal and neoliberal oppressions, and to enact social transformation.

Analyzing resistance among women leaders in Nicaragua's Movimiento Autónomo de Mujeres puts psychology at the crossroads of women's human rights, globalization, and social change by putting forth a novel model for understanding inequality and providing empirical support that provides a framework of social justice and change. In doing so, it elevates the voices of the compañeras in the production of feminist liberatory knowledge. Moreover, the findings demonstrate that women mobilized locally can take control over their own lives, rather than needing to be "rescued" by international interventionists. Given the global dominance of neoliberalism, constructing liberatory knowledge from activists within a vibrant, coordinated, and feminist movement that has survived the presence of neoliberal politics helps move oppositional methodologies from the "margins" to the "center" in a manner aimed at justice for women in far-reaching places.

APPENDIX

Timeline of Relevant Events in
the *Movimiento Autónomo de Mujeres*

1977	1979	1979	1990	1991	1992	1996	2006	2007	2012
FSLN founded the Association of Women Confronting the National Problem (*Asociación de Mujeres ante la Problemática Nacional*; AMPRONAC)	The fall of the Somoza dictatorship and the triumph of the Sandinista Revolution.	AMPRONAC change its name to the Luisa Amanda Espinoza Association of Nicaraguan Women (*Asociación de Mujeres Nicaragüenses Luisa Amanda Espinoza*; AMNLAE)	Electoral defeat of the FLSN to Violeta Chamorro	"We are 52 % Festival"	The first National Feminist Conference referred to as the "Diverse but United" meeting	Law 230, the Penal Code to prevent and punish domestic violence is passed.	*Movimiento Autónomo de Mujeres* was founded on International Women's Day March 8th 2006 Criminalization of abortion	Re-election of Ortega Political campaign against 9 feminists who protested the criminalization of abortion in the "Rosita" case	Re-election of Ortega Law 779, the Comprehensive Law Against Violence Towards Women passed.

BIBLIOGRAPHY

Agarwal, B. (1994). *Field of one's own: Property rights in South Asia.* Cambridge, UK: Cambridge University Press.

Alexander, M. J. (2005). *Pedagogies of crossing: Meditations on feminism, sexual politics, memory, and the sacred.* Durham, NC: Duke University Press.

Alexander, M. J., & Mohanty, C. T. (1997). *Feminist genealogies, colonial legacies, democratic futures.* Abingdon, UK: Routledge.

Alexander, M. J., & Mohanty, C. T. (2010). Cartographies of knowledge and power: Transnational feminism as radical praxis. In A. L. Swarr & R. Nagar (Eds.), *Critical transnational feminist praxis* (pp. 23–45). Albany: State University of New York Press.

Alvarez, S. E. (1990). *Engendering democracy in Brazil: Women's movements in transition politics.* Princeton, NJ: Princeton University Press.

Alvarez, S. E. (2000). Translating the global effects of transnational organizing on local feminist discourses and practices in Latin America. *Meridians, 1*(1), 29–67.

Anzaldúa, G., & Moraga, C. (1983). *This bridge called my back: Radical writings by women of color.* New York, NY: Kitchen Table/Women of Color Press .

Avin, R. M. (2006). Engendering development. *Feminist Economics and the World Bank: History, Theory and Policy, 3*, 65.

Bose, C. E. (2012). Intersectionality and global gender inequality. *Gender & Society, 26*(1), 67–72.

Brodsky, A. E., Portnoy, G. A., Scheibler, J. E., Welsh, E. A., Talwar, G., & Carrillo, A. (2012). Beyond (the ABCs): Education, community, and feminism in Afghanistan. *Journal of Community Psychology, 40*(1), 159–181.

Brodsky, A. E., Welsh, E., Carrillo, A., Talwar, G., Scheibler, J., & Butler, T. (2011). Between synergy and conflict: Balancing the processes of organizational and individual resilience in an Afghan women's community. *American Journal of Community Psychology, 47*(3–4), 217–235.

Bunch, C. (1990). Women's rights as human rights: Toward a re-vision of human rights. *Human Rights Quarterly,* 486–498.

Burton, M., & Kagan, C. (2005). Liberation social psychology: Learning from Latin America. *Journal of Community & Applied Social Psychology, 15*(1), 63–78.

Chase, S. E. (2003). Taking narrative seriously: Consequences for method and theory in interview studies. In Y. S. Lincoln & N. K. Denzin (Eds.), *Turning points in qualitative research: Tying knots in a handkerchief* (pp. 273–296). New York, NY: Altamira Press.

Chaudhry, L. N., & Bertram, C. (2009). Narrating trauma and reconstruction in post-conflict Karachi: Feminist liberation psychology and the contours of agency in the margins. *Feminism & Psychology, 19*(3), 298–312.

Cole, E. R., & Stewart, A. J. (1996). Meanings of political participation among black and white women: Political identity and social responsibility. *Journal of Personality and Social Psychology, 71*(1), 130.

Collins, P. H. (1989). The social construction of black feminist thought. *Signs, 745–773.*

Collins, P. H. (1990). *Black feminist thought: Knowledge, consciousness, and the politics of empowerment.* New York, NY: Routledge.

Connell, R. (1987). *Gender and power: The society, the person, and sexual politics.* Stanford, CA: Stanford University Press.

Cornwall, A. (2003). Whose voices? Whose choices? Reflections on gender and participatory development. *World Development, 31*(8), 1325–1342.

Cornwall, A., & Brock, K. (2005). What do buzzwords do for development policy? A critical look at "participation," "empowerment" and "poverty reduction." *Third World Quarterly, 26*(7), 1043–1060.

Crenshaw, K. (1989). Demarginalizing the intersection of race and sex: A Black feminist critique of antidiscrimination doctrine, feminist theory and antiracist politics. *University of Chicago Legal Forum, 140,* 139–167.

Crosby, A. (2009). Anatomy of a workshop: Women's struggles for transformative participation in Latin America. *Feminism & Psychology, 19*(3), 343–353.

Deere, C. D., & León, M. (1987). *Series in political economy and economic development in Latin America. Rural women and state policy: Feminist perspectives on Latin American agricultural development.* Boulder, CO: Westview Press.

Deere, C. D., & León, M. (2001). *Empowering women: Land and property rights in Latin America.* Pittsburgh, PA: University of Pittsburgh Press.

De Oliveira, J. M., Neves, S., Nogueira, C., & De Koning, M. (2009). Present but unnamed: Feminist liberation psychology in Portugal. *Feminism & Psychology, 19*(3), 394–406.

Dutt, A., & Grabe, S. (2014). Lifetime activism, marginality, and psychology: Narratives of lifelong feminist activists committed to social change. *Qualitative Psychology, 1*(2), 107.

Ellsberg, M., Peña, R., Herrera, A., Liljestrand, J., & Winkvist, A. (2000). Candies in hell: Women's experiences of violence in Nicaragua. *Social Science & Medicine, 51*(11), 1595–1610.

Ewig, C. (1999). The strengths and limits of the NGO women's movement model: Shaping Nicaragua's democratic institutions. *Latin American Research Review, 34*(3), 75–102.

Fals Borda, O. (1988). *Knowledge and people's power: Lessons with peasants in Nicaragua, Mexico and Colombia.* New Delhi: Indian Social Institute.

Fernandes, L. (2013). *Transnational feminism in the United States: Knowledge, ethics, and power.* New York, NY: NYU Press.

Ferree, M. M. (2006). Globalization and feminism: Opportunities and obstacles for activism in the global arena. In M. M. Ferree & A. M. Tripp (Eds.), *Global feminism: Transnational women's activism, organizing, and human rights* (pp. 3–23). New York, NY: NYU Press.

Ferree, M. M., & Tripp, A. M. (2006). *Global feminism: Transnational women's activism, organizing, and human rights.* New York, NY: NYU Press.

Foucault, M. (2005). *The hermeneutics of the subject: Lectures at the Collège de France 1981–1982* (Vol. 6). New York, NY: Macmillan.

Foundation for Sustainable Development (FSD). (2015). *Environmental sustainability issues in Nicaragua.* Retrieved from http://www.fsdinternational.org/country/nicaragua/envissues

Fregoso, R. L., & Bejarano, C. (2010). *Terrorizing women: Feminicide in the Americas.* Durham, NC: Duke University Press.

Freire, P. (1970). *Pedagogy of the oppressed* (translated by M. Bergman Ramos). New York, NY: Continuum.

Glick, P., & Fiske, S. (1999). Gender, power dynamics, and social interaction. In M. M. Ferree & J. Lorber (Eds.), *Revisioning gender* (pp. 365–398). Newbury Park, CA: Sage.

Grabe, S. (2010). Women's human rights and empowerment in a transnational, globalized context: What's psychology got to do with it? In M. A. Paludi (Ed.), *Feminism and women's rights worldwide* (pp. 17–46). Westport, CT: Praeger/Greenwood.

Grabe, S. (2012). An empirical examination of women's empowerment and transformative change in the context of international development. *American Journal of Community Psychology, 49*, 233–245.

Grabe, S. (2013). Psychological cliterodectomy: Body objectification as a human rights violation. In M. Ryan & N. R. Branscomb (Eds.), *The SAGE handbook of gender and psychology* (pp. 412–427). Thousand Oaks, CA: Sage.

Grabe, S. (in press). Transnational feminism in psychology: Women's human rights, liberation, and social justice. In P. Hammack (Ed.), *Oxford handbook of social psychology and social justice*. New York, NY: Oxford University Press.

Grabe, S., & Arenas, C. (2009). *Promoting gender equality through development: Land ownership and domestic violence in Nicaragua* (Gendered Perspectives on International Development, Working Paper 295). East Lansing: Gender, Development, and Globalization Program, Michigan State University.

Grabe, S., & Dutt, A. (2015). Counter narratives, the psychology of liberation, and the evolution of a women's social movement in Nicaragua. *Peace & Conflict: Journal of Peace Psychology, 21*, 89–105.

Grabe, S., Dutt, A., & Dworkin, S. L. (2014). Women's community mobilization and well-being: Local resistance to gendered social inequities in Nicaragua and Tanzania. *Journal of Community Psychology, 42*(4), 379–397.

Grabe, S., & Else-Quest, N. M. (2012). The role of transnational feminism in psychology complementary visions. *Psychology of Women Quarterly, 36*(2), 158–161.

Grabe, S., Grose, R. G., & Dutt, A. (2015). Women's land ownership and relationship power: A mixed methods approach to understanding structural inequities and violence against women. *Psychology of Women Quarterly, 39*, 7–19.

Grewal, I., & Kaplan, C. (1994). *Scattered hegemonies: Postmodernity and transnational feminist practices*. Minneapolis: University of Minnesota Press.

Grigsby, W. (2003). Caribbean Coast: Multiethnic, multilingual . . . and finally autonomous? *Envio, 266, September*. Retrieved from http://www.envio.org.ni/articulo/2117

Grose, R. G., & Grabe, S. (2014). The explanatory role of relationship power and control in domestic violence against women in Nicaragua: A feminist psychology analysis. *Violence Against Women, 20*(8), 972–993.

Hammack, P. L. (2010). Identity as burden or benefit? Youth, historical narrative, and the legacy of political conflict. *Human Development, 53*(4), 173–201.

Henrich, J., Heine, S. J., & Norenzayan, A. (2010). The weirdest people in the world? *Behavioral and Brain Sciences, 33*(2–3), 61–83.

Hesse-Biber, S. N. (2007). Feminist research: Exploring the interconnections of epistemology, methodology, and method. In *Handbook of Feminist Research: Theory and Praxis* (pp. 1–28). Thousand Oaks, CA: Sage.

hooks, b. (1984). *Feminist theory: From margin to center*. Cambridge, MA: South End Press.

Hurtado, A. (1989). Relating to privilege: Seduction and rejection in the subordination of white women and women of Color. *Signs: Journal of Women in Culture and Society,* *14*(4), 833.

Hurtado, A. (1996). *The color of privilege: Three blasphemies on race and feminism.* Minneapolis: University of Michigan Press.

Hyde, J. S. (2014). Gender similarities and differences. *Annual Review of Psychology, 65,* 373–398.

Jubb, N. (2014). Feminists and Sandinistas in Nicaragua: Then and now. *Bulletin of Latin American Research, 33*(3), 257–258.

International Fund for Agricultural Development (IFAD). (2015). *Rural poverty in Nicaragua.* Retrieved from http://www.ruralpovertyportal.org/country/home/tags/nicaragua

Kabeer, N. (1994). *Reversed realities: Gender hierarchies in development thought.* Brooklyn, NY: Verso.

Kabeer, N. (1999). Resources, agency, achievements: Reflections on the measurement of women's empowerment. *Development and Change, 30*(3), 435–464.

Kagitcibasi, C. (2002). Psychology and human competence development. *Applied Psychology, 51*(1), 5–22.

Kampwirth, K. (1996). Confronting adversity with experience: The emergence of feminism in Nicaragua. *Social Politics: International Studies in Gender, State & Society,* *3*(2–3), 136.

Kampwirth, K. (2004). *Feminism and the legacy of revolution: Nicaragua, El Salvador, Chiapas* (Vol. 43). Athens: Ohio University Press.

Kampwirth, K. (2011). *Latin America's New Left and the politics of gender.* New York: Springer.

Kurtiş, T., & Adams, G. (2015). Decolonizing liberation: Toward a transnational feminist psychology. *Journal of Social and Political Psychology, 3*(1), 388–413.

Lacombe, D. (2014). Struggling against the "worst-case scenario"? Strategic conflicts and realignments of the feminist movement in the context of the 2006 Nicaraguan elections. *Bulletin of Latin American Research, 33*(3), 274–288.

Latina Feminist Group. (2001). *Telling to live: Latina feminist testimonios.* Durham, NC: Duke University Press Books.

Lira, E. C., & Martinez, J. J. (2009). *Social movements and citizenship in Central America: The women's movement and the struggle for their rights in Nicaragua 1998–2008.* Retrieved from Hivos Knowledge Program website: https://hivos.org/social-movements-and-citizenship-central-america-womens-movement-and-struggle-their-rights-nicaragua

Lorde, A. (1984). *Sister outsider.* Freedom, CA: Crossing Press.

Lugones, M. (2010). Toward a decolonial feminism. *Hypatia, 25*(4), 742–759.

Lykes, M. B. (1997). Activist participatory research among the Maya of Guatemala: Constructing meanings from situated knowledge. *Journal of Social Issues, 53*(4), 725–746.

Lykes, M. B., Beristain, C. M., & Pérez-Armiñan, M. L. C. (2007). Political violence, impunity, and emotional climate in Maya communities. *Journal of Social Issues, 63*(2), 369–385.

Lykes, M. B., & Coquillon, E. (2006). Participatory and action research and feminisms: Toward transformative praxis. In S. Hesse-Biber (Ed.), *Handbook of feminist research: Theory and praxis* (pp. 297–326). Thousand Oaks, CA: Sage.

Lykes, M. B., & Moane, G. (2009). Editors' introduction: Whither feminist liberation psychology? Critical explorations of feminist and liberation psychologies for a globalizing world. *Feminism & Psychology, 19*(3), 283.

Maddison, S., & Shaw, F. S. (2007). Feminist perspectives on social movement research. In S. Hesse-Biber (Ed.), *Handbook of feminist research: Theory and praxis* (pp. 391–408). Thousand Oaks, CA: Sage.

Madrigal, L. J., & Tejeda, W. V. (2009). Facing gender-based violence in El Salvador: Contributions from the social psychology of Ignacio Martín-Baró. *Feminism & Psychology, 19*(3), 368–374.

Mahalingam, R., Balan, S., & Haritatos, J. (2008). Engendering immigrant psychology: An intersectionality perspective. *Sex Roles, 59*(5–6), 326–336.

Marecek, J. (1995). Gender, politics, and psychology's ways of knowing. *American Psychologist, 50*, 162–163.

Martín-Baró, I., Aron, A., & Corne, S. (1994). *Writings for a liberation psychology.* Cambridge, MA: Harvard University Press.

Menchú, R. (1984). I . . . Rigoberta Menchú. *Index on Censorship, 13*(5), 18–20.

Mendez, J. B. (2002). Gender and citizenship in a global context: The struggle for *maquila* workers' rights in Nicaragua. *Identities: Global Studies in Culture and Power, 9*(1), 7–38.

Mendez, J. B. (2005). *From the Revolution to the maquiladoras: Gender, labor, and globalization in Nicaragua.* Durham, NC: Duke University Press Books.

Mendez, J. B., & Wolf, D. L. (2007). Feminizing global research/globalizing feminist research: Methods and practice under globalization. In S. Hesse-Biber (Ed.), *Handbook of feminist research: Theory and praxis* (pp. 651–662). Thousand Oaks, CA: Sage.

Milchman, A., & Rosenberg, A. (2007). The aesthetic and ascetic dimensions of an ethics of self-fashioning: Nietzsche and Foucault. *Parrhesia, 2*(55), 11.

Moane, G. (1999). *Gender and colonialism: A psychological analysis of oppression and liberation.* Basingstoke, UK: Palgrave Macmillan.

Moane, G. (2003). Bridging the personal and the political: Practices for a liberation psychology. *American Journal of Community Psychology, 31*(1), 91–101.

Moane, G. (2010). Sociopolitical development and political activism: Synergies between feminist and liberation psychology. *Psychology of Women Quarterly, 34*(4), 521–529.

Moghadam, V. M. (2005). *Globalizing women: Transnational feminist networks.* Baltimore, MD: Johns Hopkins University Press.

Mohanty, C. T. (1984). Under Western eyes: Feminist scholarship and colonial discourses. *Boundary 2*(12), 333–358.

Mohanty, C. T. (2003a). *Feminism without borders: Decolonizing theory, practicing solidarity.* New Delhi, India: Zubaan.

Mohanty, C. T. (2003b). "Under Western eyes" revisited: Feminist solidarity through anticapitalist struggles. *Signs, 28*(2), 499–535.

Molyneux, M. (1985). Mobilization without emancipation? Women's interests, the state, and revolution in Nicaragua. *Feminist Studies, 11*(2), 227–254.

Montenegro, S. (2002). Our Weak Civil Society Has Been Weakened Further. *Envío, #250, May.* http://www.envio.org.ni/articulo/1580

Montenegro, M., Capdevila, R., & Sarriera, H. F. (2012). Editorial introduction: Towards a transnational feminism: Dialogues on feminisms and psychologies in a Latin American context. *Feminism & Psychology, 22*(2), 220–227.

Montero, M. (1994). Consciousness-raising, conversion, and de-ideologization in community psychosocial work. *Journal of Community Psychology, 22*, 3–11.

Montero, M. (2009). Community action and research as citizenship construction. *American Journal of Community Psychology, 43*(1–2), 149–161.

Naples, N. A., & Desai, M. (2002). *Women's activism and globalization: Linking local struggles and transnational politics.* New York, NY: Routledge.

Narayan, U. (1997). *Dislocating cultures: Third world feminism and the politics of knowledge.* London, UK: Routledge.

Peña, N., Maiques, M., & Castillo, G. E. (2008). Using rights-based and gender-analysis arguments for land rights for women: Some initial reflections from Nicaragua. *Gender & Development, 16*, 55–71.

Perkins, D. D. (1995). Speaking truth to power: Empowerment ideology as social intervention and policy. *American Journal of Community Psychology, 23*(5), 765–794.

Prilleltensky, I. (2008). The role of power in wellness, oppression, and liberation: The promise of psychopolitical validity. *Journal of Community Psychology, 36*(2), 116–136.

Prilleltensky, I. (2012). Wellness as fairness. *American Journal of Community Psychology, 49*(1–2), 1–21.

Prilleltensky, I., & Prilleltensky, O. (2003). Synergies for wellness and liberation in counseling psychology. *The Counseling Psychologist, 31*(3), 273–281.

Randall, M. (1981). *Sandino's daughters: Testimonies of Nicaraguan women in struggle.* New Brunswick, NJ: Rutgers University Press.

Randall, M. (1994). *Sandino's daughters revisited: Feminism in Nicaragua.* New Brunswick, NJ: Rutgers University Press.

Renzi, M. R. & Arguto, S. (1993). ¿Qué hace la mujer Nicaragüense ante la crisis económica? Managua, Nicaragua: FIDEG.

Riessman, C. K. (2005). Narrative analysis. In N. Kelly, C. Horrocks, K. Milnes, B. Roberts, & D. Robinson (Eds.), *Narrative, memory, and everyday life* (2nd ed., pp. 1–7). Huddersfield, UK: University of Huddersfield.

Riger, S. (1993). What's wrong with empowerment? *American Journal of Community Psychology, 21*(3), 279–292.

Rocha, J. L. (2002) Rural women in Nicaragua: "Anything is possible … ." *Envio, 246, January.* Retrieved from http://www.envio.org.ni/articulo/1558

Ryan, P. (1995). *Fall and rise of the market in Sandinista Nicaragua.* Kingston, ON, Canada: McGill-Queen University Press.

Sandoval, C. (2000). *Methodology of the oppressed* (Vol. 18). Minneapolis: University of Minnesota Press.

Sen, G., & Grown, C. (1987). *Development, crises, and alternative visions: Third World women's perspectives.* New York, NY: Monthly Review Press.

Shayne, J. D. (2004). *The Revolution question: Feminisms in El Salvador, Chile, and Cuba.* New Brunswick, NJ: Rutgers University Press.

Shayne, J. D. (2009). *They used to call us witches: Chilean exiles, culture, and feminism.* Lantham, MD: Rowman & Littlefield.

Sudbury, J., & Okazawa-Rey, M. (2009). *Activist scholarship: Antiracism, feminism, and social change.* Boulder, CO: Paradigm.

Swarr, A. L., & Nagar, R. (2012). *Critical transnational feminist praxis.* Albany, NY: SUNY Press.

Taylor, V. (1998). Feminist methodology in social movements research. *Qualitative Sociology, 21*(4), 357–379.

United Nations. (1995). *Beijing Declaration and Platform of Action, adopted at the Fourth World Conference on Women, 27 October 1995.* Retrieved from http://www.refworld. org/docid/3ddeo4324.html

United Nations. (2012). Statistics and indicators on men and women. Retrieved from http:// unstats.un.org/unsd/demographic/products/indwm/

United Nations. (2014). *Women's rights are human rights.* Retrieved from the Office of the High Commissioner on Human Rights website: http://www.ohchr.org/Documents/ Publications/HR-PUB-14-2.pdf

U.S. Agency for International Development (USAID). (2011). *USAID country profile: Nicaragua. Property rights and resource governance.* Retrieved from the USAID land tenure website: http://www.usaidlandtenure.net/nicaragua

Walker, T. W. (1985). *Nicaragua: The first five years.* Westport, CT: Praeger.

Walker, T. W. (2003). *Nicaragua: Living in the shadow of the eagle.* Boulder, CO: Westview Press.

White, A., & Rastogi, S. (2009). Justice by any means necessary: Vigilantism among Indian women. *Feminism & Psychology, 19*(3), 313.

White, A. M., & Dotson, W. (2010). It takes a village to raise a researcher: Narrative interviewing as intervention, reconciliation, and growth. *Journal of Black Psychology, 36*(1), 75–97.

Zimmerman, M. A. (2000). Empowerment theory. In *Handbook of community psychology* (pp. 43–63). New York, NY: Springer.

Zimmerman, M. A., & Rappaport, J. (1988). Citizen participation, perceived control, and psychological empowerment. *American Journal of community psychology, 16*(5), 725–750.

INDEX

Note: Page numbers in italic refer to photos.